CHILD-CENTERED
COUNSELING AND PSYCHOTHERAPY

CHILD-CENTERED COUNSELING AND PSYCHOTHERAPY

By

ANGELO V. BOY

Professor of Education
University of New Hampshire
Durham, New Hampshire

and

GERALD J. PINE

Dean, School of Education
Boston College
Chestnut Hill, Massachusetts

CHARLES C THOMAS • PUBLISHER
Springfield • Illinois • U.S.A.

Published and Distributed Throughout the World by

CHARLES C THOMAS • PUBLISHER
2600 South First Street
Springfield, Illinois 62794-9265

© *1995 by* CHARLES C THOMAS • PUBLISHER

ISBN 0-398-06521-7   (cloth)
ISBN 0-398-06522-5   (paper)

Library of Congress Catalog Card Number: 95-13348

Printed in the United States of America
SC-R-3

Library of Congress Cataloging-in-Publication Data

Boy, Angelo V.
    Child-centered counseling and psychotherapy / by Angelo V. Boy and
Gerald J. Pine.
        p.   cm.
    Includes bibliographical references and index.
    ISBN 0-398-06521-7 (cloth). — ISBN 0-398-06522-5 (pbk.)
    1. Client-centered psychotherapy.   2. Child psychotherapy.
3. Children—Counseling of.   I. Pine, Gerald J.   II. Title.
RJ505.C55B69   1995
618.92'8914—dc20   95-13348
                                                                       CIP

PREFACE

Child-centered counseling and psychotherapy is the application of client-centered counseling and psychotherapy to children. The client-centered viewpoint first appeared in 1942 with the landmark book by Carl R. Rogers, *Counseling and Psychotherapy* (Houghton Mifflin). Prior to 1942, children and adults undergoing counseling and psychotherapy were subjected to analytic, diagnostic, directive and counselor-centered procedures. The child or adult client was viewed as incapable of understanding and solving a problem. The counselor or psychotherapist controlled the relationship. The client was expected to respond to the counselor's explanation of the causes of behavior and change that behavior by following the counselor's suggestions or directions.

The 1942 book by Rogers revolutionized counseling and psychotherapy. The ownership of the counseling relationship was returned to the client. The client was treated with dignity and respect and the counselor's behavior was built on an attitude of warmth, empathic understanding, and unconditional positive regard. The client assumed responsibility for determining the causes and solutions to problems and the counselor facilitated the client's involvement in that process.

Through the years the client-centered viewpoint has been further clarified and expanded. It has become applicable in a widening variety of situations in which effective interpersonal relationships are crucial: teaching, organizational behavior, families, parenting, groups, marriage and its alternatives, leadership, and pastoring. A theory which began modestly within the context of a one-to-one counseling relationship suddenly attracted the attention of persons and professionals involved in other kinds of interpersonal relationships. Research indicating the effectiveness of the Rogerian view developed quickly and today more research evidence supports its effectiveness than any other theory of counseling and psychotherapy. In the past decade the viewpoint has also served as a process for communicating peaceful intent between and among nations.

The authors of this book have been identified with the client-centered literature of counseling since 1963. We worked together as counselors to initiate and develop a client-centered counseling program among sixth, seventh, and eighth grade pupils. Our counseling also brought us into contact with children in elementary schools and the counseling programs serving those children. We sensed then that a book needed to be written which showed how client-centered counseling could be applied to children but other professional and family responsibilities interfered. We did satisfy our need to contribute to the literature of child counseling by coauthoring a number of articles on the subject.

This, then, is a book we've wanted to write for a number of years. We're pleased with the outcome. The process of child-centered counseling has evolved over the years and we hope that this book contributes to that evolution. Previously, the child-centered counselor was only concerned with the effectiveness of one-to-one counseling with children. Today's child-centered counselor is not only committed to improving that process but also in a wider range of responsibilities which contribute to improving the child's psychosocial environment.

We're pleased that this book has taken some time to develop. It's now far more comprehensive. It contains material which has been refined over the years. It represents the present status of child-centered counseling while also identifying ideas which can influence its future.

ANGELO V. BOY
GERALD J. PINE

CONTENTS

CHILD-CENTERED
COUNSELING AND PSYCHOTHERAPY

Chapter 1

INTRODUCTION TO
CHILD-CENTERED COUNSELING

Client-centered counseling was founded and developed by Carl R.
Rogers (1942, 1951, 1970, 1975, 1977, 1978, 1980, 1984). Hart (1970)
identifies three historic periods in its development:

Period 1 (1940–1950): The nondirective period in which the counselor
essentially formed a relationship with the client based upon acceptance and clarification.

Period 2 (1950–1957): The reflective period in which the counselor
essentially responded to the client's feelings by reflecting those feelings back to the client.

Period 3 (1957–present): The experiential period in which the counselor
goes beyond reflecting the client's feelings and engages in a wider
range of responses in order to meet the needs of the client (pp. 3–22).

This book combines the three periods into one integrated child-
centered counseling process. The viewpoint presented in this book corresponds to the experiential third period of client-centered counseling
without giving up what was developed during the first two periods of its
history. Our viewpoint is consistent with what has always been the open
quality of client-centered theory (Rogers & Wood, 1974):

> ...willingness to change, an openness to experience and to research data has
> been one of the most distinctive features of client-centered therapy. The
> incorporation of this element of changingness has set it apart, almost more
> than anything else I know, from other orientations to therapy (p. 213).

Corsini (1984) acknowledges the evolving nature of client-centered
counseling when he points out Rogers' insistence that the theory and its
application should be open to alteration whenever the facts so dictated.
Corey (1985) indicates that Rogers always viewed his theory as a tentative
set of principles and not as dogma.

Wexler and Rice (1974) indicate that a rigid interpretation of client-centered counseling would be in contradiction to the developmental nature of both Rogers and the theory:

> Fortunately there has not grown up around Rogers the kind of orthodoxy that would require his formulations to be the last word on any issue. Rogers certainly would not welcome this kind of blind devotion, and would in fact view it as a failure in actualization (p. 9).

Brown and Srebalus (1988) indicate that "counseling theories mature over time" (p. 46). The authors hope that the perspective presented in this book is a contribution to that maturing process and that we have not sacrificed the humanistic principles of client-centered counseling in making it adaptable to the more complex needs of clients in today's world.

CHILD-CENTERED COUNSELING: AN INTEGRATED PROCESS

In the authors' application of child-centered counseling there are three phases which correspond to the three historic periods of client-centered counseling identified by Hart (1970). In the first historic period the "counselor essentially formed a relationship with the client based upon acceptance and clarification." Our corresponding first phase focuses on the quality of the counselor as a person. This quality is known to the child and is especially prevalent in the counselor's *attitude* of empathy, genuineness, and unconditional positive regard toward the child. The child is able to sense whether or not these qualities exist in the helping relationship. When they exist, the child has a positive response to the counselor and the helping process. The child senses whether or not the counselor has the capacity to help by the counselor's attitude. During the first historic period of client-centered counseling, Rogers put heavy emphasis on the counselor's caring attitude as the catalyst for the help-ing process. Without the human caring qualities contained in the counselor's attitude, child-centered counseling cannot work. They need to be truly present in the counselor. When they are, the child client trusts the counselor and the helping process.

The second phase in our application of client-centered counseling to child counseling corresponds to the second historic period of its develop-ment (Hart, 1970). This historic period and our second phase both focus on the reflective process as the fundamental way of responding to the client's feelings. All clients with problems have unexpressed (repressed or in the subconscious) feelings about their problem. These unexpressed feelings have contributed to the formation of a problem and their expression is necessary for the solution of a problem. The counselor helps the client to clarify and express these feelings through the skillful application of the process known as "reflecting feelings." The reflective process was historically important in the development of client-centered counseling in its second period and it must not be abandoned today if child-centered counseling is to be successful. It is too powerful a therapeutic tool. It possesses immense power not only for helping the client to express feelings but for bringing the client and counselor together in a relationship which the client trusts. The relationship enables the client to feel that at last there is someone, the counselor, who respects the child's feelings and perceptions about a problem and is not analyzing, defining, or explaining the problem.

The counselor's entry into the child's world of feelings, through the reflective process, may sometimes need to be aided through the use of play materials if the child is excessively withdrawn or without the language needed to describe or express feelings. Since play is the child's natural language it can become the vehicle for some children to express feelings. When the child expresses feelings through play materials, the counselor acknowledges and reinforces their expression through the reflective process. The authors' second phase of child counseling, then, emphasizes the skilled application of the reflective process. There is no abandonment of a process that has proven itself to be effective and remains vital in our concept of child-centered counseling.

The third historic period in the development of client-client counseling is the experiential period in which "the counselor goes beyond reflecting the client's feelings and engages in a wider range of responses in order to meet the needs of the clients." Our third phase of counseling corresponds to this third historic period. During this third phase, the counselor is able to use techniques and procedures drawn from other theories of counseling and which meet the needs of clients. These techniques will work in the third phase of counseling because of the influence of phases one (the counselor's human attitude) and two (the counselor's use of the reflective process) on the client's acceptance of phase three. The child will cooperate with phase three because the child has learned to trust the counselor during phases one and two. The counselor does not betray that trust in phase three. The counselor only uses techniques and procedures designed to amplify the client's understanding of the problem and encourage movement toward a concrete solution that is acceptable to the child. These phase three techniques and procedures are always respectful of the child's rights and dignity as a person and are never applied without the child's consent. When the child is not responsive to these techniques and procedures, the child-centered counselor always remains willing to return to reflecting the child's feelings in order to understand the lack of response. The reflective process, in its respect for the client's feelings and rights, becomes a useful replacement for techniques and procedures which do not elicit a positive response from the child in phase three. This lack of a positive response tells the counselor that the child is not ready to understand or solve a problem through these more directive techniques and procedures. The child needs more time to process feelings. At a later time in the counseling relationship, a client is usually more willing to accept and cooperate with the more directive techniques and procedures of phase three. For the time being, and perhaps for the remainder of the counseling relationship, the counselor may need to rely exclusively on the reflective process as the foundation for helping a client solve a problem. This is not a great loss, however, since the reflective process, by itself, does have the potential to produce the therapeutic gains needed by a client.

In phase three, then, our application of child-centered counseling enables the counselor to build upon what was accomplished with the client in phases one and two. When the counselor's attitude is genuine and can be felt by the client (phase one), and when the counselor is able to empathically understand the child's problem and accurately apply the reflective process (phase two), the child is usually ready to work on the concrete dimensions of solving a problem (phase three). The child moves toward a trust in the counselor and the counseling process.

Other more directive theories of counseling will become more effective when the counselor delays the implementation of strategies and interventions until after the relationship with the child has been established through phases one and two. Often these approaches are "too much too soon" for the child to accept and absorb. Counselors diminish the potential effectiveness of directive approaches when they tend to apply them too quickly; the typical child is not ready to accept a counselor who is overly directive in the beginning phases of counseling. Initially, the child desires to be received as a person, accepted and understood on the child's terms and from the child's internal frame of reference.

More directive theories of counseling will produce more positive results when they are founded upon the existence of a close, human, and empathic relationship with the child. It is the existence of such a relationship which ultimately enhances the effectiveness of *any* counseling process.

When the practicing counselor has developed a substantive relationship with a child in phases one and two, any approach can be implemented in phase three which is appropriate to the needs of the child. Without a relationship based upon the client's trust, the counselor's effectiveness is greatly diminished in the concrete third phase of counseling.

Children respond to counselors who are persons. When the counselor is able to develop an affective bond with the child in phases one and two, it is the counselor's authenticity, in the child's mind, which enables the third phase to be effective. Many novice counselors abandon a directive approach to counseling when it is resisted by the child. If these counselors *first* apply the fundamentals of phases one and two, they would increase the potential of their approach having a positive effect in phase three.

The development of an effective helping relationship requires that the counselor possess identifiable positive attitudes (phase one) which can be communicated to children through the reflective process (phase two). An ownership of these attitudes and their application through the reflective process, does much to insure the success of phase three.

Setting the stage for phase three is one beneficial outcome of phases one and two. Another valuable outcome of phases one and two is the full and accurate assimilation of the child by the counselor. By assimilating or absorbing the child's personality, attitudes, values, and behavior, the counselor is able to gain an accurate and full picture of the child. Such a picture enables the counselor to more accurately understand which techniques and procedures will produce the best results in phase three.

Through assimilation, the counselor develops a more accurate approach for assisting a particular child because of the counselor's more sharpened and focused understanding of the child's full range of attitudes, values, and behaviors. Without this level of understanding, the counselor often makes the mistake of dealing with the child's presenting problem while the child's deeper and more incapacitating problems go unattended; they were never identified by either the child or the counselor because of the superficiality of their relationship. Superficial relationships with children are usually established when counselors do not take the necessary time to penetrate and absorb the inner, deep, and more influencing dimensions of the child's personality, attitudes, values, and behavior. Phases one and two enable the counselor to do that.

Therefore, two distinct advantages of phases one and two are that they provide the counselor with a meaningful vehicle for building a therapeutic relationship with a child while also enabling the counselor to more deeply and accurately assimilate the full range of the child's personality, attitudes, values, and behavior; and a deep and accurate assimilation of the child contributes significantly to the counselor's ability to *accurately* meet the needs of the child in phase three.

The evidence currently available indicates that children still respond to traditional Rogerian counseling. This is a confirmation that most children desire to be treated as human beings rather than as objects. They respond positively when they have an equalized relationship with a counselor who is empathic, acceptant, genuine, liberating, involved, and is a sensitive listener. These relationship building attitudes have proven to be effective in establishing the foundation for a productive counseling relationship. Indeed, for many children, these phase one attitudes are sufficient to positively affect attitudinal and behavioral changes.

For many children, however, phases one and two don't seem to be enough. Children respond well to the phase one, child-centered attitudes of the counselor and the phase two reflective process. Many other children, however, also need to move toward a more concrete counseling process so that their individualized needs can be realistically met. Children outside the mainstream often need more than the counselor gives in phases one and two. They often need the direct intervention of a counselor to achieve a basic need or solve a problem.

It is important to receive children with the sensitivity of phases one and two. Phase three of our approach enables the counselor to go beyond phases one and two and be more flexible and concrete in meeting the needs of children.

WHY CHILD-CENTERED COUNSELING?

In this section, the authors identify those objective and subjective reasons which have influenced them to support the theory and practice of child-centered counseling.

1. It possesses a positive philosophy of the person.

Client-centered counseling views the person as having basic impulses of love, belonging, and security which influence one to be cooperative, constructive, trustworthy, forward-moving, rational, socialized, and realistic. These human qualities tend to become actualized in environments which encourage their emergence and tend to be dormant in environments which repress them. Counseling, then, is the process of liberating a natural inclination in the child which has become repressed because of environmental influences. The counselor enables this positive inclination to emerge by creating a relationship which focuses on respect, the child's capacity for self-direction, and a prizing of the worth of each child (Patterson, 1980).

2. It articulates propositions regarding human personality and behavior.

These propositions regarding human personality and behavior (Rogers, 1951, pp. 483–524; Rogers, 1959, pp. 184–256) form the philosophic core of child-centered counseling and provide the counselor with a general conceptual framework for understanding human motivation and behavior. These propositions view the person as:

— being the best determiner of a personal reality
— behaving as an organized whole
— desiring to enhance the self
— goal-directed in satisfying perceived needs
— being behaviorally influenced by feelings which affect rationality
— best able to perceive the self
— being able to be aware of the self
— valuing
— interested in maintaining a positive self-concept
— behaving in ways that are consistent with the self-concept
— not owning behavior which is inconsistent with the self-concept
— producing psychological freedom or tension by admitting or not admitting certain experiences into the self-concept
— responding to psychosocial threat by becoming attitudinally and behaviorally rigid
— admitting into awareness experiences which are inconsistent with the self if the self is free from threat
— being more understanding of others if a well integrated self-concept exists
— moving from self defeating values toward self-sustaining values

We are attracted to a child-centered approach to counseling. We are congruent with its theory of human personality and behavior which serves as the foundation for the process of child-centered counseling.

3. It possesses achievable goals for the child.

The goals of child-centered counseling are very personalized and human goals *for the child* rather than being goals designed to simply support the theory, society, or its institutions; but in achieving these personalized goals, the child will behave in ways that contribute to the well-being of society and its institutions (Ellinwood, 1989). Although the goals of child-centered counseling are general, they are interpreted and translated by the individual child within the process of counseling and can become applicable to the child's life outside of counseling. Child-centered counseling is aimed at helping the child to:

— engage in behavior which liberates, actualizes, and enhances the self
— engage in the discovery of previously denied feelings and attitudes
— become more acceptant and trustful of the self
— engage in self-assessment
— engage in reorganizing the self
— become more self-reliant
— become more responsible for the self
— engage in self-determined choices, decisions, and solutions
— achieve individuality while being conscious of social responsibilities
— becomes sensitive to the process of becoming a person which involves a new and self actualizing way of being.

Our experience as counselors indicates that these goals represent a process which can bring the child closer to an optimum level of psychological wholeness and stability. We have experienced children achieving these goals in proportion to the quality of the child-centered counseling relationship.

4. It possesses a definition of the counselor's role within the counseling relationship.

The counselor's child-centered attitude finds its expression in the following behaviors. The counselor is understanding, liberal, acceptant, empathic, a sensitive listener, authentic, and possesses a sense of involvent while equalizing the relationship.

The authors add the term "concrete" (Carkhuff & Berenson, 1977), to the preceding desired counselor behaviors because in our child-centered viewpoint, after the therapeutic relationship has been established and developed in phases one and two, the counselor is able to move toward phase three procedures which are specifically related to the needs of the individual child. These phase three procedures are typically more concrete and represent an individualization of the counseling process. This coincides with the experiential third period (1957 to present) in the historic evaluation of client-centered thinking (Hart, 1970; Corey, 1991).

While identifying the necessary counselor behaviors for effective counseling, the child-centered viewpoint also indicates counselor behaviors which must be avoided. The counselor is not a moralist, questioner, or diagnostician.

An enlightening aspect of child-centered counseling is that it defines the counselor's role in terms of attitudes and behaviors which will both facilitate and inhibit the child's progress in counseling. The authors' experience as counselors confirms that when we exhibited the desired counselor attitudes and behaviors our counseling was beneficial to children. When we exhibited undesirable attitudes and behaviors the outcome was to inhibit the child's progress.

In the third phase of child-centered counseling, the counselor tends to be more concrete and open to personal reactions to the child and is more comfortable in expressing these reactions; but these reactions are always focused on the person-centered needs of the child rather than being expressions of the needs of the counselor to be a moralist, questioner, or diagnostician.

5. It has research evidence supporting its effectiveness.

Any theory of counseling must satisfy the requirements of being both an art and a science by possessing both qualitative and quantitative research evidence which confirms the effectiveness of the theory. In this area, client-centered counseling does not disappoint. It does possess the desired research evidence which supports its effectiveness. In fact, it goes far beyond the requirements in this area. Patterson (1980) and Corey (1991) conclude that the client-centered approach has generated, and is supported by a greater amount of research than any other approach to counseling and psychotherapy.

From our own investigations and research into the effectiveness of client-centered counseling (Arbuckle & Boy, 1961; Boy & Pine, 1963; Boy & Pine, 1968), its application to learner-centered teaching (Pine & Boy, 1977), and its influence on fostering psychosocial development (Boy & Pine, 1988), plus the far more voluminous investigations and research of others, we feel that client-centered counseling has more than met its obligation to have its effectiveness supported by research evidence.

6. It is comprehensive.

Client-centered counseling has the substance needed to be applied beyond the one-to-one counseling relationship. The comprehensive nature of the client-centered view is evident in its application to teaching, organizational behavior, family relationships, parenting, groups, marriage and its alternatives, leadership, pastoring, and the process of peaceful communication between and among nations.

Another indication of its comprehensiveness is that client-centered counseling can be applied to "normals," "neurotics," and "psychotics" (Corey, 1991). The comprehensiveness of client-centered counseling enables it to be applied in a variety of settings which deal with a wide range of human problems: elementary, middle, and high schools; mental health centers; colleges and universities; rehabilitation agencies; prisons and halfway houses; pastoral counseling centers; marriage and family centers; human development centers; employment service agencies; youth centers; and religious seminaries.

The depth and range of the client-centered viewpoint enables it to be applied in any agency which deals with human problems. In the lives of the authors we have been able to apply it to our individual and group counseling, consultation, staff relations, teaching, family living, friendships, administrative functions, and interpersonal relationships, in general. Whenever it has been well applied we were in attitudinal and behavioral congruence with the philosophy and process of client-centered counseling. Whenever we stumbled or failed it was because we were detached from its philosophic and process cores. We do sense, however, that the client-centered theory has the necessary comprehensiveness to be applied even further in interpersonal relations that have yet to be identified.

7. It can be applied.

Child-centered counseling is clear and precise enough so that it can be applied. At the process level, the counselor's reflections of the child's feelings is an understandable concept that is applicable in proportion to the counselor's grasp of *why* it is done and *how* such reflections contribute to the child's self-awareness. The authors see no difficulty in applying child-centered counseling when the counselor is *attitudinally* child-centered. When a counselor is not *attitudinally* child-centered then that counselor has difficulty in intellectually absorbing, and applying, the reflective process. Such a counselor typically repeats the surface content of what the child is saying rather than reflecting the feelings behind the surface content. When the counselor repeats the surface content the results are innocuous and the counselor eliminates the therapeutic potential of child-centered counseling.

To the authors, the process of reflecting feelings appears simple on the surface while actually being quite complex. A counselor's ability to accurately reflect feelings depends upon the counselor's ability to read and absorb those feelings, the ability to accurately represent those feelings back to the child, and a vocabulary which is sensitive to the child's world of feelings and which can reflect a core feeling in a number of descriptive ways. And once again, the quality and depth of a counselor's reflections are proportional to the degree to which the counselor is *attitudinally* child-centered.

The third phase of child-centered counseling has utility in proportion to the quality of phases one and two. If phases one and two are based on qualitative interactions between the child and the counselor, then phase three is a natural sequence of events; phase three flows easily and well from phases one and two because these phases were qualitative and, hence, effective.

The only potential problem in our concept of phase three is the possibility that the counselor's needs for domination, moralization, or righteousness could influence the counselor's phase three procedures. The result could be the creation of a forum for the counselor's expression of personal ideologies and needs rather than the development of a phase three which meets the needs of the child. But once again, this will not occur in phase three when the counselor is *attitudinally and reflectively* child-centered.

Our experience in the preparation of counselors for employment in a variety of settings indicates that our concept of child-centered counseling is both teachable and applicable. It becomes teachable and applicable in proportion to our modeling of the attitudes and behaviors which characterize child-centered counseling.

8. It has an expansive intellectual and attitudinal substance.

Intellectually, client-centered counseling keeps us alert to better understanding its philosophy, process, goals, and outcomes. On some days there are rays of intellectual insight which give a wholeness to the viewpoint. On other days, a personal experience, or the reading or experiencing of another very different viewpoint, cause us to wonder about the viability of client-centeredness. From these insights and uncertainties emerges a clarity or synthesis which serves to energize our intellectual understanding. We are always alert to, and challenged by, the ability of client-centeredness to be intellectually stimulating. It possesses an intellectual *gravitas* which can sometimes exceed our grasp but we appreciate the viewpoint's ability to keep our brain cells excited.

Another intellectually stimulating aspect of client-centeredness is its connection with other past and present systems of thought. The writings of existentialists, humanists, phenomenologists, theists, rationalists, and politicians take on a clarity because we have a point of reference—the client-centered viewpoint—from which to better understand these views. Without this point of reference our understanding would be superficial, partial, and segmented.

Attitudinally, client-centeredness gives us a process structure by which our caring tendencies can be expressed. Those who possess a caring attitude toward others often have difficulty in identifying a career or role by which that caring can be expressed. Client-centeredness appears to be the bridge which connects our caring to the real world of human problems; it enables us to express values which deal with truth, honesty, beauty, justice, love, human rights, and peace. The congruence between client-centered counseling and these tendencies give a fuller meaning to both.

9. It focuses on the child as a person rather than on the child's problem.

In terms of the philosophy, process, and goals of client-centered counseling, it has much to say about the person and the improvement of the human condition. It is person-centered rather than problem-centered. It focuses on *the child as a person* rather than on the client's problem, and this, to us, is where the focus should be.

When the counselor is able to assist a child to become a more adequate and better functioning person, this improvement will enable the child to solve and resolve both current and future problems. When the child is psychologically stable, that child is able to deal with problems because that stability produces the insight needed to develop solutions. Psychological stability produces the insights and behaviors needed to deal with specific problems (Ellinwood, 1989).

Since child-centered counseling focuses on the child rather than the problem, it possesses a deeper potential for assisting a child to become more adequate, *as a person*, in dealing with a range of problems. When the child becomes more psychologically stable, the child is more free to deal with, and find solutions to, specific problems.

10. It focuses on the importance of the counselor's attitude.

The counselor's facilitative attitude flows from the personhood of the counselor. If we desire children to develop themselves as persons then we must also expect the counselor to do the same if the counselor is to be influential in affecting behavioral change among children. We cannot expect the child to become better functioning if the counselor does not model attitudes which encourage these behaviors to emerge from the child.

The personhood of the counselor, when expressed through a qualitative counseling relationship, becomes the primary influence on the child's cooperation in the counseling process. Counseling theories have neglected to focus on the therapeutic influence of the counselor as a person. They have instead influenced the development of mechanical techniques to induce behavioral change. These techniques can sometimes be useful if they are used *as an adjunct* to the personhood of the counselor. In too many cases, however, such techniques are the core of the counseling process and the therapeutic influence of the *counselor as a person* is neglected.

If one listens to children describe how a counselor has helped them, one will hear the counselor's personhood as the *fundamental influence* rather than the techniques which the counselor used.

11. It provides the counselor with a systematic response pattern.

Most theories of counseling make insightful statements regarding their philosophy, goals, process, and outcomes. Their philosophic, goal-oriented, and outcome statements are noble and sometimes border on the poetic when describing the human condition and its improvement. Other counseling theories do not provide the counselor with a systematic response pattern which will induce the client to gain insight and improve behavior. These theories address themselves to the "why" of counseling but provide the counselor with little regarding the process or "how" of counseling.

Child-centered counseling presents the most clear and well defined response pattern to guide the child-centered counselor in the process of counseling: reflecting the child's feelings. This response pattern enables the counselor to assimilate and absorb the child's perceptions, values, and attitudes; it enables the child to develop an awareness of how these perceptions, values, and attitudes affect the child's behavior; it enables the child to perceive the counselor as a caring person who is able to understand the child and the child's problem from the child's viewpoint; it frees the child to disclose information which the child was not able to share in other interpersonal relationships; and it serves to establish a bond of trust between the child and the counselor.

Although reflecting the child's feelings may be sufficient and effective throughout a counseling relationship, the third phase of child-centered counseling enables the counselor to go beyond reflecting feelings *when doing this more adequately meets the needs of child clients.*

Further, if this process change does not produce results, the counselor is able to return to reflecting the child's feelings.

Reflecting the child's feelings, then, affords the counselor with a systematic response pattern which serves as the core of the counselor's responses in phase two of child-centered counseling but is not the only response pattern available to the counselor in phase three.

12. It provides flexibility for the counselor to go beyond reflection of feelings.

In the second historic period of client-centered counseling, perhaps some child-centered counselors were in a verbal straight jacket when they only reflected the child's feelings. During this period, however, other child-centered counselors felt comfortable with reflecting the child's feelings and saw evidence that such a process was effective.

The authors believe in, and have continually experienced, the therapeutic effectiveness of reflecting feelings. Reflecting the child's feelings does not have to be bland; the process can be lively, penetrating, and expanding in proportion to the counselor's ability to read feelings and the counselor's disciplined commitment to the process. A pure reflection of the child's feelings does possess therapeutic impact. It prompts the child to investigate previously denied feelings and bring them into conscious awareness.

In the third historic period of client-centered counseling, counselors went beyond merely reflecting the client's feelings if doing that was needed. In our concept of child-centered counseling the counselor has four choices in phase three. The counselor can continue to engage in pure reflections of feelings if doing this best meets the needs of the child, (2) the counselor can make additives (Turock, 1978) to basic reflections of feelings if doing this best meets the therapeutic needs of the child, (3) the counselor can incorporate techniques from nonclient-centered theories of counseling if doing this best meets the therapeutic needs of the child, and (4) the counselor can make a natural and responsible judgment to do something natural, intuitive, and eclectic, if this best meets the therapeutic needs of the child.

Child-centered counseling is not a set of static and hardened principles of application. It gives the counselor a high degree of flexibility if one is willing to absorb the implications of what it means to be *child-centered*. The child-centered counselor's behavior is within the bounds of the theory when it is child-centered *and* meets the needs of the child. The counselor's behavior is outside the bounds of the theory and is *counselor-centered* when it instead meets the needs of the counselor.

13. It can be individualized according to the particular needs of a child.

Child-centered counseling's third phase flexibility enables it to be tailored to the needs of the individual child. It has the malleability to be shaped toward a child's unique needs. Phase three enables the process to fit the child rather than forcing the child into a predetermined process.

Some children can be manipulated by the requirements of a theory. If a theory requires that children behave realistically then children must be molded to behave realistically; if a theory sees problems rooted in the child's experiences with parents then the child must be prompted to talk about these experiences; and if a theory postulates that repressed anger is the cause of a child's problem then the child must be confronted in order to release that anger. Counseling according to a narrow theoretical bias can result in a particular theory being thrust on all children regardless of their individualized needs or problems. The child whose problem is far from the need to be realistic is molded to be realistic; the child with an interpersonal relationship problem with peers, which is far removed from the child's relationship with parents, is prompted to delve into the relationship with parents; the child whose problem is far removed from the need to express anger is confronted to release a nonexistent anger.

The flexibility of the child-centered approach enables it to be individualized according to the needs of the child in phase three. The theory has no grandiose concepts which the counselor imposes on children. What the theory does require is the development of a relationship in which *the child* can identify the problem and a relationship in which *the child* can choose the behaviors that will enable the problem to be solved. A child-centered relationship is an open and flexible relationship because the child is the one who determines the scope and depth of a problem, and once this has occurred, the child is in the best position to explicitly or implicitly identify the process for solving the problem. Such an individualization of counseling enables child-centeredness to be a highly accurate approach in its ability to be congruent with the needs of children.

14. It enables a child's behavior to change in a natural sequence.

A child who enters a counseling relationship typically has an interpersonal communication problem with a person or persons in their lives. The cause of the problem is usually an inability to communicate feelings. As a result, a number of negative feelings become repressed and this repression often produces tension, behavioral confusion, and physical symptoms.

In phases one and two of child-centered counseling, the counselor establishes a relationship with the child in which these repressed feelings can be released. In phase two the counselor accomplishes this by reflecting whatever feelings the child may present. If the counselor's reflections are accurate the child becomes more comfortable in the relationship and describes these feelings more deeply.

Once a child has fully expressed repressed feelings (because of phases one and two) the child's natural inclination is to seek a solution to the problem which initiated counseling. At this stage the child no longer has feelings which need to be released. The child is, therefore, ready to develop a rational solution to the problem. Because the child is no longer frustrated by feelings, the child can begin to work toward an objective solution. The child's intellect, previously clouded by emotions, is now free to function clearly and move toward a rational solution. All persons are both emotional and rational and problems often develop because our emotions overpower our ability to think. Once we have expressed our emotions, we free our intellect to function clearly and bring us to a reasonable solution.

In child-centered counseling the counselor can follow this natural sequence of events by basically reflecting the child's feelings in phase two. As the child becomes more rational the counselor can begin to respond to the child's needs by using more rational and objective responses in phase three.

An important aspect of effective counseling, regardless of theory, is that a counselor should respond affectively to an emotionally burdened child and rationally to a child who communicates rationally. Child-centered counseling indicates that children are generally emotional at the beginning and middle stages of counseling (phases one and two), and are more rational during the later stages of counseling (phase three), in proportion to the quality of phases one and two.

15. It can draw from the process components of other theories of counseling and child development.

As was indicated earlier, in phase three of child-centered counseling, the counselor has four basic response patterns for meeting the individualized needs of children: (1) a continuation of reflecting the child's feelings started in phase one, (2) making additives to reflections of feelings, (3) incorporate techniques from nonchild-centered theories of counseling, and (4) make a natural and responsible judgment to do something intuitive if this best meets the therapeutic needs of the child.

We wish to emphasize that in phase three, the child-centered counselor can use procedures suggested by other theories when they meet the needs of the individual child. A child-centered counselor does not have to believe in the philosophy of another theory in order to use procedures from that theory.

It appears that child-centered counseling has failed to develop such techniques because these techniques have been traditionally inamicable with the relationship centered philosophy of client-centered counseling; namely, that the *relationship itself,* if of sufficient quality, can influence behavioral change on the part of the client.

Such closed mindedness on the part of some child-centered counselors has resulted in the theory not developing a useable set of techniques. The one exception being the counselor's reflecting of the child's feelings, which some do classify as a technique. Since the child-centered approach is basically without techniques and relies more on the counseling relationship itself as the vehicle for behavioral change, the counselor who is at phase three of child-centered counseling must look to other theories in order to identify useable techniques such as role playing, fantasizing, desensitization, goal identification, modeling, encouragement, and confrontation. But if the child-centered relationship developed in phases one and two is of sufficient quality, the counselor should be able to utilize modified versions of these techniques in phase three. The essential criterion in selecting a phase three technique is the degree to which it will be helpful in meeting the individualized needs of the child (Thompson and Rudolph, 1992).

In phase three of child-centered counseling the counselor is also able to make a natural and responsible judgment to do something intuitive if this best meets the therapeutic needs of the child. This judgment may prompt the counselor to utilize the techniques and process components of play therapy, art therapy, music therapy, or recreational therapy if techniques associated with these therapies have the capacity to meet the individualized needs of children.

The counselor's phase three process judgment can also be concrete and based upon common sense as in the following illustration. A counselor had counseled a preadolescent female client on a weekly basis for about nine months. The client had a poor self-concept and felt that she was physically unattractive and unable to feel comfortable in her relationships with peers. The client became isolated, lonely, shy, and depressed. The counselor responded to her feelings by reflecting those feelings and although the client felt close to the counselor and appreciated the counselor's genuineness and warmth, there was no improvement in her self-concept and, hence, no improvement in her behavior. As the counseling relationship developed the counselor became more sensitive to the potential influence of the client's decayed and broken teeth on her self concept. The client eventually progressed beyond her presenting problem and began to express negative feelings about her teeth. The counselor made an intuitive common sense judgment that her poor self-concept was due to the condition of her teeth. Since the client had no finances and came from an economically deprived family, she felt that she was forever doomed to carry a negative self-concept and become more introverted.

The counselor decided to intervene by telephoning a local school of dentistry and inquiring about the possibility of free dental work for the client. The dental school was cooperative, and, with the consent of the client and her parents, the counselor arranged a series of visits for the client to the school's dental clinic which was staffed by dental interns. After the client completed her dental work, there was a dramatic improvement in her self-concept. She became friendly and gregarious and was no longer isolated, shy, and depressed. Her improved teeth gave her confidence in meeting people and she became confident and alive.

The counselor in this case might not ever have helped the client develop a positive self concept by using standard child-centered procedures. Instead, the counselor made a direct intuitive judgment which produced a dramatic improvement in the client's self-concept.

Such intuitive interventions can be introduced in phase three when the child-centered counselor is flexible enough to match the helping process with the individualized needs of clients.

In summary, we believe that an effective child-centered counselor both believes and doubts. Within the framework of our concept of child-centered counseling there is much that is applicable; but there are certain other aspects of the viewpoint which we must be willing to doubt in order to shed new light on the process of helping children through counseling. A competent counselor believes in a theory but also maintains a tentativeness regarding the theory and its application. This cautious attitude is necessary in order to shape a theory to meet the individualized needs of children rather than shaping clients to meet the needs of a theory (Bohart & Todd, 1988).

The flexibility needed by a counselor is aptly represented by the following two historic statements:

> No scientific investigation is final; it merely represents the most probable conclusion which can be drawn from the data at the disposal of the writer. A wider range of facts or more refined analysis, experiment, and observation will lead to new formulas and new theories. This is the essence of scientific progress (Pearson, 1897).

and

> Knowledge progresses by stages, so that the theory one holds today must be provisional, as much a formulation of one's ignorance as anything else, to be used as long as it is useful and then discarded. Its function is to organize the available evidence. It is really a working assumption which the user may actively disbelieve (Hebb, 1958).

REFERENCES

Arbuckle, D. S., & Boy, A. V. (1961). Client-centered therapy in counseling students with behavior problems. *Journal of Counseling Psychology,* 8, 136–139.

Bohart, A. C., & Todd, J. (1988). *Foundations of clinical and counseling psychology.* New York: Harper and Row.

Boy, A. V., & Pine, G. J. (1963). *Client-centered counseling in the secondary school.* Boston: Houghton Mifflin.

Boy, A. V., & Pine, G. J. (1968). *The counselor in the schools: A reconceptualization.* Boston: Houghton Mifflin.

Boy, A. V., & Pine, G. J. (1988). *Fostering psychosocial development in the classroom.* Springfield, IL: Charles C Thomas.

Brown, D., & Srebalus, D. J. (1988). *An introduction to the counseling profession.* Englewood Cliffs, NJ: Prentice-Hall.

Carkhuff, R. R., & Berenson, B. G. (1977). *Beyond counseling and therapy.* (2nd ed.). New York: Holt, Rinehart, and Winston.

Corey, G. (1991). *Theory and practice in counseling and psychotherapy.* (4th Ed). Monterey, CA: Brooks/Cole.

Corsini, R. (1984). *Current psychotherapies.* (3rd ed.). Itasca, IL: F. E. Peacock.

Ellinwood, C. (1989). The young child in person-centered therapy. *Person-Centered Review,* 4(3), 256–262.

Hart, J. (1970). The development of client-centered therapy. In J. T. Hart, & T. M. Tomlinson (Eds.), *New directions in client-centered therapy.* Boston: Houghton Mifflin.

Hebb, D. O. (1958). *A textbook of psychology.* Philadelphia, PA: Saunders.

Patterson, C. H. (1980). *Theories of counseling and psychotherapy.* (3rd ed.). New York: Harper and Row.

Pearson, K. (1897). *The chance of death and other studies in evolution.* London: E. Arnold.

Pine, G. J., & Boy, A. V. (1977). *Learner-centered teaching: A humanistic view.* Denver, CO: Love.

Rogers, C. R. (1942). *Counseling and psychotherapy.* Boston: Houghton Mifflin.

Rogers, C. R. (1951). *Client-centered therapy.* Boston: Houghton Mifflin. (Renewed 1979)

Rogers, C. R. (1961). *On becoming a person.* Boston: Houghton Mifflin.

Rogers, C. R. (1970). *On encounter groups.* New York: Harper and Row.

Rogers, C. R. (1975). Empathic: An unappreciated way of being. *Counseling Psychologist,* 5, 2–10.

Rogers, C. R., & Wood, J. (1974). Client-centered theory: Carl Rogers. In A. Burton (Ed.), *Operational theories of personality.* New York: Bruner/Mazel.

Rogers, C. R. (1977). *On personal power.* New York: Delacorte.

Rogers, C. R., & Dymond, R. F. (1978). *Psychotherapy and personality change.* Chicago: University of Chicago Press.

Rogers, C. R. (1980). *A way of being.* Boston: Houghton Mifflin.

Rogers, C. R., & Meador, B. (1984). Client-centered therapy. In R. Corsini (Ed.), *Current psychotherapies.* (3rd ed.). Itasca, IL: F. E. Peacock.

Thompson, C. L., & Rudolph, L. B. (1992). *Counseling children.* Pacific Grove, CA: Brooks/Cole.

Turok, A. (1978). Effective challenging through additive empathy. *Personnel and Guidance Journal,* 57, 144–149.

Wexler, D. A., & Rice, L. N. (Eds.). (1974). *Innovations in client-centered therapy.* New York: John Wiley and Sons.

Chapter 2

CHILD-CENTERED COUNSELING
AS A THREE-PHASE PROCESS

The authors see child-centered counseling as a three-phase process. In phase one the counselor works to develop caring and helpful human qualities that can be sensed by the client. In phase two the counselor is attentive to the client's feelings and reflects those feelings back to the client so that the client will come to better know those feelings which are influencing behavior. In phase three the counselor can continue the reflective process started in phase two if it is working, can use procedures from other theories or can make a common sense judgment regarding how best to help the client.

PHASE ONE: A PROFILE OF
FACILITATIVE COUNSELOR ATTITUDES

The following phase one counselor attitudes are fundamental. They need to be present in phase one of counseling if phases two and three are to be successful. They need to be identified and become part of the counselor's personhood if counseling is to be effective. In a society which insists on becoming more hurried, mechanical, and superficial, they represent human qualities which need to be preserved by those committed to child-centered counseling. The first phase of child-centered counseling requires the counselor to own attitudes which will influence the degree to which phases two and three are effective. For some counselors, the acquisition of these attitudes will require fundamental attitudinal changes. For others, their acquisition will mean consciously nourishing some basic human qualities which have always sought to be expressed. They represent where the counselor begins if he or she expects counseling to be effective in phases two and three.

Empathy

Empathy occurs when the counselor is emotionally congruent with the feelings of a child (Rogers, 1975; Egan, 1973; Bergin & Garfield, 1985). An empathic attitude enables the counselor to feel the pain, the sorrow, the disgrace, the rejection that the child has felt. It is the placing of one human spirit within another so that there is an emotional congruence. The counselor must be selfless and not allow personal negative life experiences and problems to interfere with or influence the counseling relationship. The more selfless the counselor, the deeper the empathy. Empathy enables the counselor to experience the child's reactions. Instead of evaluating the accuracy of the child's feelings, the counselor experiences, however imperfectly, the same emotions and feelings as the child. To be emotionally close to a child's feelings and reactions enables the counselor to experience them from the child's viewpoint. A child-centered counselor knows that empathy can occur again and again in proportion to the counselor's willingness to enter the perceptual world of the child.

When counselors empathize with troubled children, they recognize that empathy as the core of the attitude needed to be a counselor. The counselor's sensitivity to the child's feelings enables the child to see the meaning and cause of those feelings. Counselors develop empathy when they diminish and eventually eliminate the intrusion of their own thinking when communicating with children in the first phase of counseling.

To be truly empathic, a counselor needs to be selfless. Selflessness requires a willingness to identify with the child's being so that the counselor can feel as the child feels rather than as the counselor might feel. This giving of self by the counselor is very real for the child client. The child senses that the counselor cares about learning about the child's problem from the child's viewpoint. The counselor who deeply penetrates the child's feelings will be respected by the child and will be regarded as possessing helping skills (Mock, 1982).

Acceptance

The counselor's acceptance of the child is another facilitating characteristic of a substantive relationship (Rogers, 1951; Polster & Polster, 1973; Boy & Pine, 1990). Acceptance means many things to many counselors, and even within a counselor it varies in degree. For one counselor acceptance may mean that as part of the counselor's work a certain number of children have to be seen; this counselor accepts children just as an accountant accepts numbers as part of being an accountant. For another counselor acceptance means that the counselor is in a full respectful contact with the child.

The latter counselor does not feel that the child is just another person. The child is an individual, unique among all others, and carrying a very special problem. The counselor receives whatever the child says without judgment. The counselor indicates to the child that no barriers exist between them simply by the counselor's acceptant attitude. The child can sense this counselor's acceptance, and the child, in turn, is willing to accept the counselor as a helper.

True acceptance is unaffected by the child's reputation or diagnostic label. It is unconditional. It does not depend upon the child behaving or communicating in a certain way, upon the child's family background, values, economic status, or intelligence. It is not dependent upon the child meeting certain moral, ethical, or behavioral criteria. It is unconditional.

Child-centered counselors put a heavy emphasis on the importance of an acceptant attitude. They know that without acceptance counseling cannot occur. They believe in this simple principle and understand that the helping process cannot occur unless one can be genuinely acceptant. The depth of true acceptance can be felt by a child. The child will have a positive response to the counseling process when the counselor possesses an acceptant attitude toward the child.

Genuineness

At the beginning of a counseling relationship, a child is typically unauthentic. The child will not become more authentic until he or she feels that the counselor can be trusted. Counseling becomes the process of the child moving away from unauthentic self-statements and moving toward more genuine self-statements. Troubled children live in a world where they have learned to engage in unauthentic patterns of response. They learn to speak the words that others expect to hear rather than to genuinely express feelings and attitudes. Such children have some difficulty in the beginning of counseling because of the tendency to be personally evasive rather than honest. It is a typical defense which enables the client to protect inner feelings which might not be acceptable to adults.

The child's movement toward genuineness is characteristic of successful counseling. The child moves from an unauthentic representation of the self to a more authentic self. The quality of the counseling relationship furnishes the child with the safety to take an uninhibited look at feelings and behavior. The counselor's authenticity produces authenticity in the child; and the child must achieve authenticity if counseling is to be successful.

The counselor's genuineness is imperative if the child is to achieve genuineness. If the counselor is truly genuine, the counselor engages in behaviors which express that genuineness. The authentic counselor feels compelled to express that authenticity rather than becoming involved in superficial and mechanical behaviors which contribute little to the relationship needed for successful counseling.

For many counselors a movement toward genuineness means discarding superficial and hollow attitudes and behaviors. When one takes a close look at the requirements of authenticity, one becomes involved in eliminating attitudes and behaviors which do not contribute to that authenticity. Philosopher Wild (1965) indicates this when he says:

> Authentic action is the expression of a very finite freedom. But it does not enslave us to norms that are externally imposed, since it takes them over, and lifts them up into a world of meaning that we have thought through and authorized for ourselves. There is a real sense in which these meaningful acts are mine. But they have not been laid down by an arbitrary decree, since they take account of the facts and make them meaningful precisely as they stand. Acts demanded of me by external norms, which I do not understand, are not mine. I am not the author of them. Hence they are unauthentic. Meanings which fail to take account of real conditions and existent facts make lasting action impossible. Hence they also are unauthentic—a hollow pretense and a sham (p. 77).

Rogers (1951) views the counselor's behavior as primarily an expression of personal authenticity. The counselor provides a substantive counseling relationship in which the counselor is: genuine (internally consistent); acceptant (prizing the client as a person of worth); and empathically understanding of the client's private world of feelings and attitudes.

Liberality

Liberality is a quality needed for an effective counseling relationship. The child must feel free to reveal innermost feelings without fear. In a truly liberal atmosphere the child can explore innermost feelings, sift them, accept them, or reject them. The child can run the gamut of feelings about persons and events in the child's life.

The counselor does not create this liberal atmosphere by telling the child that freedom of expression exists. If the child expresses anger the counselor does not block its expression. In a liberating atmosphere the child is not afraid to reveal feelings.

Counselors can interrupt the child's focus on feelings by asking questions. Such questions are usually only important to the counselor and carry little or no meaning for the child. The counselor may also steer the counseling session in a direction which the counselor thinks is best rather than allowing the child the freedom to choose the subject matter of counseling. If we accept the principle that each person knows the self better than anyone else, and is, therefore, in the best position to reveal and understand the self, we see that counselor direction of a counseling session is nonproductive. A counseling relationship based on the counselor's needs will produce superficial outcomes which make sense to the counselor but have no meaning for the child.

A child responds to a liberating atmosphere by exploring feelings with a depth that may not have been previously experienced. In effective counseling, children often have their first experience in gaining an awareness of themselves and why they behave in a particular way. Outside of counseling, children have been conditioned to hide their inner feelings. This seems to be a safer way to exist. Revealing feelings involves a risk. Children know this all too well.

The degree to which a counselor creates a liberating atmosphere is directly related to the degree of counselor security. The secure counselor enables children to engage in freedom of expression because the counselor is not threatened by what they may say or do. Less secure counselors inhibit the child's free expression, not just by words, but by a generally restrictive attitude. If the counselor is restless, embarrassed, angered, moralistic, or judgmental, the child will not disclose inner feelings.

A counselor's tightly guarded value system will often make the counselor insensitive to children whose values are quite different. The mark of an effective counselor is not the counselor's ability to deal with children who share the same values, but rather the ability to communicate with children who have values which are vastly different from the counselor's.

Involvement

The counselor's sense of presence is essentially a cognitive and visceral involvement—involvement with the child in the child's private perceptual world and with the child's struggle to become a more adequately functioning individual.

The counselor who achieves a sense of involvement is able to enter the child's attitudinal and behavioral life. This means more than sitting waiting for the child to pause so that the counselor may interject a judgment or moralization. It means to be attuned to the child's feelings— hopes, desires, frustrations, fears, defenses, anxieties—those feelings which make the child unique and different from any other person who has existed or will exist. The depth of this type of involvement demands a giving of self—a putting aside of one's ego needs and forming a counseling relationship which exists for the evolvement and development of the child (Bugental, 1978).

The ineffective counselor is unable to achieve a sense of involvement. Such a counselor introduces information from an external frame of reference, makes suggestions, supports or criticizes the child, or may ask irrelevant questions. Each of these responses detracts from the counselor's involvement. Whenever the counselor engages in such responses, the counselor diminishes the possibility of true involvement. Involvement for the child-centered counselor means feeling the child's feelings and responding to them. Such responses exclude the use of rehearsed and superficial remarks. In phase one of counseling, when the counselor is deeply present in the child's inner world of feelings and is not afraid to be there, it is impossible to retreat into a pattern of routine questioning and information gathering. To do so would indicate that the counselor is not really involved. When the counselor is deeply communicating with the child, the counselor's needs are all but lost because of the deep involvement with the needs of the child.

Becoming involved requires that the counselor attain such a deep level of communication that the counselor's own values and opinions are put aside and replaced with the process of understanding the child's values and opinions. Such a giving of self by the counselor is difficult because life has often taught us to be more interested in listening to ourselves than in listening to another person. We tend to be more interested in judging than in understanding. We tend to think that a child's psychological growth can be achieved only if it is guided by the omniscience of the counselor. Such attitudes make it difficult to be involved because they give more importance to the counselor's opinions than the needs of the child. In relationship building, when the counselor assumes an evaluative attitude, the counselor is in effect diminishing the possibility of receiving communication from the child. Evaluation requires a judgmental attitude toward the child. A sensitive counselor finds it impossible to be listening to the feelings of a child while at the same time evaluating the child. In a sense, the counselor attempting to do both communicates to the child that neither is taking place. Either the counselor is involved or the counselor is distant from the child because of the different requirements of an evaluative attitude. Child discomfort and early termination of counseling occurs when the child senses that the counselor has lost a sense of involvement. Such a loss occurs when the counselor loses contact with the child's internal frame of reference and reverts to the counselor's evaluative or external frame of reference.

Sensitive Listening

The counselor's ability to listen is often taken for granted. Certainly an effective counselor should be a good listener. But the requirements of *sensitive listening* are often more demanding than merely listening. Sensitive listening is nonevaluative listening. Listening to a news broadcast or a lecture is often partial listening; we listen with one ear, as it were, while structuring our opinion about what is being said. But sensitive listening requires the counselor to feel the child's emotions as if they were the counselor's own. The existential philosopher Marcel (1963) indicates this when he says:

> . . . there is a way of listening which is a way of giving and a way of listening which is a way of refusing (p. 40).

In describing the effective counselor, Maslow (1965) indicates his awareness to sensitive listening when he says that the counselor:

> . . . must be able to listen in the receiving rather than in the taking sense in order to hear what is actually said rather than what he expects to hear or demands to hear. He must not impose himself but rather let the words flow in upon him. Only so can their own shape and pattern be assimilated. Otherwise one hears only one's theories and expectations (p. 182).

The kind of listening we do while engaged in conversation with acquaintances and colleagues is often very superficial. We listen in a way, but we don't get the full message because we are still involved with ourselves. We all have encountered persons who look over our shoulder or glance around as we talk. They are indulging in social listening, which would have no value in a counseling relationship. The child wants the counselor's complete attention. A counselor who half listens, only waiting until the child takes a deep breath so that the counselor can get a point across, is not really listening; the counselor is tolerating the child's talk. The troubled child is aware of this and won't bother to respect or deepen the relationship.

Children who consider the counselor a poor listener will terminate the association unless, as in some situations, the counselor insists that the fruitless relationship continue. Too often this is the case. If the counselor has some sort of vested authority the child continues the relationship, fearful that terminating it will have an adverse effect.

Sensitive listening demands that the counselor not only hear the child's words but also the feelings behind the words. The words are important but the more hidden emotional tones and underlying feelings behind them are the focal point of the child-centered counselor's listening. Listening indicates to the child that the counselor cares and the caring counselor will be valued by the child.

Equalizing

Equalizing is the process whereby any human relationship is made more equal. That is, the relationship is brought into balance, accord, parity, or mutuality. Any human relationship which is equalized has the potential to be productive. Any human relationship which is unequalized has the potential to be nonproductive (Boy & Pine, 1976). An equalized counseling relationship is one in which the counselor is not dominant. The counselor and child engage each other at equal levels of authority in the helping process.

An effective marriage is basically equalized. Both marriage partners equally share rights and responsibilities and have developed an intuition regarding the process whereby the relationship is kept in balance. When this balance is struck, the marriage is a personally rewarding and a positive experience for both partners. When the relationship is not balanced, the groundwork is laid for the deterioration of that marriage.

When the relationship between labor and management is equalized, the work incentive and level of productivity is higher than when the relationship is unequalized. Both labor and management behave productively when there is a balance between the groups in their trust, positive regard, and concepts of justice.

When the relationship between and among nations is equalized there is a tendency toward peaceful coexistence. When the relationship between and among nations is not equalized there is a tendency toward distrust which can eventually lead to war. When nations are economically, territorially, politically, and militarily equalized, they possess the psychological security to deal with each other in an atmosphere of mutual trust.

In any human relationship, then, the equalizing principle is of paramount importance in the development of that relationship. Whether the relationship is between friends, worker and supervisor, genders, marriage partners, child and counselor, or nations, it is the equalizing principle which prompts the relationship to be productive.

Within any human relationship the process of equalization is the undergirding factor which serves as the catalyst for a substantive relationship. The concept of equalization is especially important in successful counseling. When children sense that their relationships with counselors are equalized, they can trust those relationships. This trust develops because children realize that they are respected coparticipants in counseling. The child feels accepted, understood, free, trusted, and motivated to communicate feelings honestly. The counselor is perceived as someone who is equally involved in the process and outcomes of the relationship. The child senses the cooperative quality of the relationship and there is no need to be evasive, defensive, or vague.

Once the counselor internalizes the importance of equalizing the counseling relationship the counselor can implement the following activities which can do much to equalize the counseling relationship.

Develop an awareness program to help children understand counseling.

Before a child enters counseling there is a desire to have an awareness of what to expect from that relationship. This is a very human attitude. Persons desire to know what they're getting into before they move ahead with any experience; and the counseling profession has an obligation to satisfy the child's right-to-know.

Satisfying the child's right-to-know can be achieved by counselors who develop an awareness program which introduces potential clients to what takes place in a counseling relationship. Through such a program the child is able to gain a vicarious sense of what to expect from the counselor. When children understand that what transpires in counseling is founded upon the principle of equalization, they will feel more comfortable with the counselor and the process. No child wants to be lessened as a person in counseling. Children want their human rights and integrity respected. An awareness program will help clients to be more receptive to the idea of counseling.

Involve clients voluntarily.

An equalized counseling relationship can more easily occur if the child is voluntarily involved. When children make the decision to voluntarily enter a counseling relationship, their personal sense of being an equal to the counselor is enhanced. A child who is voluntarily involved retains more personal rights than the child who is required to engage in counseling. The child intuitively knows this. In required counseling relationships, the child is usually less than cooperative because the child does not own the decision regarding whether or not to enter counseling. For this child, an involuntary association with the counselor will lead to an unequalized and nonproductive relationship which will especially interfere with progress during the second and third phases of counseling.

Forming voluntary relationships with children has become more difficult in an era in which the rate of referrals to counselors is increasing. This increase is due, in part, to the bureaucratizing of human services. The counselor must counterbalance this tendency by developing creative and child-centered awareness programs whereby children will be drawn to the voluntary use of a counseling service. A child's voluntary participation in counseling will do much to insure successful outcomes.

Demystify counseling.

If potential child clients perceive counseling to be a deep, dark, and mysterious experience with an authority figure, and if the counselor's attitude and behavior reinforces such perceptions, then any hope of equalizing the counseling relationship will be lost.

Through awareness programs, children should perceive counseling for what it is—an equalized human relationship between persons who invest themselves in the process of solving or resolving a human problem. Counseling is an understandable process and should be represented as such to children. They should see that counseling is not a threatening human relationship filled with counselor intrigue and power. The Freudian parenthood of counseling has done much to contribute to public myths about counseling. Children need to see counseling as a helpful human relationship in which their personhood will be treated with dignity and respect.

Develop a positive image of the counselor.

Children want to associate with counselors who possess human attitudes which contribute to their psychological growth. Children feel more comfortable with a counselor who has a reputation as a facilitative person.

In the name of professionalism, some counselors have inhibited the feeling of security on the part of children. They have been bureaucratic in their attitudes and behaviors and have been perceived by children as anything but facilitative. Awareness programs should cultivate an image of the counselor which is positive and encouraging. The counselor's general reputation will also be enhanced when the word-of-mouth messages transmitted in the community are positive. When a positive image of the counselor exists, children will be more easily drawn to the helpful potential of counseling.

Own attitudes and behaviors which increase the potential for equalizing the counseling relationship.

Some counselors assume too much power. They perceive themselves as being able to determine the child's proper attitudes and behaviors. Such counselors tip the relationship's balance of power toward themselves. When a counselor behaves this way, there is little hope that the child will perceive that he or she has much power in the relationship. Children, covertly or overtly, rebel against such a counselor because they sense that their personal rights and power are being eroded. They feel that they really can't communicate with the counselor because the counselor has fixed personal standards about how human beings should and should not behave.

In such an unequalized relationship, the child engages in a struggle to resist the counselor's power. When both the child and counselor engage in a power struggle, they place themselves in a win-lose position and the potential for a positive outcome becomes lost in the struggle. The counselor needs to be sensitive to the importance of creating an equalized relationship with the child and its contribution to successful outcomes. The desired equalization can be achieved when the counselor owns human attitudes and behaviors which are real to the child.

In summary, phase one of our concept of child-centered counseling rests upon the counselor's ownership of facilitative attitudes. These attitudes can't be manufactured. They cannot be built into the counselor's repertoire of skills and techniques. They must be developed over a period of time through the counselor's diligent involvement in the process of becoming more human. When these attitudes are owned and part of the counselor's way of being, their existence shows through to the client and the client becomes a cooperative participant in the second and third phases of child-centered counseling.

PHASE TWO: THE REFLECTIVE PROCESS

This section will present the most fundamental element of phase two of child-centered counseling: *reflection of feelings.* Through the reflective process, the counselor assimilates the psychosocial needs of the child, builds an affective and facilitative relationship, and lays the foundation for judging which process will best meet the needs of the child in phase three.

Reflection of feelings is a concept not well understood at the application level. Through this section we hope that it will be applied with more skill and accuracy. When applied well, reflection of feelings will enable the counselor to dramatically improve phase two of child-centered counseling. And as Hansen, Stevic, and Warner (1986) have indicated, reflection of feelings contributes to the basic requirements of all effective counseling.

Background for the reflective process.

Reflection of feelings has been traditionally used by many counselors and psychotherapists in their work with clients. It was first identified as a powerful therapeutic process in 1942 in the landmark book by Carl R. Rogers, *Counseling and Psychotherapy* (Rogers, 1942). This book was the foundation for the development of other humanistic concepts of counseling and it still serves as a fundamental viewpoint for the successful application of counseling. Through the years the process of reflecting feelings has also been applied to improving interpersonal communication in a variety of situations. Rogers recently identified its newest and most important application: as a foundation communication process which can lead to international understanding, so vital to harmony and peace among nations (Rogers, 1982).

Rogers (1942), in his first major contribution to our understanding of reflection of feelings, let us know that the process is not easy:

> Probably the most difficult skill to acquire in counseling is the art of being alert to and responding to the feeling which is being expressed (p. 133).

Rogers (1942) also helped us to understand that reflecting a feeling is not responding to the logical content of what a client is communicating.

> If the counselor is to accept these feelings, he must be prepared to respond, not to an intellectual content of what the person is saying, but to the feeling which underlies it (pp. 37–38).

In his second book, Rogers (1951) added to our understanding of the process of reflecting feelings by indicating that the counselor's function is to assume:

> ... the internal frame of reference of the client, to perceive the world as the client sees it, to perceive the client himself as he is seen by himself, to lay aside all perceptions from the external frame of reference while doing so, and to communicate something of this understanding to the client (p. 29).

Rogers (1951) elaborated further when he said:

> Essentially what the therapist attempts to do is to reconstruct the perceptual field of the individual, at the moment of expression, and to communicate this understanding with skill and sensitivity (p. 289). Rogers (1951) concluded that the counselor: ... tries to adopt the internal frame of reference of the other person, to perceive what the other person perceives, to understand what is in the central core of the speaker's conscious awareness—in a sense, to take the role of the other person (p. 352).

Why reflect feelings?

Brammer and Shostrom (1977) have identified the advantages accruing to the counseling process when the helper is able to successfully reflect the client's feelings. Their view is summarized as follows:

1. Reflection helps the individual to feel *deeply understood.*
2. The reflection technique helps to break the so-called neurotic cycle, often manifested in marital counseling and expressed by such phrases as, 'She won't understand me, and therefore I won't understand her.'
3. Reflection impresses clients with the inference that *feelings are causes of behavior.*
4. Reflection causes the *locus of evaluation* to be in the client.
5. Proper reflection gives ... the feeling that [the client] ... has the *power of choice.*
6. Reflection *clarifies the client's thinking so that* ... the situation [can be seen] more objectively.

7. . . . It helps communicate to the client the idea that *the counselor does not regard him (or her) as unique and different.* (The counselor is not shocked.)
8. Reflection helps clients to *examine their deep motives* (pp. 189–191).

An inner core of feelings contributes to our self-concept and it is our self-concept which influences us to think and behave as we do. If our inner feelings about ourselves are positive, then our self-concept will be positive. We'll think well of ourselves and have confidence that we can improve the quality of our psychosocial experiences. A positive self gives us a sense of personal power and decreases the possibility of being psychosocially victimized. On the other hand, a set of negative feelings about ourselves will produce a self-concept which feels powerless in its ability to control reactions to threatening psychosocial experiences. We then perceive ourselves as victims who have little or no control over what happens to us.

Feelings have an enormous impact upon our thinking and behavior. They form the critical core which influences our thinking and behavior. Therefore, in any effective counseling the client's inner world of feelings must be entered in order to understand what motivates the client's thinking and behavior.

The process of reflecting feelings is both an attitude toward the client and a learnable skill. As an attitude it emanates from an identification with the human principles of client-centered counseling. Rogers (1975) has indicated that when the counselor is deeply committed to respecting the client as a person, and believes in the client's capacity to improve and change, then the counselor forms a helping relationship characterized by an empathic understanding of the child's inner world of feelings. From an attitude of empathy the counselor easily moves toward the skill of reflecting feelings since the skill is a natural extension of an empathic attitude. Once the reflective process is understood and learned, its application occurs in a natural, human, and facilitative manner, and it flows easily. If the counselor is attitudinally empathic then the ability to reflect feelings is not awkward. It is a way of entering the child's inner world of feelings, feelings that influence the child's behavior. Being attitudinally empathic and caring makes reflecting feelings a natural process.

A counselor without a commitment to the importance of empathy and caring, can still use the reflective process. It can be used as a therapeutic technique or skill rather than as a natural application of one's empathic and caring attitude. As a technique, the reflective process will lose some of its helping potential, but it will still work. The child will have a better response to its empathic application but the child will still respond well to its application as a technique. It will serve either helper well. It will not only facilitate the building of a counseling relationship, but the reflective process will also enable the counselor to learn about the child's inner world of feelings and perceptions which have contributed to the development of a problem. Reflecting the child's feelings, then, produces two clear results. It enables the helping relationship to develop while at the same time enabling the counselor to learn about those feelings which influence the child's behavior.

CONDITIONS FOR REFLECTING FEELINGS

In order for feelings to be reflected well, certain conditions must first be met. The effectiveness of the reflective process occurs in proportion to the existence of these conditions. If they exist maximally, then the counselor is able to apply the reflective process in a natural way. If these conditions exist minimally, then the reflective process loses its potential to be effective (Boy & Pine, 1988).

Be convinced that the child has the power to change.

Reflecting feelings occurs well when the counselor is convinced that the child has the capacity to change feelings and behavior. When the counselor is convinced of this, the reflective process is applied because of the conviction that it will produce positive results. The child will change. The child needs to feel the stimulus of the reflective process in order to talk about those feelings which are influencing behavior. Once the child realizes the contribution of these feelings to one's behavior, the child is in a position to do something about that behavior; and changing one's behavior will mean that the child needs to change the feelings which cause the behavior. Understanding and improving those feelings is the catalyst for understanding and improving one's behavior.

Be convinced that feelings influence thinking and behavior.

Once the counselor realizes the powerful influence of the child's feelings upon behavior, the counselor becomes committed to utilizing reflection of feelings as a process for helping the child get in touch with those feelings. Once the child becomes sensitive to how feelings influence behavior, the child can begin to change those feelings; and once those feelings change, the child's behavior will also change, much like a chain reaction.

In order for the counselor to be sensitive to feelings, two pitfalls must be avoided. The first is the temptation to be an analyst; the tendency to try to analyze the child's feelings and put them in some known diagnostic framework and attempt to explain the meaning of these feelings to the child. The second is the temptation to be solution-oriented, to listen to and reflect the child's feelings for a while and then revert to offering the child a solution to the problem. Both temptations are indicative of our natural desire to want to do something to help the child, but doing either or both will interfere with the child's ownership of how one's feelings are affecting one's behavior. This realization puts the child in control of doing something about these feelings rather than waiting for someone else to solve the child's problems. Self-resolution of a problem is deep and long-lasting. Resolution by others is superficial and short-term.

Be aware of the veracity of the client's presenting problem.

Too many counselors listen to the child's presenting problem and quickly begin to work on that problem and its solution. Even if a solution is developed that appears reasonable, the problem solved is often superficial. Children, and all clients, tend to begin a counseling relationship with superficial concerns. They try to present themselves as reasonable people who don't possess serious problems. They typically talk about a class "D" problem. They sometimes do this because all they're aware of is the class "D" problem. The counselor who quickly responds and begins helping the child with the class "D" problem may appear to be efficient. In reality, however, this child has not been given the opportunity to move beyond a class "D" problem toward a class "A" problem. The counselor moved so quickly toward responding to the class "D" problem that the child doesn't have the time to consider that a class "A" problem exists.

Experienced counselors realize that what the child talks about in the early sessions of counseling is not what is talked about in the middle or later sessions. Children, and all clients, need a period of time to warm up, to feel comfortable with the counseling process. After they have warmed up, they feel comfortable enough to talk about more serious class "A" problems. Other children don't realize that they have a class "A" problem until they're well into a counseling relationship. As they begin to peel back layers of feelings, they typically go from class "D" to "C" to

"B" to "A" problems. It takes time for a child to get in touch with feelings which affect behavior; especially those feelings which are repressed.

Be especially empathic.

In the phase one section of this chapter, a number of counselor attitudes are identified that are critically important if the second and third phases of child-centered counseling are to be successful. From these attitudes, one, empathy, is identified by Rogers (1975) as being the most important. The genuinely empathic counselor is best able to enter the deeper recesses of a child's world of feelings. Empathy is that quality which enables a counselor to feel, just as deeply as the child, the very same feelings that the child is feeling (Gordon, 1980). A counselor cannot do this as well when the reflective process is mechanically applied as a technique. As a technique, there is some penetration of the child's inner world of feelings but the penetration is superficial when compared to what the child experiences with a counselor who is also attitudinally empathic (Rogers, 1975).

The attitudinally empathic counselor penetrates the child's feelings more deeply because the reflective process is being used in a natural rather than a mechanical manner. What to say next is not difficult for the empathic counselor. And what is reflectively said is congruent with what the child is feeling and prompts the client to examine those feelings with greater care.

Empathy is at the core of the counselor's humanness. Reflecting the child's feelings is the process for expressing that empathy. All counselors consider themselves to be empathic, to a degree. Feeling empathy is one thing, expressing empathy is another. Empathy expressed within the disciplined framework of the reflective process enables the counselor to steadily express that empathy in a way that is known to the child. Feeling empathic toward the child without a vehicle, reflecting feelings, for consistently expressing that empathy leaves the counselor frustrated. The empathy is not expressed and its therapeutic potential lies dormant. Empathy toward the child needs a vehicle for its expression, and the most scientifically accurate and humanistic vehicle for its expression is the reflective process.

Possess an affective vocabulary.

Many counselors who are attitudinally empathic and understand the reflective process still experience difficulty in expressing that empathy.

This is a simple technical problem that can be overcome by expanding one's affective vocabulary.

Most people have reasonable vocabularies. We can easily discuss, clarify, and reach conclusions about a rational topic. Schools, families, and society have trained us to do this reasonably well. We do, however, have difficulty in expressing affect or feelings. Schools, families, and society have been deficient in expanding our affective vocabularies. Perhaps not purposely deficient but deficient all the same. So much of life is concrete that we become conditioned to use words and phrases which represent that concrete reality. To many, the vagueness of feelings prompts us not to have much experience in using words which accurately describe feelings. We prefer to use concrete words since they appear to describe a precise reality. We tend not to use abstract words, the words which convey feelings, simply because such words often sound vague.

The counselor who expects to reflect feelings well, however, must devote time and energy to expanding one's affective vocabulary since the possession of such a vocabulary will facilitate the process of reflecting feelings. Danish, D'Augelli, and Hauer (1980) have produced a list of 377 words designed to help expand one's affective vocabulary (p. 40–42). Some time spent with such a list will improve the counselor's ability to reflect feelings.

Be patient with the reflective process.

Some counselors have said, "I tried the reflective process and gave it up. It didn't work." The authors' observation is that the process will work if the counselor gives it the time to work. You can't expect to apply reflection of feelings for ten minutes and see magnificent results. You must patiently and steadily apply it over a series of meetings before the process begins to produce results. It takes time to apply the reflective process and it takes time for the child to respond to the process.

We live in a society in which "doing it quickly" is too often the goal. We are surrounded by fast food enterprises, microwave ovens, jet travel, quick divorces, and computers that promise to process information more quickly than their competitors. If we apply this attitude of quickness to reflecting feelings, then the process will fail. Reflection of feelings requires the utmost of patience in steadily applying it and making it work. There are no short-cuts, gimmicks, or tricks which will speed up the process. It takes time to do it well. The outcomes of its application are more than well worth the effort.

The time required to reflect feelings well and produce results should not be surprising if one looks at the typical problems possessed by children. They didn't develop yesterday or the day before. The problems have developed over a period of time. It seems logical, then, that time will also be needed in order for the child to identify the cause of a problem and the best way to solve it. A child's problem that has developed over a period of two years will not be resolved by a counselor in one reflective counseling session.

THE PROCESS OF REFLECTING FEELINGS

Once the counselor has internalized the preceding conditions for reflecting feelings, the process can begin. These conditions alert the counselor to focus on the feelings of the child. The process cannot be effectively implemented, however, until the counselor is attitudinally ready to hear the feelings which accompany the words; and it is this special kind of listening which enables the reflective process to occur. Following are some important elements of the reflective process.

Read the child's feelings accurately.

Beneath almost everything a child says is a set of feelings. These feelings are not often well verbalized but they exist. Regardless of what the child may choose to discuss, feelings accompany that discussion. Even what appears to be an innocuous statement regarding snowfall will, more often than not, also contain feelings about the snowfall. The child may either feel elated about the snowfall because of the opportunity to use a new sled, or the child may be terrified about driving conditions during the mother's trip home from work.

Almost everything we say has two dimensions. The content dimension and the feeling dimension. The content dimension consists of the facts contained in a client's statement. The client may say, "I'm five feet two inches tall, weigh 175 pounds, and live in a three room apartment on Elm Street. If I could lose some weight I'd feel a lot better about myself." The facts contained in the statement are the client's height, weight, size of apartment, and its location. The feeling contained in the client's statement is the dissatisfaction regarding being overweight and the effect of that added weight upon the client's self-image. The reflective counselor pays no attention to the facts contained in the statement. The client's feelings are heard, absorbed, and internalized by the counselor and reflected back to the client with a statement approximating the following: "You don't feel good about how you look. You'd like to lose some weight." Such a reflective statement will prompt the client to continue talking about feelings. Such a continuation will give the counselor additional feelings to reflect and will encourage the client to explore the same feeling more deeply or become comfortable enough to move on to other feelings. Each time the child makes a statement containing a feeling, the counselor recognizes the existence of that feeling by reflecting it. Reflecting feelings can be viewed as a conditioning process whereby the child is encouraged to express feelings because of the stimulus provided by the reflective responses.

The reflective counselor must hear what the child is feeling rather than what the child is saying; and these feelings must first be identified before they can be reflected. An accurate reading of the child's feelings will enable the counselor to make accurate reflections.

Be sensitive to same, new or conflicting feelings.

The reflective counselor stays attentive to the child's feelings. Those feelings often remain the same, especially at the beginning stages of counseling, but as counseling progresses those feelings often undergo obvious or subtle changes. The counselor must be alert to these changes.

A child may spend a number of early counseling sessions talking about how much a recently deceased single parent is missed. The counselor stays attentive to these feelings of loss and reflects them. As the child deepens the relationship with the counselor, the child begins to uncover feelings of resentment and anger toward the deceased parent. The resentment and anger is over being left alone in what the child perceives to be an uncaring world. Toward the later stages of counseling, the child's feelings move toward forgiveness and renewed love for the parent since the parent had no control over the timing of death's visit. Three separate and distinct feelings characterize the beginning, middle, and later counseling sessions for this child: feelings of loss, feelings of resentment and anger, and feelings of forgiveness and renewed love. The counselor who is sensitive to hearing feelings knows that three distinct feelings are present in the relationship and reflectively responds to these differences. The counselor who is superficially sensitive to feelings helps the child deal with the feelings of loss but doesn't provide the child with reflections that are deep enough to allow the child to move on to feelings of resentment and anger, and eventually, renewed love. That child may become an adult and never have the opportunity to express that resentment and anger, thereby never having the opportunity to feel a renewal of love for that parent. The processing of feelings for this client is incomplete. The processing never went beyond expressions of loss because the counselor's reflections were not deep enough to enable the feelings of loss to turn to feelings of resentment and anger, and eventually to renewed love.

The child-centered counselor needs to respond well to the child's basic feelings in order to set off a chain reaction whereby the child can go on to other feelings.

Each child has a unique set of feelings and gets in touch with them in a very individualized way with a reflective counselor. The counselor must be sensitive to that fact that clients do move from one set of feelings to another and must be prepared to respond to these changes throughout the reflective process.

Reflect primarily, but also clarify.

When the counselor has achieved a reflective tempo in response to the child's feelings, that tempo has to be maintained in order for the child to receive help. When the counselor is able to steadily reflect the child's feelings, the child will have a release from those feelings and be able to move toward rational conclusions regarding how to solve a problem. Along the way, however, the child sometimes stumbles, becomes confused, and gives the counselor feelings which are confusing, complex, and contradictory. Some inexperienced counselors, who are overly committed to the reflective process, feel that every expression of feeling must be matched with an appropriate and accurate reflective response. Not all statements of feelings, however, are made with full clarity. Some feelings are couched in hesitation and uncertainty. Others are ambiguous and contradictory. When the child is expressing feelings which fall into these categories, the reflective counselor asks the child to clarify the intended feelings with statements like, "I don't quite understand that," "You're confusing me . . . please help me understand what you're feeling," "You're not quite certain how you feel and so am I," and "I'm confused . . . I don't know whether you feel good or bad about that."

If the child leads the counselor down a path of hesitant, uncertain, ambiguous and contradictory feelings, and the counselor follows, then we have two confused participants in the counseling process. When hearing confused feelings, the counselor realigns, refocuses, and expedites the reflective process by requesting that the child clarify these feelings (Egan, 1973, 1985).

Be sensitive to the child's corrections of reflections.

Reflecting a child's feelings is virtually a fail-proof process. The counselor can afford to be occasionally inaccurate when reflecting, because the counselor's greatest ally for improving the accuracy of a reflection is the child.

After an affective communicating process has been established, the child begins to listen very carefully to what is being reflected. The child is essentially monitoring the counselor's reflections and judging their empathic content and accuracy. When the child hears the counselor responding with an inaccurate reflection, the child usually responds with, "That isn't quite what I feel. What I'm feeling is . . . " Such corrections serve the reflective process well. They enable the counselor to correct the accuracy of a reflective statement.

At the beginning of a counseling relationship, however, the child is unsophisticated regarding the reflective process and may not have the sensitivity to correct a process which the child has not yet sufficiently experienced. It is, therefore, crucial for the counselor to be highly accurate with reflective responses at the beginning of a counseling relationship. Once the child begins to understand what the counselor is trying to accomplish by using the reflective process, the child will have enough understanding of the process to make corrections when the counselor's reflections are inaccurate.

Be disciplined in applying reflective responses.

In reflecting feelings, the counselor assumes the internal frame of reference of the child and perceives experiences as the child perceives them.

When the counselor makes this identification with the child's feelings, the counselor translates that identification into words that accurately represent the child's feelings; and mirrors back to the child those feelings so that the child may evaluate their accuracy and meaning.

When the counselor accurately identifies with the child's feelings and wants the child to know this, the counselor prefixes the reflection of feeling with such phrases as:

You are saying . . .
You feel . . .
If I understand you . . .
I'm not sure I follow you, but you seem to feel that . . .
I gather that you mean . . .
Let's see if I really understand that . . .

Some counselors so deeply identify with the feelings of a child that their reflections of feelings gradually move from saying, "You feel that . . ." to "*I* feel that. . . . " This kind of transition takes place when the counselor develops such a deep and empathic identification with the feelings of the child that it becomes more natural to use "I feel . . ." rather than "You feel . . ." when responding. Using "I" rather than "You" is a quantum step forward for the counselor; but when the step is taken, it occurs in a natural manner when the counselor feels so closely drawn to the feelings of the child that the most natural response involves the use of "I." The following *counselor* reflections of feelings convey the depth of empathic identification that can occur when responding to feelings by the use of "I:"

I can't speak to her. . . . I'm always afraid that I'll be criticized.
It's hard to be me. . . . I want to but I never seem to be able to say what I want.
I wish I could get mad . . . but I don't want to get into even more trouble.
I feel myself becoming a better friend and I like it!
Sometimes I feel that if I could like me then things would improve.
I don't know what to do. . . . I was never like this before . . . before I seemed to know what to do.
If I could only do it then maybe I wouldn't be so shy.
There are times when I don't understand myself . . . times when all I know about me is my name!

Once again, the preceding statements are counselor reflections to the feelings of children. They are responses that counselors can comfortably make after they have accurately heard the feelings of child clients (Boy & Pine, 1990).

REFLECTING FEELINGS: EXPANDING ITS APPLICATION

Reflecting the child's feelings also has another potential—it can incorporate "additives," a procedure that has been found to be an effective expander of the reflective process (Egan, 1975; Carkhuff & Berenson, 1977; Turock, 1978). That is, a pure reflection of the child's feelings can be expanded to include an additive that is confrontative, interpretive, or challenging.

When well timed, such additives can give the child an added dimension of self-awareness not typically included in a standard reflection of feeling. For example, a standard reflection by a counselor might be: "You feel discouraged and lonely." A counselor additive that is *confrontative* would be: "You feel discouraged and lonely *and don't seem to want to do anything about it.* An additive that is *interpretive* would be: "You feel discouraged and lonely *and would feel much better if you only knew that your parents loved you.*" An additive that is *challenging* would be: "You feel discouraged and lonely *and it's OK with you to stay this way.*"

Reflecting the child's feelings can be done in a standard way or with additives that can be tacked on to a basic reflection. An additive can be used on certain occasions when such an additive gives the child a new insight that could not be achieved if the counselor's response was just a basic reflection (Boy & Pine, 1990).

To continue or limit the reflective process?

Many children make progress in solving their problems when the counselor does nothing more than empathically reflect their feelings. When the counselor only uses reflection of feelings throughout a counseling relationship, the counselor is a classic representation of the second historic period in the development of client-centered counseling. To just reflect feelings is to incorporate a process for which there is more than ample research evidence indicating its effectiveness. If the counselor, however, decides that with another child the reflective process has taken the child just so far and the child needs to go beyond that point, then the counselor can apply a different approach because that different approach better serves the child's needs. The following guidelines will enable the counselor to judge when to move beyond reflection of feelings in the counseling process. The counselor does this (Boy & Pine, 1990) when the child:

1. Has achieved an emotional catharsis and is no longer overwhelmed by incapacitating feelings.
2. Is more open and honest in assessing the self and the attitudes and behaviors which constitute the self.
3. Shows a movement from emotionally-based communication to rationally-based communication.
4. Is motivated and willing to energize the self toward solving or resolving a problem rather than blaming others for its existence and solution (pp. 47–48).

A counselor's commitment to, and accurate application of, the reflective process will enable the counselor to possess a helping skill that has enormous potential. When applied well, the reflective process will improve a counselor's ability to help children solve, resolve, and deal with psychosocial problems on a deeper and more permanent basis.

PHASE THREE GUIDELINES

Phase three of our child-centered approach to counseling is not for all children. Those who respond well to the reflective process of phase two should not have that process interrupted or changed. If the reflective process is producing the desired insights and behavioral changes, then it should be continued until those clients are no longer in need of counseling.

For other clients, however, the reflective process may have achieved all that it can without the child's problem being solved or resolved. When this is the case, the counselor can utilize nonreflective techniques and procedures drawn from other theories of counseling, the behavioral sciences, developmental psychology, or good common sense.

Whatever is done in phase three that proves to be effective will have its effectiveness based upon the quality of what the counselor did in phases one and two. What was learned about the client in phases one and two becomes the foundation for deciding what techniques and procedures to use in phase three.

Before the counselor reaches the phase three point of meeting the specific needs of an individual child, the counselor needs to make a transition from phase two to three. The transition necessitates making a sound judgment about which phase three process should be incorporated to accurately meet the needs of *this* child with *this* problem. The success of phase three depends upon (1) the effectiveness of phase two and (2) the accuracy of the counselor's judgment regarding which approach will be most beneficial for the child in phase three.

This transitional judgment is not difficult for the counselor because the judgment is not made in a vacuum. The judgment is based upon the counselor's assimilation of the child's feelings and behavior during phase two. The deeper this assimilation, the more accurate is the counselor's judgment regarding which counseling approach best meets the needs of the child in phase three. When the counselor has acquired only a superficial assimilation of the child during phase two then that counselor is not in a position to make an accurate judgment about what process will be best for the child in phase three.

Flexibility in responding to the child is crucial if phase three is to be effective. Corey (1991) indicates that if client-centered counselors limit their range of responses to clients to listening and reflecting feelings, then their ability to influence behavioral change is limited. Carkhuff and Berenson (1977) concur that the child-centered counselor may need to go beyond being empathic and genuine if counseling is to be effective. They suggest that the counselor also needs to be *concrete* since such concreteness encourages the client to focus on specific problems which need to be solved. Linking counselor behavior to the concrete requirements of a child's needs means that phase three may require more than reflecting feelings.

When the counselor has only a limited and partial awareness of the child's personality, attitudes, values, and behavior, the counselor does not move ahead with phase three. In such a circumstance, moving ahead with phase three is detrimental to the child because the counselor has only a limited and partial reservoir of information upon which to base a phase three process judgment. In such a case, the counselor needs to stay in phase two, reflecting feelings, for a longer period of time until a sufficient information base has been developed so that the counselor can make a sound judgment regarding which phase three process will be best for the child.

The process used with the child in phase three is not a guess. It is a studied judgment based upon an awareness of the feelings which influence the child's behavior that was acquired in the phase two reflective process.

Assuming that the counselor has had an effective phase two with a child, the counselor now moves toward making an accurate judgment regarding which phase three process will be most beneficial for the child.

The basis for this judgment must always be the therapeutic needs of the child; that is, which process will yield *the highest therapeutic gain for the child.*

The needs of the child must always remain paramount in phase three.

When constructing a phase three approach that will have a positive influence on the child's behavior, the counselor must be certain that the phase three approach meets the needs of the child. During phase three the counselor may be faced with a subconscious temptation to meet the counselor's needs rather than the needs of the child. The counselor will also need to avoid having a process bias that incorporates only one way of working with all children during phase three. In succumbing to such a bias, the counselor will lose sight of the needs of *this* child, in *this* situation, with *this* particular set of needs.

The objectivity established in phase two must not be lost in phase three. Phase two provides an opportunity for the counselor to objectively know the child. This objectivity must be continued into phase three so that the counselor focuses on the needs of the child rather than allowing the counselor's process biases to take over. Being objective requires a high level of self-discipline on the part of the counselor; being objective means that the counselor has more respect for the needs of the child than for a phase three process bias.

The child's progress in phase three is proportionably related to the counselor's success in phase two.

Phase three is not automatically productive. It is productive only in proportion to the counselor's effectiveness during phase two. If phase two was a facilitative and growthful experience for the child, then the stage is set for phase three to be effective. If phase two had little positive effect upon the child, then the stage is set for phase three to be ineffective.

An effective phase two is a catalyst for an effective phase three. Phase three is only as productive as was phase two. The success of phase two has a clear influence on the success of phase three.

The counselor must be flexible in phase three and not impose one approach on all children.

If a counselor is committed to, for example, confrontation and also sees the usefulness and desirability of phase two, that counselor must not lie-in-wait for children to come out of the phase two woods so that all clients can be confronted in phase three. *Some* children may need confrontation in phase three, but not *all* children. The counselor needs to be flexible in phase three so that the approach used with a *particular* child meets the *unique* needs of *this* child.

Counselors who are loyal to only one phase three process, will have difficulty in being flexible in phase three. It is the flexible counselor, however, who has the best chance to meet the varied needs of different clients in phase three. Such flexibility depends upon counselors becoming more knowledgeable regarding the different process models they might use with children in phase three.

The counselor must be prepared to go back to phase two if the phase three approach is not producing results.

If carefully considered and constructed, phase three generally tends to meet the needs of a child. If the evidence of the child's feelings and behavior, however, indicates that the phase three approach being utilized is not meeting the needs of the child, then a reassessment of the child's needs is required. This is best accomplished by going back to the reflective process of phase two. By returning to the reflective process, the counselor gains a more accurate and deeper understanding of the feelings which influence the child's behavior.

Counselors whose phase three approach does not yield results will often find that the necessary understanding of the child, usually acquired in phase two, did not occur deeply or well. Therefore, instead of struggling through phase three with an ineffective process, the counselor's return to phase two will put the relationship back on track until the counselor reassesses what needs to be done in phase three. By returning to phase two, the counselor acquires the additional information necessary to make a more accurate judgment regarding a more appropriate phase three approach.

The counselor's phase three approach must be based upon an accurate assimilation of the child's needs in phase two.

Phase three becomes effective because the counselor has taken the time necessary, in phase two, to understand the feelings which influence behavior. When the child has amplified feelings in phase two, then an accurate assessment of the child's needs in phase three becomes possible. Such an accurate assimilation of the child can only occur in proportion to the accuracy of the child's self-disclosure in phase two; and the accuracy of the child's self-disclosure will largely depend upon the counselor's ability to create a phase two reflective process that influences the child to be open and honest about feelings.

Phase three can include a noncounseling approach if it more accurately meets the needs of the child.

Some child-centered counselors see therapeutic benefits occurring only within the context of a person-to-person, talk-centered, counseling relationship. Some behavior modification counselors see therapeutic benefits occurring outside of the counseling relationship in behavioral experiences conceived by the counselor.

Which is generally more effective is not a valid question. The basic issue is which is the better approach for *this* child, in *this* relationship, with *this* identified set of needs. For one child the talking-out process may be the best mode for influencing behavioral change. For another child, the talking-out process yields little and this child will change behavior only as a result of being involved in concrete actions.

Knowing which approach is better for a particular child can only occur after the counselor has assimilated the child in phase two; but what is done in phase three only becomes known when we focus on what would be appropriate and effective for *this* child in phase three; and phase three for some children may not include one-to-one counseling but may include noncounseling experiences which have a better potential for helping to change the behavior of *this* child.

Regardless of which approach is used in phase three, there should be evidence that the behavior of the child has improved.

Having children feel good about themselves is a desirable goal of counseling. Having counselors feel good about the effectiveness of their work is another desirable goal of counseling. But if feeling good about oneself were the only goal of counseling we would be in trouble as a profession since there may be less expensive and more simple ways of helping children and counselors feel good about themselves.

Feeling good about oneself means that the child has an improved self-concept. An improved self concept alone, however, is not the only goal of counseling. A positive self-concept must be matched with positive behavior and there should be observable evidence that this behavior exists. A child's improved self-concept must be accompanied by observable behavior which affirms the existence of an improved self-concept.

The emotionality or rationality of the child will determine which phase three approach is best for the child.

An important contributor to the counselor's judgment about the most appropriate approach for phase three is the child's tendency to respond best to either a rationally based approach or an affectively based approach.

Some children engage in troublesome behavior because the intellectual processing of information is a certain and definite influence in the formation of that behavior. With such a child, since rational influences play such a central role in causing behavior, a rational process can be utilized in phase three to help solve the child's problem. With some children a clearly rational approach to the solution of a problem influences the child to change the behavior (Beck, 1976).

Other children engage in troublesome behavior because their affective functioning is a greater influence in the formation of that behavior (Rogers, 1951). These children intellectually know the difference between behaviors which enhance or diminish the self, but they affectively and viscerally feel compelled to engage in the troublesome behavior. With such children, the influences of emotions is so compelling in causing behavior that the phase three resolution of the child's problem lies in the counselor utilizing an affective approach.

In phase three the counselor must recognize whether a rational or affective approach will best meet the needs of a particular child; and this judgment rests upon which was the greater influence in causing the child's problem and then using a corresponding affective or rational approach in phase three.

A child inclined to be abstract will respond best to an existential approach; a child inclined to be concrete will respond best to a more specific approach.

Some children see answers to their problems in abstract terms. If they can develop a set of unified abstract constructs in order to identify a solution to their problems, such abstracting is the first requirement for a solution. Other children see answers to their problems in concrete terms and must develop a set of concrete realities which provide a realistic solution to a problem.

The counselor working with an abstracting child needs to have the inclination and patience to follow the intricacies of the child's abstractions. This is not easy for the reality-based counselor, but this ability needs to be developed in order to promote behavioral change in a child whose primary mode of feelings and understanding is through abstraction.

The counselor working with a child who is concrete needs to have the ability to penetrate the importance of concreteness for this particular child. This is not easy for the counselor who is abstractly inclined. Such a counselor, however, will need to develop the ability to see the usefulness of concrete solutions with children whose primary mode of feeling and understanding is in concrete terms.

Penetrating and understanding the abstract world of some children and the concrete world of others will require a high degree of flexibility on the part of the counselor. The accuracy of this insight, however, will be a large contribution to the success of phase three.

The child-centered approach can be applied in individual and group counseling.

The phase two and phase three components of child-centered counseling are applicable to both individual and group counseling. And of course, the success of phases two and three depends upon the counselor's ownership of the facilitative attitudes identified in phase one. In group counseling phase two influences the quality of phase three just as in individual counseling. During phase two the group counselor attempts to build relationships between and among group members by reflecting feelings and by assimilating the group's *raison d'etre,* motives, processes, and goals. By applying phase two, the counselor develops the communication network whereby children share attitudes, feelings, experiences, and personal observations.

During phase three, the group counselor accommodates the needs of the group, and individuals within the group, by engaging in processes designed to meet the specific needs of both the group and individuals within the group. The counselor also harnesses the natural and spontaneous helping behaviors which exist among some group members and which can be utilized to help other group members. In phase three of group counseling, the counselor shares the counseling role with children and creates opportunities for them to function as counselors for each other (Gumaer, 1986).

In phase three the counselor can assist the child with a problem solution that is logical, natural, spontaneous, or eclectic.

The last guideline for phase three is by no means the least important. In fact, it may be the most important. Sometimes a counselor can become too complex in attempting to identify a phase three process which will best meet the needs of a child. Often, after a successful phase two, the most helpful process for the child can be one which is logical, natural, and spontaneous. If the counselor is attitudinally child-centered and has learned to trust his or her human, genuine, and empathic qualities, the counselor needs only to respond to the child in a logical, natural, and spontaneous way. This phase three kind of responding has great therapeutic potential, but its power has been lost by counselors who have buried it with wooden and mechanical techniques.

What will be done in phase three cannot always be determined in advance. What is done in phase three takes on the characteristics of being natural when it is closely linked to the reflective process applied in phase two. What is applied in phase three should not disrupt or contradict the self understanding that emerged for the child in phase two. When there is a reasonable, complimentary, and developmental connection between phase three and two, and phase three is a natural extension of what was accomplished in phase two, then the needs of the child have been well served and the outcomes of counseling will point in positive directions.

REFERENCES

Beck, A. T. (1976). *Cognitive therapy and the emotional disorders.* New York: Meridan.

Bergin, A., & Garfield, S. V. (1985). *Handbook of psychotherapy and behavior change: An empirical analysis.* New York: John Wiley and Sons.

Boy, A. V., & Pine, G. J. (1976). Equalizing the counseling relationship. *Psychotherapy: Theory, Research, and Practice, 13,* 20–25.

Boy, A. V., & Pine, G. J. (1990). *A person-centered foundation for counseling and psychotherapy.* Springfield, IL: Charles C Thomas.

Boy, A. V., & Pine, G. J. (1988). *Fostering psychosocial development in the classroom.* Springfield, IL: Charles C Thomas.

Brammer, L. M., & Shostrom, E. L. (1977). *Therapeutic psychology.* 3rd ed. Englewood Cliffs, NJ: Prentice-Hall.

Bugental, J. F. T. (1978). *Psychotherapy and process: The fundamentals of an existential-humanistic approach.* Cambridge: Addison-Wesley.

Carkhuff, R. R., & Berenson, B. (1977). *Beyond counseling and therapy.* 2nd ed. New York: Holt, Rinehart, and Winston.

Corey, G. (1991). *Theory and practice in counseling and psychotherapy.* (4th Ed.). Monterey, CA: Brooks/Cole.

Danish, S. J., D'Augelli, A. R., & Hauer, A. L. (1980). *Helping skills: A basic training program.* New York: Human Science Press.

Egan, G. (1973). *Face to face.* Monterey, CA: Brooks/Cole.

Egan, G. (1985). *The skilled helper.* (3rd ed.). Monterey, CA: Brooks/Cole.

George, R. L., & Cristiani, T. S. (1981). *Theory, methods and process of counseling and psychotherapy.* Englewood Cliffs, NJ: Prentice-Hall.

Gumaer, J. (1986). Working in groups with middle graders. *School Counselor, 33,* 230–238.

Hansen, J. C., Stevic, R. R., & Warner, R. W., Jr. (1986). *Counseling: Theory and process.* (4th ed.). Boston: Allyn and Bacon.

Marcel, G. (1963). *The philosophy of existentialism.* New York: Citadel Press.

Maslow, A. (1965). Cognition of being in the peak experiences. In D. E. Hamacheck (Ed.), *The self in growth: Teaching and learning.* Englewood Cliffs, NJ: Prentice-Hall.

Mock, B. (1982). Analysis of therapist variables in a series of psychotherapy sessions with two child clients. *Journal of Clinical Psychology, 38,* 63–76.

Polster, I., & Polster, M. (1973). *Gestalt therapy integrated.* New York: Vintage.

Rogers, C. R. (1942). *Counseling and psychotherapy.* Boston: Houghton Mifflin.

Rogers, C. R. (1951). *Client-centered therapy.* Boston: Houghton Mifflin.

Rogers, C. R. (1975). Empathic: An unappreciated way of being. *Counseling Psychologist,* 5, 2–10.

Rogers, C. R. (1982). Nuclear war: A personal response. *Monitor,* 13, 6–7.

Wild, J. (1965). *An invitation to phenomenology.* Chicago: Quadrangle Books.

Chapter 3

SUE AND FRED:
APPLYING THE REFLECTIVE PROCESS

This chapter is designed to enable the reader to gain insight into the phase two verbal transactions between a child-centered counselor and two separate children. With the first client, Sue, counseling sessions four and nine are presented. With the second client, Fred, counseling sessions two, seven, and ten are presented. Both Sue and Fred were voluntarily involved in counseling.

With Sue and Fred, the counselor did not have to go beyond the reflective process. It was producing results. Reflecting the child's feelings well is often all that is needed to induce behavioral change. When a child's feelings are responded to in an empathic manner, this process is often all that is necessary in order for the child to gain insight into the behaviors needed to enhance the self. When the reflective process is not producing results, it still has value in its ability to help the counselor develop an affective bond with the child that will be useful as a foundation for phase three. The counselor who worked with Sue and Fred felt no need to move beyond the reflective process. It was producing results. Sue and Fred were responding to the process.

SUE

Counseling Session 4

Counselor-Client Dialogue

Co   Come in, Sue. Have a seat. How are things going?
Cl   My teacher gave me what she told me she was going to give me . . . she failed me in math.
Co   Uh, huh.
Cl   Couldn't do nothing with that.
Co   You were wondering if she would fail you in math and now you've discovered that she did. That hurts.

56

Cl   When I told her she couldn't do it with my marks, she says she would, and maybe she would get away with it. So I says you won't.

Co   Uh, huh.

Cl   So she says, "I'll try my hardest to flunk you," and so I says, "Go right ahead!"

Co   Uh, huh.

Cl   And because of my low marks my mother is going to visit school — this afternoon, of all times.

Co   Uh, huh.

Cl   And what she's going to find out is that I'm in trouble.

Co   You don't want your mother to find out that you're in trouble.

Cl   No. My teacher don't bother me as much as she used to.

Co   Things are better between me and my teacher.

Cl   Mm-mm. Like when I was coming here she says, "Where are you going?" I said, "China." So she started laughing, you know. She usually hollers at me!

Co   Uh, huh.

Cl   So I said, "China." So she says, "OK."

Co   Uh, huh.

Cl   So . . . she doesn't bother me any more.

Co   You feel that no matter what she says, no matter what she does, she doesn't bother you as much as she used to.

Cl   She don't bother me. She can say anything she wants.

Co   Uh, huh.

Cl   I don't care what she does, what she says either.

Co   Uh, huh.

Cl   It doesn't bother me in the least.

Co   I don't care what she thinks of me.

Cl   That's right. I don't.

Co   It doesn't bother me. I don't care.

Cl   I'm not worried about her.

Co   What should I worry about her?

Cl   She doesn't bother me, so I'm not going to bother her.

Co   As long as she doesn't give me a hard time, I won't give her a hard time.

Cl   If she gives me a hard time, I'm just not going to pay any attention to her, that's all!

Co You kind of feel that if you don't pay any attention to her, that's kind of the best thing for you to do.

Cl It'll have to be.

Co You kind of feel this is the only way.

Cl I'm not going to fight with her.

Co Uh, huh.

Cl She's not worth fighting with.

Co I really don't care for her. I don't even want to bother fighting with her.

Cl Because of her, I can't go out after school!

Co Uh, huh.

Cl Why should I fight with her?

Co You kind of feel that the more you fight with her, the more trouble you'll have.

Cl That's right. The less I bother with her, the better off I'll be.

Co Uh, huh.

Cl So if she wants to fight, she can fight with my mother when she visits here today.

Co Uh, huh.

Cl That's all.

Co As long as she doesn't fight with me, that's all that matters. Let her say what she wants, as long as she doesn't bother me.

Cl That's right. No one will believe a word she says anyway. So, I'm not worried.

Co I feel that people won't believe her and what she says about me, so she can say what she wants.

Cl I don't care if they believe her or not because they'll find out different for themselves. I don't care what anybody tells anybody about me, just as long as I know it isn't true.

Co You don't care what people say about you as long as you know it isn't true. That seems to be more important to you than what they think. What you really are is more important than what people think about you.

Cl Nobody can see the good things anybody does. They always think of the bad things. You do something right all along, then you do something wrong once and they don't remember what you did right.

Co You feel that there are things about you that are right, that you don't do everything wrong. There are things you do right. People just don't notice these things.

Cl That's right. And if she wants to fight, let her fight with my mother. She'll fight with her!

Co You feel that if she is looking for trouble and wants to fight, that your mother will give her the trouble she's looking for.

Cl No, not exactly. But I know that if she is going to start fighting with her, my mother will fight back!

Co You feel that your mother won't take some of the things you've taken from her.

Cl That's right. And I don't blame her. She knows that I've been fooling around in school, because I told her, and she told me if I didn't buckle down, I'd be sorry.

Co Uh, huh.

Cl So I says all right, and I guess she kind of figures I'm in trouble, but I don't worry about that. If she finds out, she finds out.

Co Uh, huh.

Cl Nothing I can do about it.

Co I figure if this thing is going to happen, it's just going to happen.

Cl That's right.

Co If she is going to find out that I'm in trouble in school, it is just going to have to happen. There is nothing I can do about it.

Cl If my brother doesn't do his homework, she thinks nothing of it. If I don't do my homework, my teacher tells my brother, he goes home and tells my mother, and I get in trouble.

Co Uh, huh.

Cl But—anybody else—they can skip their homework, but every time *I* do anything wrong, my teacher has to tell my brother!

Co Other kids do something wrong and they don't get into trouble, but I do something wrong and I always get into trouble. I think that's unfair.

Cl Like today. I didn't finish my homework because I didn't understand it. After school, my teacher calls my brother and starts telling him about it. Then if I ask my brother what's going on, he won't tell me! He tells me it's none of my business—it doesn't concern me. My teacher offered to give me help, but what's the use? I'm not going to get anywhere with it.

Co Uh, huh.

Cl My mother told me if I didn't improve she was going to send me to a private school. I told her if she sent me to a private school, I wouldn't do anything, no matter how they slapped heck out of me.

Co Uh, huh.

Cl I told her I wouldn't do it for them and then I'd get thrown out. So she said I'd do it or they'd punish me.

Co I don't care what people do to me. If I don't want to do my work, I'm not going to.

Cl That isn't the right attitude, but I told her before I didn't want to go to private school. She thinks that just because she went, I'd have to go, too!

Co You figure that maybe this attitude might not be right, but still you don't want to be forced into anything you don't want to do.

Cl That's right. Because she knows that when I say I don't want to do it, I'm *not* going to do it!

Co Once I make up my mind, I'm just not going to do it no matter what anybody says.

Cl I don't think it's fair that if a person doesn't want to go some place, they have to go anyway, especially if it's to private school!

Co Why should she make me do something I don't want to do? It's unfair.

Cl It would be different if it was something—you know, like I was going someplace with my mother and I didn't want to go—and I had to go. But it's different when you *have to go* to private school.

Co Uh, huh.

Cl I told her I wasn't going to go. She told me I was going to go if I didn't buckle down, and I told her I wasn't going to go—I said I'd go there, but I wouldn't do anything! So she told me she'd make sure I'd go to a private school where I stayed overnight and I didn't come home! So I says, send me and you'll see how fast I'll get out of there.

Co I don't want to be forced into anything.

Cl I told her I don't want to be kept anywhere I don't want to be.

Co Uh, huh.

Cl And like right now, my teacher says, "What are you going to do—go to our vocational school when you're in the seventh grade next year?" I says, "No, my mother won't let me," and she says, "Well, that's your only chance." I think my only chance *is* to go to vocational school, but my mother won't let me go! She told me all the bums go there, you don't learn nothing. I figure what am I going to learn here that I'm not going to learn at vocational school?

Co Out of all these places that people want me to go, I kind of think that vocational school *would be* the best.

Cl That's right.

Co But still my mother thinks she is going to make me go to a private school . . . if she does make me go there, I'm not going to do anything.

Cl That's right. I'm not going to be forced into anything. Why should I be forced into something I don't want to do?

Co If I don't want to do something, nobody should force me into it!

Cl Like my older brother. My mother and father are trying to make his career choice for him, and I don't think that is right. So my brother was talking about what he was going to be last night and my mother and father started butting in, so I says, "Let the kid decide for himself," and my mother says, "We're only helping him."

Co Uh, huh.

Cl Like my mother, she's been pushing the idea of being a school teacher and I told her I wasn't going to be one, I was going to be what I felt like!

Co Uh, huh.

Cl So she asks me what I was going to be and I says, "A hairdresser!" So she says, "You are, huh?" So I says, "Yeah, I am!" So she didn't say anything after that. So I says I am going to be one and that's all there is to it! My brother chose his career last night, and my mother got mad because she didn't want him to go into the one he picked. So—I mean—she is always going to make up her mind for both of us!

Co I want to make up my own mind . . . I don't want anybody else making up my mind . . . I want to do what I want to do.

Cl Why should I have my mother tell me what kind of a life I want to lead ahead of the time that I get out of school! She told me that if I went to vocational school, I wouldn't get a decent job! She says it isn't worth going to school if you are going to vocational school. To her, vocational school is nothing! Plenty of girls go there! She says she can see it for boys, but she can't see it for girls.

Co Uh, huh.

Cl If it is good for boys, it is good enough for girls, too! We're no different!

Co I want to be able to make up my own mind in this thing. If I want to go to vocational school, I want to be able to go!

Cl But she won't let me go. She told me it is no good for me. She says I got the brains to do the regular school work, so why don't I do it?

Co But still my mother won't let me go.

Cl That's right. I've told her I want to go. I told her last year I wanted to go and she said she would see about it, but then when this year came and I asked again, and I said I wanted to go next year, she said I couldn't! She told me it was no good!

Co Uh, huh.

Cl She said that the only reason I want to go there is because all the boys are there!

Co Uh, huh.

Cl She says that it's still no good. I says, "I'll be 95 walking down the aisle with a cane when I graduate from high school!" She told me she didn't care how old I was when I got out of high school, but I was going to graduate because she did.

Co I wish my mother would stop pushing me and making me do things I don't want to do.

Cl I mean, I don't see anything wrong with vocational school. Some of my cousins go. All my girl friends go there! There's nothing wrong with it.

Co Uh, huh.

Cl No, but not me; I can't go. I mean, I don't see nothing wrong with vocational school—you learn a good trade there! They teach you all you have to know in the trade you want!

Co You feel you can get a lot out of vocational school, but still your mother doesn't realize this. She thinks it would be a waste of time.

Cl I know I can get a lot out of vocational school, more than I can get out of this school!

Co There would be a lot more there for me to learn—things that I can really use.

Cl Yeah, but she won't let me do it!

Co Uh, huh.

Cl She says it's not good for me. She says I got the brains, why don't I do the work in regular school? I told her I wanted to go to vocational school, but she says she won't let me. Even my math teacher said she thinks vocational school would be a lot better for me than this school.

Co Uh, huh.

Cl I said that at least I would learn something there. I'd learn a trade and I would be out of this school! Even Miss Brown said I'd be better off in a trade and Miss Green and Miss White said I would be better off in vocational school than here.

Co Everybody says I'd be better off in vocational school, but still my mother doesn't understand this.

Cl She does now, because I told her Miss Brown said I'd be better off in vocational school and she said it is none of Miss Brown's business! She says, "It's *my* business what you do and you're not going to vocational school," and every time I mention it she gets mad at me! She tells me she graduated from high school and I'm going to, too.

Co Every time I mention going to vocational school, my mother just gets mad at me!

Cl She thinks that just because I didn't make honors here that I'm dumb. My cousin, she's in the 5th grade, and she's made honors from the first grade up and my mother thinks my cousin is so smart just because she did it! But last year, in the fifth grade, I made honors, too, maybe only a couple of times, but at least I made honors. Just because my cousin made honors this year, my mother makes fun of me. She tells me I'm stupid.

Co My mother makes a big deal out of her, but she makes me look stupid because I didn't make it, but I could make it if I wanted to!

Cl Then she tells all my aunts I flunked five subjects. She makes me feel like two cents! She says my brother got a good report card. One A, a couple of Bs, and C and a couple of Ds—and that's a good report card to my mother because at least my brother improved. Now she says to me, "You're headed down." But that's Miss Brown's fault, not mine.

Co I wish she wouldn't make fun of me because it isn't my fault. I could make it if I wanted to. It's just Miss Brown's fault . . . she's the one that keeps me from honors.

Cl And Miss Green keeps me from honors. I can't do Miss Green's work and she knows it. I've tried and tried and tried and tried—I can't do it! No matter what she asks me to do, I can't do it. I can read the questions and I can answer them out loud, but I can't write them on paper and I can't pass a test.

Co Uh, huh.

Cl It's all up here in my head . . . I can't write it on paper.

Co You feel you know the school work, that you could pass it, but it just seems to stick in your head and never gets on paper.

Cl I can't do anything on paper for her. I don't know whether I'm coming or going in her room.

Co She's got me so mixed up that I don't know how to do it.

Cl I know I'd be better off at vocational school and I would be happier there than I am here.

Co Uh, huh.

Cl I don't know if you can still go to vocational school if you don't pass the sixth grade . . . I think you can, I'll get the teachers to convince her. Maybe Miss Brown will tell her . . . I hope! I mean I would feel so much better at vocational school than I would here because I know I can do the work at vocational school . . . I know what it's like. All it is is learning a trade—what you are going to be, what you are going to do. Then after you get out of there, they help you get a job.

Co Uh, huh.

Cl She tells me that vocational school is no good, you don't get a regular high school diploma. You don't get this and you don't get that! I says, "Maybe you don't get a regular high school diploma, but you *do* get a job!" She says, "Yeah, you get a job breaking your back."

Co I feel that trade school would be good for me, but my mother just doesn't go for it.

Cl She won't let me go! Even Miss Green said I'd be better off at vocational school learning a trade than I would be here. She says I am not learning a single thing.

Co Even the teachers say I'd be better off there and I know I would be.

Cl Miss Brown says, "If you don't pass this year, you'd be better off at vocational school than repeating the sixth grade here."

Co Uh, huh.

Cl If I stayed here, I'd have at least six years to go and that would be just a waste of time for me because I'd just be staying back and staying back, because I couldn't do the work. What do you want to do schoolwork for if you can't go where you want to go?

Co Uh, huh.

Cl If I finish the year off, and say I pass and my mother makes me stay in this school next year, I know I won't pass because I'll forget everything I learned this year. I know myself . . . I'll be better off at vocational school learning a trade.

Co In my own mind, I know that I'd be better off—I'd be learning a trade that I could use; but my mother just doesn't understand that. She just doesn't want me to go.

Cl   I mean, they teach you a good trade there. They teach you a good trade you can use!

Co   I wish my mother could understand this. If she could only realize that it is not a waste of time! I could learn something there.

Cl   She says, "But you wouldn't get a regular high school diploma. You don't get a good job." She says, "What happens if you get married; you have to keep the same old job again."

Co   Uh, huh.

Cl   I says, "Ma, at least wait until I'm 19 or 20 years old before I get married." I mean, you'd think I was going to get married as soon as I got out of school. It isn't worth it, going to school, if I can't go where I want to go. It isn't worth it because I know I won't learn anything here. I know that if I could go to vocational school next year, I could do the work.

Co   Uh, huh.

Cl   I mean, I want to be with kids my own age, not with kids younger than me! I feel like a jerk in my room. I am the oldest kid there!

Co   I really feel out of place. They are all so young and I'm so much older.

Cl   I feel like a jerk!

Co   I want to get out of this school so that I can go to vocational school and be with kids my own age.

Cl   It isn't only the ages. I know I could learn something at vocational school if I could go, but my mother won't let me. She tells me it isn't worth it. She says, "You don't learn nothing there because you need a regular high school diploma to get a job."

Co   Uh, huh.

Cl   She says, "I graduated from regular high school and you'd better do the same."

Co   I don't think going to regular school is that important. Why are they pushing me on it? I could go to vocational school and learn just what I have to, and then go out and get a job. That's just what I want.

Cl   At vocational school, they help you get a job . . . they help you find one.

Co   Uh, huh.

Cl   If I can get a job, then I'm all right. If I am going to be just pushed into going to this school if I don't want to go, for crying out loud, before you know it I'll be 105 before I finish school!

Co If they keep pushing me through school, I'll never make it because I can't do the work.

Cl Even if it means that I won't become a hairdresser, it's worth it. At least I know that I'll learn something. It is better than being stuck in this school and learning nothing. By the time I'd finish high school, I'd be too old to be a hairdresser!

Co If they make me go through high school, I'll be too old to be anything. At least if I go to vocational school, I'd be out of there in three years and then I can get a job.

Cl They help you get a job. I know kids that graduated last year. They helped them all to find jobs.

Co If they'd only let me do what I want to do.

Cl At vocational school, in a way it's easy; in a way, it's hard. You have to learn your trade—they teach you the easiest way possible. If my mother would let me go to vocational school I'd be all right because I'd learn something there. I'd learn a trade. If it was good for me, I'd learn it.

Co Uh, huh.

Cl No teacher has ever brought up the subject that I should go to vocational school, but if they ever do, I know my mother is going to go crazy. There's only one teacher who can talk my mother into letting me go to vocational school and that's Mrs. Amber. She's the only one who can do it. Or Miss Brown. They are the only two who can do it.

Co Uh, huh.

Cl And maybe Miss Green, I don't know. Maybe just those three teachers. They're the ones that can do it.

Co Uh, huh.

Cl I know that Miss Brown can because her and my cousin once worked together. My mother thinks it would be very embarrassing if I went to vocational school. She figures that she would be embarrassed; that she'd be ashamed of it because everybody in her family graduated from regular high school.

Co Uh, huh.

Cl She probably thinks it would be dirt on my name because I went to vocational school. There is nothing wrong with it. Everybody goes there.

Co Uh, huh.

Cl It's for girls just as well as boys.

Co I kind of feel my mother doesn't want me to go because she'd be ashamed of me at vocational school. She'd want me to graduate from regular high school because everybody else in my family went to high school.

Cl My mother tells me I've got the brains and I know I've got the brains, but I can't use them.

Co Uh, huh.

Cl If I don't go where I want to go, I can't use my brains.

Co Uh, huh.

Cl Why should I be stuck someplace where I don't want to be; where I won't do nothing?

Co Uh, huh.

Cl If you can't be where you want to be, why should you do anything for anybody. If they are going to throw you off your course, then you throw them off their course, too.

Co If they are going to make me stay here, I'm not going to do a thing. If I can be where I want to be, at the vocational school, then I will do something.

Cl I'll learn something there.

Co Uh, huh.

Cl My mother wants me to be an old lady when I get out of school.

Co My mother just doesn't understand that I can get more out of vocational school than this school.

Cl My mother says, "Your brother's doing all right in regular school." I says, "I know he's doing all right, but he's different than I am." I says, "I want to be where I know I can study."

Co Uh, huh.

Cl They teach you your trade while you're in school.

Co Uh, huh.

Cl She says, "All they teach you is cooking; they don't teach you nothing down there." I says, "Ma, they teach you your trade."

Co Uh, huh.

Cl I'm getting tired of being pushed. Like, something goes wrong in my house. Who gets blamed for it? I do. Anything goes wrong and I get blamed for it. Like my mother, she leaves some money around the house for us in the morning; but we're not supposed to touch it unless she hands it to me and my brother. If the money is missing, she comes to my room and she goes through my drawers, through my things, through everything of mine. She tells me I took it . . . she blames it on me.

Co I am always getting blamed for things I don't do. I don't like that.

Cl If anything happens, it's always my fault. And then when they find out I didn't take it, they sit and sympathize with me. I tell them not to try to sympathize. Then my mother tries to give me money and I tell her, "Listen, keep your money. I don't need any money from you. Why should I take any money from anybody that thinks I am stealing it from them?"

Co First they think I'm a crook, and then they give me money. Why should I take it from them when they make me feel so low?

Cl Why should I take money that they think I stole? Like sometimes my mother misplaces her change purse and where do they find it? On the floor. After they go through my room and throw everything up in the air. Where do they find it? In my mother's room and then they come around sympathizing.

Co I don't want their sympathy.

Cl "And don't go out," she says. "You are being punished for taking the money." I says, "You found the money, I didn't take it!" She says, "I still don't believe it, you're staying in the house, anyway." So I says, "Why don't you treat me a little *more* like dirt, huh?" Then she tried to love me up and I tell her, "Get out of here!" Then I go out of the house. But she tells me that if I don't get right back in the house, then I'll *never* go out. Every time something goes wrong in the house, I get blamed for it. The same thing happened this morning when she handed me my money. "I don't want any money from you," I says, "I don't want any money from you after you make me feel so low. Keep your old money, I don't want anything from you!" And when I go home, she will try to love me and make me eat supper, but I won't eat it. I don't care. I'll starve myself.

Co I don't like her treating me like that. She mistrusts me first and then she feels sorry and tries to pity and love me. I don't want that. I want to be treated one way.

Cl From what my girlfriend tells me about her home life, I've got it easy. But still I don't like the way my mother treats me. She tells me I can't go here, I can't go there; and then something goes wrong, I get blamed for it.

Co I am always the one who has to take it. I am always the one who gets blamed. Me. Always me. I don't like that.

Cl My mother is starting to get like my girlfriend's mother. She's not letting me out. I can't use the phone. I can't watch TV. I got to do my homework until I turn blue. I have to do it over and over; and then I still can't go out. My cousin said that if I pick up in school, my mother would let me out once a week. What good is once a week? I might as well stay in the whole week. Like yesterday, she let me go up to my girlfriend's house to finish my homework. That was all right. I mean, she let me out and everything—sometimes—lets me out at quarter of 4 and tells me to be in the house at quarter of 5. I came home and asked if I could go out again the next day and my mother said, "No." I says, "I'm not going to stay in the house all alone just for you . . . why should I be bored to death?"

Co Uh, huh.

Cl She tells me she doesn't want me out of the house and starts yelling at me and everything. She thinks I am just going to sit there and twiddle my thumbs.

Co My mother just doesn't understand me. I try to be good but she doesn't believe me.

Cl She doesn't believe me. She don't believe a word I say. Everybody else is right but me.

Co If only she'd believe me once in a while instead of everybody else.

Cl My mother says, "I believe you." I says, "You don't believe a word I say. Maybe if I told you a lie, you'd believe me!"

Co I don't lie to her, but still she doesn't believe me.

Cl I told her, "I'm not coming home from school. You can do anything you want, but I am not coming home from school." She says, "I'll pick you up in school." So I says, "Go right ahead because I ain't going to be there." She says that if I don't come home from school then she'll go looking for me. So then she says that she'll send me away. I says, "Go right ahead. I'm willing just to get away from you!" She says, "What do you mean?" I says, "I am not going to be treated like dirt." Why should I be accused of something and when they find it isn't true, then they try to make up to me. I told her one of these days I was going out of the house and I wasn't coming back!

Co I'm fed up with her and the way she treats me. I've had enough!

Cl I mean, that isn't fair. Like the money, I told her, "I haven't got it!" I says, "Don't ask me, because I haven't got it!" So she goes through my drawers, my closet, my wallet. She goes through everything that belongs to me. Even my personal stuff. She don't leave my mail alone. She's got to read every piece of mail that comes into the house for me.

Co I have no privacy. She thinks she can do just about anything with me.

Cl I suppose she's got a right to go through my things and read my mail, I know, but I asked her if she'd leave my mail alone. Every little thing I get in the mail, she's got to open it and read it. Like money, if I get it on my birthday, she keeps it all, then she buys me something with it and what's left, she keeps. Then she tries to tell me that she spent some of her money, too! The money that a relative may send me in the mail, she takes it away from me.

Co She acts as if she just doesn't trust me, as if I'm a nobody. She thinks she can take things away from me. It makes me feel awful.

Cl Then some of my jeans. My mother claims my jeans are tight. Some of them are—but not bad tight, though. Just as tight as anybody else would wear them, anyway. Then, I got jeans that need to be fixed. She won't have them fixed for me. She tells me to wear what I have and I wear the same things over and over again. Then you go into her closet and you find plenty of clothes. Every time she goes out I think she buys something new. Last time she went out, she comes home with five sweaters and five skirts. Then she tells me she hasn't got any clothes!

Co My mother has a lot, but I don't have much of anything, but she is always saying that she has nothing and I have a lot. I just wish she'd spend some money on me instead of herself.

Cl She tells me that I get too much money during the week. She tells us she spends too much money on us.

Co No matter what I do at home, it always turns out that my mother is going to have her way and I can never have my way. She is always going to be treating me like dirt.

Cl Every time there is something missing, I did it. She did it. She did it. She did it. Everybody points to me!

Co It's always my fault and never anybody else's fault.

Cl Then after my mother gets mad at me, someone tells her that they did it. After I go through it all. Then she tries to love me up.

Co If she can't love me from the start, then I don't want her to love me.

Cl Like this morning, when she found the money where she had dropped it, she says, "Here's your money for school." I says, "I don't want it." So she says, "Come back here." But I walked out and slammed the door and told her I wasn't coming home from school.

Co First she treats me like dirt and then she expects us to be friends.

Cl First she tells me we'll be friends, then she tells me I'll have to stay home all afternoon. "Come home and stay in," she says.

Co I never know where I stand with my mother.

Cl And they say your mother is supposed to be the closest person to you. She don't let me do a thing.

Co She is always on my neck. She never lets me do a thing.

Cl She always says I am too young to go out at night. Like on Friday and Saturday night a bunch of girls and a couple of boys, they go to the movies. "You're just a baby." I says, "Kids younger than I am go." She says, "You aren't kids younger than you. You are my daughter and you are staying in this house."

Co I wish she'd let me do some of the things other kids do.

Cl And I can't go out at night. I have to be in the house at a quarter to five and we don't eat supper until 7. In the house by quarter to five. If I'm not there, I get killed. My brother, he can go out after supper. I get all my homework done and I say, "Ma, can I go out?" She says, "No, you're staying in."

Co She never lets me out, never lets me do the things I want to do. I have to be in and other kids get out.

Cl Sometimes she lets me stay up until 9:00. If I want to get out, I have to lie to her . . . but she won't let me out if she knows that I lied to her. The first time I lied to her was the last time. I don't remember where I went or what time I got home. She told me to come home at 8:00 and I probably came into the house at about 9:00. No matter what I do, I'm a liar, I'm a sneak, I'm no good.

Co I never do things right. She just doesn't trust me. Doesn't believe anything I say.

Cl The other night—I don't know what I did, but she talked to me from 4:30 in the afternoon until about half past seven, until my father came home. I was actually bored and then she talked about it all during supper and then she talked about it until 9:00 and then she said, "Get to bed."

Co If she would just leave me alone instead of talking and talking about whatever I do wrong.

Cl She's getting to be like my girlfriend's mother. Can't do this, can't do that.

Co Getting so that I can't move.

Cl I can't go anywhere without a definite reason. If I want to go with the kids she says, "Where are you going? Who are you going with?" Those are the first words that come out of my father's and mother's mouths.

Co Uh, huh.

Cl All I have to say is I'm going with so and so and she says, "You can't go!"

Co Uh, huh.

Cl My mother makes up everybody's mind for them!

Co I can't have a mind of my own. She is always telling me what to do and what is right and wrong.

Cl Whenever my brother starts doing something wrong, my mother starts yelling at *me*. She calls *me* stupid and everything, and all I have to do is complain and my father starts yelling at me!

Co She can tell you off, but you can't tell her off.

Cl I wish I could tell her off!

Co If I could only tell her off, I'd feel better.

Cl I am not going to get picked on from her! Everything that goes wrong, I get blamed for it!

Co It is always me. Never anybody else. I am always the one to get blamed for anything that happens in my house.

Cl Because I am the one that is nothing in my house.

Co I am nobody. Everybody else is smart and I am nobody.

Cl My father always says that I'm stupid. As though I wasn't even living there. And if I had my choice, I'd get out of there.

Co I'd like to get away from them all, if I only had the chance. They all make me feel like I am nothing. They think I lie and steal and I'm stupid.

Cl One day I was going to run away, but I know my mother would catch up with me before I did. Like plenty of times, when she is sleeping and the kids are waiting for me—I have to climb out the back window just to get out.

Co Uh, huh. I can never do anything right. Everything that I do is wrong. I get blamed for everything.

Cl Everything that goes wrong, I get blamed for it!

Co It is always me and never anybody else.

Cl I told her some one of these days, when I get older, I am going to go out of the house one morning for school and I wasn't going to come home. I told her I didn't know where I was going to go, but I wasn't going to come home.

Co I'm fed up. I told my mother that someday I'm just going to run away.

Cl I'm just going to leave.

Co Just get away from it all. If they are going to treat me that way, I'm just going to leave.

Cl I *am* going to leave. My mother says, "If you leave, you'll break my heart!" I says, "Good, that'll teach you something!" Another day she says to me, "If I died, you'd be the happiest person in the world." So I said, "That's right. I would be. Anything to get away from you!"

Co Anything to get away from my mother and all the things she does to make my life miserable. Even if she dies, I wouldn't care.

Cl I don't *want* her to drop dead! She is just a pain in the neck!

Co A real big pain. I can never have a life of my own. I can never do what I want to do.

Cl I can never be with the friends I want to be with. My mother tells me they are all no good! And if I hang around with them anyway, my mother calls me no good.

Co I never have a life of my own. My mother is always going to have something to say about me.

Cl I don't want anybody leading my life.

Co I want to live my own life. I don't want my mother to try to live it for me.

SUE

Counseling Session 9

Counselor-Client Dialogue

Co Come in. How are things going?

Cl Fine. Everything is turning out perfect now. Miss Brown and I are getting along fine. Things are working out all right now.

Co Uh, huh.

Cl If I want to do something, she says O.K. Like if I want to change my seat, she says, "Go ahead."

Co Uh, huh.

Cl Things are going along all right, thank God. I don't feel like fighting with her all year.

Co You kind of feel better about that.

Cl She says that because of my improved behavior, my marks are going up. She says my behavior was the only thing that brought my marks down. Things are going along all right. We only fight once in a while, if she's in a bad mood.

Co Most of the time I find that it is easier to get along with Miss Brown.

Cl If I don't bother her, she won't bother me.

Co I kind of find that if I manage not to bother her, she in turn doesn't bother me.

Cl If I feel like fooling around with her, I'll ask a silly question. She doesn't mind. She's O.K. if you can get along with her. My mother says I've got to buckle down because Miss Brown will keep me in the sixth grade because of my poor conduct.

Co Uh, huh.

Cl I know, and all my teachers know, I have the brains to do the work, but I just don't want to do it. Like Miss Brown gave us 17 examples for homework and I did them in ten minutes. She checked them and I got them all right. She says, "I told you I thought you could do the work." Because the first quarter she gave me either an A or a B, I forget which, but the second quarter she gave me a failing mark. When we were fighting, I didn't do my homework. Now when I finish my homework, I ask her for some of the assignments I didn't do, and now I did three of them and she's marked me in the book for having finished them.

Co But now that I'm doing my homework and getting better marks and not fooling around, I find that it's easier to get along with Miss Brown.

Cl I knew I was wrong about her. I know that ever since I came to this school, I thought I was a big deal. Just because I was older than everyone else, I thought I was some sort of queen. Now I see that some of the fights might have been caused by Miss Brown, but most of the time they were by both of us—by me, mostly.

Co I'm willing to take some of the blame for the trouble I was getting into.

Cl I started part of them but she did her share, too. Like I'm supposed to stay after school thirteen times more, and I skipped, and Miss

Green gave me some more days to stay after school. The principal saw me and says if I skip staying after school, he'll throw me out. He says if I stay after school for three weeks, he'll clear my school record. Also, he wants me in school ten minutes before school starts. I think this is pretty fair, because I'm the one that was skipping out after school. Even when I stayed after school I fooled around and got in trouble.

Co I was kind of responsible for getting into trouble.

Cl In ways I was, in ways I wasn't.

Co It wasn't always my fault. Mostly my fault, but sometimes someone else's.

Cl My mother says I'm old enough to take care of myself. She says if I fool around now, I'll never get out of school.

Co I'm glad I listened to my mother and did these things that have helped me to improve.

Cl She's given me good advice. I go home and do my homework. Then I ask my mother if I can go out to eight o'clock. She says, "No." and then I drop the thing. Last night I was studying for a test today and I asked her if I could go to my girlfriend's house. She says, "O.K., but leave me the telephone number." I did and she called me up there. She's got a right to know where I was. I was telling the truth. I called her at ten minutes of eight and said we weren't through with the questions. She says, "O.K., but I want you home by 8:30." I was in the house by 8:20. She says, "If you want to go to your girlfriend's house tomorrow night, you can go."

Co Uh, huh.

Cl I do a lot for my parents and they do a lot for me. Even my father used to get himself in trouble giving me breaks. My mother used to chase him around the house saying, "Don't you give her any breaks."

Co If I can only keep it up . . .

Cl I know I have the will power. Like I tried to keep these two boys from skipping out to early recess, and one of them shoved me and Miss Brown took my side and told them not to touch me. I was really surprised. She says, "Just keep out of trouble." And then when there's trouble in the room and she says, "Was it you?" and I say, "No." Now she believes me and she never used to believe me.

Co Now I feel that Miss Brown trusts me and it feels pretty good. I can get along with her.

Cl She seems like a new person to me. Like any other teacher. She fools around with me and seems pretty good, now. She's funny when she's out of school. But in school, she gets mad with kids when they do something wrong, but I suppose they deserve it. I've learned my lesson.

Co It's rough being in trouble. I went through a lot. I've had a horrible time. Now I want to stay out of trouble.

Cl I don't know what got into me when I got into all that trouble with Miss Brown. I guess I wasn't thinking. I was just going ahead and doing things so I could bother Miss Brown because she was giving me trouble. But now I'm getting along good with Miss Brown . . . I sort of don't have to keep fighting with her. I can sort of have fun in school, and learn more.

Co I hope this good feeling of getting along with Miss Brown lasts.

Cl It is good. She's really a nice teacher. She loses her temper and gets mad if you cause trouble; and in a way, I can't blame her. My class fools around a lot and makes her nervous. She has to do what she does to make us respect her. My mother says she has to. She says, "Don't treat a teacher like dirt." She gave me a hard math problem to do in three minutes. I got it done in two and a half. She made a mistake in checking it, and I found her mistake for her. She said my answer was right. She said it was a very, very hard math problem. Everybody was surprised. If I do what's right, I can stay out of trouble with her.

Co I have a different feeling inside. I find it easier to get along with Miss Brown.

Cl It was hard at first, but it became simpler. She never gave me trouble when I told her the truth.

Co I feel better now that I know that when I tell the truth, I can get along with her.

Cl She told me if I don't fool around, I'd have no trouble. I told her if she would call on me when I raise my hand, she'd have no trouble with me, either.

Co It is a nice feeling to know that she trusts me.

Cl It *is* nice that she trusts me. She told me to forget the past and think about the future. If I'd been in my grave when she said that, I'd have turned over three times! She sent me upstairs on an errand to get a girl, and the girl says, "How come *you're* on an errand?" I says, "My friend, Miss Brown, sent me."

Co Uh, huh.

Cl   Miss Brown said that my girlfriend was a bad influence on me. My mother says as long as I don't get into trouble with her I can see her and I think that's fair.

Co   I get the feeling that my mother is beginning to trust me.

Cl   My mother says I can make all my own decisions except when I go out. I have to ask her if I can go out.

Co   I like it this way, making my own decisions.

Cl   I'm glad I'm getting along because it's the third marking period and Miss Brown says she'd give me a C just because of my improved attitude. We're getting along fine, now.

Co   As long as I don't give her a hard time, we'll get along.

Cl   Some kids say I'm foolish to be friends with her after the trouble she gave me. "Listen," I says, "that's my business." I won't let anybody use bad language talking about her. Whatever I felt about Miss Brown before is all over.

Co   I can leave all I had against Miss Brown behind me.

Cl   I can forget it. Anything, except if she had gotten me thrown out of school! Even keeping me after school helps me. I study after school, but at home I'd be watching TV while I was trying to do my homework. I get my homework done now. At home, all the kids come over. We have our own little group. Last night was my birthday and they all chipped in and bought me a bracelet.

Co   Things are going pretty good for me now.

Cl   I'm doing fine now. I don't have the worries I had before.

Co   I feel that getting along with Miss Brown is very important; it was important to get myself out of this trouble.

Cl   It was hard, but it had to be done, and I did it, and I'm glad I did!

Co   I'm happy about the fact that I've changed.

Cl   I thought I was a big shot, but I learned. It pays in the end to smarten up. I'm satisfied with myself.

Co   I decided that I wanted to do the right thing.

Cl   Miss Brown was sometimes unfair but lately she's understood my side of things. Like that time I tried to stop the kids from going out to early recess, they were boys, but they felt it when I belted them. Miss Brown broke it up. I would have really gotten into trouble if Miss Brown had blamed me!

Co   I was glad Miss Brown didn't blame me for the whole thing and get me into trouble. It felt good to have her on my side.

Cl   She says to them, "Take her advice; she's been through it and she knows what she's talking about." She left me in charge when she went out of the room. Harry started walking around the room, and I made the shrimp sit down.

Co I really felt good that she left me in charge, because I never thought she'd trust me enough to do that!

Cl I think both of us will be very sad if trouble comes between us again.

Co She respects me, and I can respect her.

Cl Right now I think she's O.K. When she gets mad, I shut my mouth and don't say anything. There's nothing to argue about. I've got a fresh start, and I'm not getting into any more trouble.

Co It really all depends on me.

Cl It does. It depends on me to keep this friendship. Everything will go up in flames if I don't. She tries to help me. She'll give me help when I need it. It's working out. I enjoy being in her room now.

FRED

Counseling Session 2

Counselor-Client Dialogue

Co Hi, Fred . . . come in. How are things going?

Cl Well . . . O.K. Pretty good. There's one thing I don't . . . what kind of advice could you give me on this thing? I was absent one Friday so I'm way behind . . . the teacher . . . she was way ahead . . . other kids were way ahead of me and she was busy with them and then I don't know what to do. So now I'm mixed up. They'd be going on to another thing and I'd just be sitting there blank. I wouldn't know what to do.

Co Uh, huh, I was absent that Friday and it seems that I'm behind. I don't know where I am or where I'm supposed to be.

Cl Yeah. She did show me what to do, but I just couldn't remember.

Co Uh, huh, I just couldn't understand.

Cl Yeah. I tried but I forgot what to do.

Co I just couldn't remember what I was supposed to do.

Cl Um, that's right. So I'd get mixed up some more . . . I wouldn't know what to do. I'd be scared to death.

Co I'm afraid to go into that room now because I just don't know what to do . . .

Cl I don't know . . . I don't know what to do . . .

Co Uh, huh. Tomorrow I won't know what I'm supposed to do.

Cl I wonder what I'll do. I wonder what she'll do. What would she do? I just don't know what she'll do.

Co I'm so far behind I wonder what's going to happen to me.

Cl Yeah . . . that's right . . . I don't know . . . I don't know what to do.

Co What shall I do when I go in there tomorrow? What could happen?

Cl Yeah . . . what'll happen to me? I'm stumped.

Co Uh, huh.

Cl I'm almost afraid to go to school tomorrow because I don't know what'll happen to me. I don't know what she'll do.

Co Uh, huh.

Cl What would she do?

Co I wonder just what she's going to do and sometimes it upsets me so that I don't even want to come to school.

Cl I wonder . . . I don't know what I could do. I've been sick for a while. I might be too sick to come to school tomorrow.

Co Uh, huh.

Cl I was sick and out of school on Monday and Tuesday. I was thinking that maybe I'd be too sick for school tomorrow.

Co Uh, huh.

Cl I don't know what I'm going to do.

Co Uh, huh.

Cl I wonder what I should do?

Co Maybe tomorrow I'll be too sick to come to school.

Cl Yeah, maybe . . . but I doubt it . . . I don't think I'm *that* sick.

Co Uh, huh . . . looks like I'm just going to have to come.

Cl Yeah.

Co And find out just what's going to happen.

Cl Yeah, sometimes I do stupid things. Sometimes I don't pick up what the teacher is saying.

Co Uh, huh.

Cl Like sometimes I make stupid mistakes and she tells me not to do it and she bawls me out.

Co Uh, huh . . . I just don't hear some of the things she says. Why does she have to bawl me out just because I don't hear her?

Cl I'll just have to see what's going to happen to me.

Co I wonder what tomorrow will bring.

Cl I haven't the slightest idea of what she'll do. I don't think she'll go back and explain all those things because she thinks that I'm stupid.

Co Uh, huh.

Cl I don't know what she'll do to me.

Co Uh, huh.

Cl Maybe she'd make me ah . . . I don't know what she's going to do.

Co I wonder just what she's going to do. I think she thinks that I'm too stupid to help . . . I wonder just what she's going to do.

Cl I don't know if I've gotten any worse (referring to cold) since I got sick. I went out yesterday and I don't know if I'm any sicker.

Co Uh, huh.

Cl Maybe I'm just not going to get any worse.

Co Uh, huh.

Cl There's no use in trying to pretend that I'm sick because . . .ah . . . they won't believe me.

Co I could pretend that I'm sick and not have to come to school tomorrow but they wouldn't believe me.

Cl My parents know me better than that.

Co My mother and father would be able to see right through me . . . they'd know I wasn't sick . . . they'd make me go to school.

Cl Yeah . . .

Co So I really can't get out of tomorrow by pretending that I'm sick.

Cl At least I don't think so. Maybe I'll have a bad headache or somethin' . . . but I don't get many of them.

Co But I wish that I could come up with something . . . I wish I could be sick so then I wouldn't have to come to school.

Cl I'm well enough to come to school. But I don't know what'll happen tomorrow.

Co I wonder what'll happen . . . I guess I'm well enough . . . I guess I'll just have to come and find out . . . but still I wonder.

Cl Maybe . . . I might get torn to pieces for it.

Co Something bad can really happen to me tomorrow.

Cl Yeah . . . I might get yelled at.

Co I won't like that.

Cl Yeah . . . and all the kids . . . I'd probably get laughed at.

Co Uh, huh . . . the kids will laugh at me and the teacher will yell at me . . . it'll be the same old thing.

Cl Yeah . . . I have trouble with the ruler. I can't measure very good . . . especially on rulers with lots of marks on them . . . I can tell pretty good . . . a half or a quarter inch but those little ones like five-sixteenths or seven-eighths . . . those are kinda hard.

Co Uh, huh.

Cl I was never good with a ruler . . .

Co Uh, huh. Doing well depends on my using a ruler and I've just never been able to really know how to use it.

Cl Measure . . . with rulers and stuff . . . and be able to draw a lot of lines. I'm not even allowed, in measuring stuff, to use the end . . . always the middle. That's a little harder.

Co Uh, huh.

Cl I kinda . . . ah . . . I just don't know what's going to happen tomorrow . . . I won't know until tomorrow.

Co I kind of wonder what's going to happen.

Cl Yeah.

Co But I just won't know until tomorrow.

Cl Yeah . . . hmmm . . . maybe it'll be embarrassing.

Co I hate to be embarrassed.

Cl Yeah . . . because it means you do something that seems very ridiculous.

Co When I get embarrassed I do things that are ridiculous. I don't want to do them but because I'm embarrassed I do them.

Cl I guess I'll have to wait and see what'll happen tomorrow. I just don't know what to do to solve it. What would she do?

Co What are some of the things that she could do to me?

Cl Well . . . she could make me just stay there and do nothing. Too bad none of the boys don't live near me . . . if they lived near me I could borrow their papers and copy them.

Co Uh, huh.

Cl The trouble is that none of them live near me, so I'm stumped.

Co If some of those kids in the class only lived near me then I could go to their houses and find out how to do it.

Cl Yeah. When using a ruler and measuring I'm really kinda nervous.

Co Uh, huh.

Cl Yeah . . . I'm nervous . . . I'm so afraid of making mistakes.

Co Uh, huh. I'm really afraid to make a mistake.

Cl Yeah. I just don't know. I guess there are just some things that you'll have to wait until tomorrow to find out.

Co Uh, huh.

Cl I've got to wait until tomorrow to find out what will happen.

Co I can't figure out today what's going to happen tomorrow. I guess I'm just going to have to wait.

Cl Yeah . . . I'm just going to have to wait.

Co I can't do anything about it. I guess I can wonder what's going to happen but I'll just have to wait.

Cl I don't know . . . nobody can think of a way . . . nobody's a magician . . . they can't think of a way. Nobody can help me.

Co I can't really think of anyone who can tell me what's going to happen tomorrow.

Cl Yeah, that's right. There's no one to help me . . . if there's something that I could do to avoid tomorrow but there's no way of avoiding tomorrow.

Co Uh, huh. Tomorrow is just going to be trouble to me but I can't see any way out of it.

Cl Yeah . . . I can't see any way out of it.

Co I just know and feel that it's going to be one of those days.

Cl Yeah . . . with ease. With ease unless I can fool someone . . . maybe get sick.

Co It's going to be a bad day, unless I can pretend that I'm sick.

Cl Yeah . . . sure . . . I'll just have to take the consequences.

Co Whatever happens, happens.

Cl Yeah . . . whatever happens, happens. I don't remember being stumped in anything like this before.

Co Uh, huh.

Cl I've always found a way to get out of things.

Co Uh, huh.

Cl I always got out of it. Maybe I'll find a way to get out of it tomorrow.

Co I've always been able to get out of things before . . . I've been able to do things that would get me out of bad things; but tomorrow, I don't know . . . but still maybe something will come up.

Cl Yeah . . . it always does. You never know what's going to happen.

Co There's a chance that before drawing tomorrow, I may find an excuse to get out of it.

Cl I can't think of any ideas. I just can't throw any light on anything.

Co Uh, huh.

Cl Like up there [pointing to head].

Co I can't figure out a way to avoid tomorrow.

Cl I guess I can't . . . well, at least I don't think so.

Co Uh, huh.

Cl 'Cause I . . . I think I'd be sent to school.

Co Uh, huh.

Cl I don't think they'd believe me . . . they'd probably know I was faking being sick.

Co Uh, huh . . . my parents would know I was faking.

Cl Yeah . . . my father always says, even if I did have a headache, he says to me, "When I get a headache, I don't get a day off from work."

Co Uh, huh.

Cl But, ah . . . maybe I'd get sent to school tomorrow.

Co Uh, huh.

Cl But working is different. A working man has to support a family and get paid for it.

Co My father has to go to work but . . .

Cl Yeah . . . they have to do that. Lots of times when the school gives you days off, fathers have to be at work . . . they have to be out working.

Co Uh, huh.

Cl People who work get a lot less days off than school kids do.

Co Uh, huh.

Cl Yeah . . . like a mailman. They know the mail must go through . . . I just don't know what's gonna happen tomorrow.

Co Uh, huh.

Cl I'm gonna have to keep guessing.

Co Uh, huh.

Cl Maybe something will happen.

Co Uh, huh.

Cl I don't know what.

Co I know tomorrow is gonna be a bad day. I wonder what's gonna happen to me?

Cl Yeah . . . I'm pretty sure it will be a bad day because if I do stay home, I'll have to hide in the house all day.

Co Uh, huh.

Cl I'd have to stay in the house and not go out. If I wanted to go to the store to buy something, there's a girl who lives right next to it and she might see me, and then I'd be caught.

Co Uh, huh.

Cl I just don't know how to escape tomorrow.

Co Uh, huh.

Cl I'm kinda tired worrying about it . . . what would the teacher do?

I wouldn't know what to say to the teacher. Maybe there's nothing I could say.

Co It's hard to know what to do.

Cl And I know . . . no one can tell me what to do. That's something that I'm just stuck with.

Co Nobody can tell me what I should do tomorrow.

Cl That's right.

Co Guess I'm just kind of stuck with the day . . . it's just going to have to come and I'm going to have to see what's going to happen.

Cl It's very doubtful that I'd get a headache.

Co Uh, huh . . . there seems to be no way of my getting out of tomorrow.

Cl No way.

Co Looks like I'm going to have to face it.

Cl Yeah. My father thinks that I should be brave enough to face things . . . but . . . I'm not.

Co I'm not brave. I just can't face it, even though my father thinks I should.

Cl I should be brave enough to face it but . . . I just don't seem to be brave.

Co Uh, huh.

Cl Sometimes I can be a real coward.

Co Uh, huh.

Cl Yeah . . . sometimes I can be a real coward . . . and be scared of lots of things.

Co Uh, huh.

Cl Like that Miles Standish, in that story, "The Courtship of Miles Standish," he wanted to propose to Priscilla and he asked John Alden to do it for him. He said he wasn't afraid when the enemy had guns all around him in a circle . . . but he was scared of a "no" from a woman . . . that she'd say, "No." He was scared of that . . . so there are some things that you can be awful scared of.

Co Uh, huh . . . I'm not the brave type. I can't be brave even though my father thinks I should be.

Cl I'm not going to think about it.

Co I'll just push it out of my mind.

Cl Maybe she'll just let me sit and do nothing . . . then I'd be laughed at. I wouldn't care for that very much.

Co Uh, huh . . . I hate to have people laugh at me.

Cl   Yeah . . . I wouldn't be very comfortable.

Co   It'll be embarrassing. It'll be so uncomfortable if that happens.

FRED

Counseling Session 7

Counselor-Client Dialogue

Co   Hi, Fred. How are things going?

Cl   My mother tried to put me on a diet, but somehow or other, I always find a way to cheat. It's hard to diet. It's hard to keep food out of my reach . . . there is always some way I can get food. Maybe the doctor could give me some pills. The pills make you feel too full to eat.

Co   I'd like to diet, but I just don't have the will power. I can't resist. I have to eat . . . I find ways to get food.

Cl   I think my mother is right about being fat. Fat people haven't got long to live.

Co   I can't seem to diet. It's too hard.

Cl   I always find something to eat. I'm allowed to have fruit and skim milk. I don't like the taste of skim milk and fruit. Fat people know fruit isn't as filling as something with salt and sugar in it. I have no way of sticking to a diet. I hope the doctor gives me pills. I need them.

Co   I can't do it on my own.

Cl   A candy bar fills me more than a banana or apple.

Co   I wish the doctor would give me pills. I don't have any will power.

Cl   My mother says I wouldn't mind it after a few days. But I feel so uncomfortable the first few days, I have to eat. I have nothing to do, so I eat because I'm bored.

Co   I'm bored. I have nothing to do, so I eat.

Cl   Something I do is lie down when I have nothing to do. I sometimes sleep when I have nothing to do. That passes the time.

Co   I'm bored and when there isn't anything to do, I sleep.

Cl   I can't find anything to do and now I'm fat and nobody wants me because I'm no good at anything.

Co   Nobody wants me because I'm fat I can't do anything.

Cl   It's awfully hard for a fat person. You have to take a lot when you're fat. You don't have many friends.

Co   Because I'm fat there aren't kids to do things with.

Cl There just aren't any kids to be with. Even if I wasn't fat, maybe there wouldn't be much to do. It happens to a lot of kids my age. I don't have a bunch to hang around with. I wish I just had somebody to hang around with. That would keep me out of the house and away from eating.

Co I'm really lonely. Who wants to have anything to do with me?

Cl Nobody lives near me, and I can't do anything, anyway.

Co Nobody lives near me, but even if they did, I wonder if they'd have anything to do with me because I'm so fat and can't do anything.

Cl I'd be afraid to run around the block, afraid I'd drop dead!

Co Hard to do anything when you're fat.

Cl I know Mr. Ron. He's six feet tall and weighs 300 pounds. I said to my mother, "He's all right." My mother says, "Who knows when he's going to drop dead?"

Co I know I shouldn't be fat, but I can't do anything about it.

Cl My mother says fat people could drop dead overnight. I got to thinking maybe I'm leading a dangerous life. Could that be true, I wonder? I don't want to die early. I hope things will improve so I can live a happier life. Life isn't over yet. I hope for the very best in the future. I'll ask the doctor about it. My mother says I have to lose 20 pounds. My mother doesn't know how hard that is! I tell her what you do as a counselor . . . help me learn more stuff about me. My mother doesn't get the point. But she says you must know what you are doing. I think you help me pretty good. It's good to have somebody to talk to. My mother couldn't understand me like you do. She isn't trained to. She couldn't understand me like you do.

Co It's comfortable to be here. At home my mother never really understands what I think or how I feel about things.

Cl I guess no one can understand you unless they are trained, like a counselor.

Co My mother has never been able to understand me.

Cl I guess it is hard. I couldn't understand anyone else. When I said I was bored, my mother just said next year I'd be older and could do more things and I wouldn't be bored. Who cares about next year? I'm worried about this year.

Co This is what I mean about my mother not understanding that I'm bored and worried about being fat.

Cl Yes, she says next year I won't be bored.

Co My problem is now, not then.

Cl   What do I do now, when things are bad?

Co   I wish my mother would understand.

Cl   She thinks everyone should have the guts to diet. My uncle and my cousin's wife lost a lot of weight, but I don't have the guts. No one in the family ever ate as much as I do. Maybe they don't miss food as much as I do. When there's a night when my mother doesn't have anything good in the house to eat, I really miss it. I feel uncomfortable. I find it hard to go without eating after supper.

Co   My mother doesn't understand that I'm not the type to diet. I haven't got the courage or the guts.

Cl   Here's what happened when I went on a diet before. I lost just about all the weight I needed to. Then I just gained it back again. I was able to diet then, but now I'm bigger and I miss food more. I hope you can understand this. Maybe I don't have will power. I just have to eat. I dieted when I was much younger, but I can't do it now!

Co   Just because I did it before doesn't mean I can still do it. My mother doesn't understand this . . . I just don't have the will power.

Cl   Now that I'm older, I eat more and that makes it all the harder to diet. She says I should have more will power now that I'm older. But she doesn't understand . . . but I hope I do lose weight because if I don't, it won't be too good for me.

Co   But I just don't seem able to do it.

Cl   I can't. Most of the doctors just say, "Go on a diet!"

Co   Easy for them to say, but hard for me to do.

Cl   I asked the doctor about just taking tablets, but he said I'd have to diet, too. Maybe those people in the magazine ads dieted and took pills, too. Maybe the pills that make you feel fuller would work. At least, I hope so. I hope they can find some reducing pills that would fit me. It sure is hard.

Co   I want something to help me . . . I can't do it myself.

Cl   All I can do is hope that diet pills will work.

Co   I can't do it myself.

Cl   I don't want to stay fat all my life.

Co   Imagine going through life fat. I couldn't take it.

Cl   I'd rather be thin. I'd be happier thin!

Co   I'd be better off thin, but I don't have the will power. I'd be happier, but I can't. I can't diet.

Cl   I can't diet. I just can't. I hope something will happen so I'll be able to.

Co It will have to be a miracle to make me diet!

Cl Maybe a scientist will invent a pill that will be good for me.

Co I like that feeling of having lots of food inside of me.

Cl Sure is a good feeling.

Co I know I shouldn't eat so much, but it's a good feeling to have the food inside.

Cl To feel full inside is great. I can't diet, but maybe there'll be some diet pills. I'd be happier.

Co I've got to find the pill that will help me.

Cl Yes.

Co I can't do it myself.

Cl I know I can't so I'll have to find that pill. I wonder if I'll find it. I guess I thought of it before. I just can't diet, it's just too hard. What could I do if I don't find a pill? Maybe I'll have to exercise. A lot!

Co Maybe exercise will be the thing for me, if I don't find a pill. I want to feel full. I just don't want to cut out good food.

Cl If I had enough money to go out to the Southwest and live on a ranch as a cowboy or on a farm doing chores or herding cows, it would keep me away from food and give me exercise. I could wrestle with calves to get them branded.

Co I'd have to just keep busy because when I'm bored, I start eating.

Cl That would give me some exercise. There's no exercise living around here.

Co The main problem is that I have nothing to do and I'm bored, and when I have nothing to do, I eat. If I had friends or something I could do, I'd stay away from food.

Cl When I have nothing to do, I have to eat.

Co I eat when I have nothing to do.

Cl What else can I do but eat? Without eating, I don't know what I'd do. Sometimes I'd like to sleep all day.

Co I don't get much fun or pleasure out of life. I'm pretty bored.

Cl The first thing to do is to lose weight.

Co I know it is hard to do, but I know it is the thing I have to do.

Cl I don't want to do it . . . it's too hard!

Co It is a lot easier for me to eat when I am bored.

Cl Yeah. I guess fat people have that trouble. Nothing to do but eat, because they're bored. My mother says I'd have things to do when I get a flat stomach. But what about now?

Co My mother doesn't understand how it feels to be fat and want to eat . . . how it feels not to have will power.

Cl She just doesn't understand. She tries but it's just too hard for her to understand how I feel.

[long pause]

Remember when I told you about the crushed horn on my train set? Well, know what? I fixed the horn! I worked on it and made it work. There are lots of things that I've done to fix broken parts of my train.

Co You feel good about fixing your train set. You feel very proud.

Cl My mother didn't think that I should bother fixing the horn. She thinks I'm too fussy about little things.

Co To you, fixing that horn was an important thing to do.

Cl It sure was. It made me feel that there was something I could do right! Because I'm fussy and want things right, I took the time to fix the horn.

Co You're very proud of what you did.

Cl Fixing that horn and other things on my train made me feel good. I don't do many things right, but I can fix my trains.

Co It gives you a nice feeling to know that you can do something. [Another long pause]

Cl I hope things improve for me. Being fat, and bored, and lonely is hard. I don't look forward to growing up being this way.

Co You wish things could get better for you. You're tired of being this way.

Cl I sure am. I think that wishing things were better is kind of a waste of time. Maybe there are things I can do to help myself. It will be hard, but I don't have a magic wand to make things get better. Maybe I'll have to begin to do some of the things I don't want to do.

Co It seems that I can't wait. I'm going to have to begin doing things I didn't want to do before.

Cl Things will improve, I hope! Even when I have bad days I'm beginning to think that there are things I can do. If I can fix my trains then maybe I can do other things. Some of the kids are starting to know that I can fix trains. They're asking me questions and things like that. One of them asked me to come over to his house and look at his broken train.

Co You sound more hopeful, Fred. It seems that you're realizing that there are things you can do. It must feel good to be invited to fix someone's train.

Cl   It does. You know there's always—well, maybe not always...but there are things people can do. Like me. I didn't think I could do anything right but I can fix trains. Me! I can do something right.

Co   That's a new feeling for you. A good feeling about something you can do. You sound excited!

Cl   Well, I never really have been invited to anyone's house for anything important. I hope I can fix his train. Maybe other kids will find out that I can and they'll ask me to fix something for them.

Co   You feel that it's a good chance to show that you can do things.

Cl   Things will get better for me, I hope. I have bad days, but I'm beginning to feel O.K., too—about me, I mean. Sometimes I think I have a bad habit of not thinking good things about myself. I don't want to do that any more. I want to feel good about me. I think I can. It'll be a different feeling—a new feeling. [Pause] It seems that I find out about myself when I talk to you. I feel better because I tell you what's on my mind. I learn a lot.

Co   It feels good to feel good about myself.

FRED

Counseling Session 10

Counselor-Client Dialogue

Co   Come in, Fred. Have a seat. How are things going?

Cl   I've been looking in stores at parts for my train. I'm kind of fussy about things like that. A part broke, just a little thing on the forklift platform. I couldn't find it in the stores. The man at one store said you couldn't buy the part separate. Maybe there's a factory where they make the part...where I could get the part I need. I must be smart at something, I thought of that.

Co   I must be smart at something. I really want my trains to be O.K.

Cl   Yeah, like they were when they were new.

Co   Sometimes I think I'm too fussy about my trains.

Cl   I just had another thought. I don't have a good place for them. Maybe I could find a safer place for them. I want things to be like they should be.

Co I want things in my life to be just right.

Cl I don't think everyone would think like that, so there must be some good in me.

Co Uh, huh.

Cl I really felt good when the people in the train store really thought it was smart of me to be so interested in my trains. I had to think and ask them good questions.

Co Uh, huh.

Cl There must be something good about me. I can't be all that bad. I can ask good questions about my trains.

Co Uh, huh.

Cl I can't be all bad if I can think up good questions about my trains.

Co Sometimes I think there are things about me that are O.K. Especially this. My interest in trains is a good thing. I know something.

Cl They couldn't help me. I had to figure it out for myself.

Co I was pleased with myself that I thought about it and came up with the answer.

Cl There's another thing. I'll have to make a part I need. There's a kid I'm kind of friendly with, maybe I'll ask him to help me. Maybe other kids will come to me with train problems. Maybe I can give them some answers.

Co Uh, huh. That would be a good feeling . . . to be able to help other kids.

Cl It would make me feel good to have someone come to me with their train problems, because it would show I know something about something.

Co That would show I know something. Make me feel important. Maybe if I helped kids to get their trains fixed, they'd think I was pretty good.

Cl Maybe I'll be famous. I don't know. That'd be a funny thing.

Co Uh, huh.

Cl You know, sometimes you think you've discovered something, but someone else did it before you. Like my mother thought when she put a candle in a jack-o-lantern on Halloween, she was inventing it, but I found out that everyone else has been doing that every year. When I asked her about it, she said, "Oh, I thought I had invented it." I told her, "Oh, no." I did some thinking on my own. I'm not dumb. I'm thinking up things.

Co I'm not bad. I'm not dumb. There are good things about me.

Cl   I can think. Maybe I'm not good at sports, because I'm fat, but I'm not lazy. I can think things up. When you really want something, you can do it. Maybe you can help other people. Maybe I could throw a light on someone's train problems. That means I'm not all bad.

Co   This is good for me, to know that I can help others. It makes me feel that I can do things.

Cl   Even if I don't get to be a discoverer, I'd be happy just to fix my trains and have them like they were when they were new. That's all I really want. I won't feel too bad if I'm not a discoverer. Being here with you helps me think of lots of stuff about myself . . . the good stuff.

Co   Uh, huh.

Cl   I could go on all day. I could think of a lot of good stuff about me here.

Co   I feel good about me!

Cl   I could be a discoverer, too, but I don't really care. It's just that I'm talking here in counseling and it came out. But I don't really care about being a discoverer!

Co   It isn't too important if I become a discoverer. What is important is that I know that I can fix my trains and can help other kids fix theirs.

Cl   I don't care about being a discoverer. I want my trains to be like they were. I'm very happy with myself.

Co   I feel good about me—what a nice feeling!

Cl   My mother helped me with the trains, a little bit. I thought about the main things. It was me, not my mother, that really thought about how to fix the trains.

Co   It's good to know I can do things.

Cl   She just gave me some little tips.

Co   This feeling of doing something on my own is new and it's a good feeling.

Cl   Not many of the kids bother me now. Maybe they'll think I'm O.K. now. I think I'll tell the kids I can help them fix their trains.

Co   I'd like the kids to know that I can. Then they'd know that there is something good that I can do.

Cl   I was afraid to go into the train store because I thought they'd laugh at me. But they didn't laugh at me. It taught me to do something that I was afraid to do.

Co If I want to do something I should just go ahead and do it!

Cl If it doesn't work, that's O.K. It's a good try!

Co At least I tried!

Cl At least I tried. Me! Fred! I'm not used to trying.

Co This is a good feeling. To at least try to do things.

Cl Even if I'm not good at something I can try to do it.

Co Uh, huh.

Cl Maybe I'll ask a boy in my room who's smart. I'll tell him my idea about trying and see what he thinks.

Co Just to see how good my idea about trying is . . . to find out if he thinks that trying would be good for me.

Cl Maybe this kid's brain is better than mine. I'd like him to judge if this is a good idea. Then I'd know more about whether it's a good idea. But I get the feeling it *is* a good idea. It would be nice to say I did my best . . . the best I could.

Co I think the idea about trying is a good one . . . I just hope that other people think it's a good idea, too!

Cl I'll feel good if my idea about trying is a good one. That'll prove that there's good in me. Maybe it won't be important to the kids that bother me. But to the kids who are friendly, they'll think it's good for me to try.

Co I've thought of something good for me to do, on my own, and I want the kids in my class to know about it.

Cl I don't seem to be good in many things. I'm lower than average — but trying would show some good in me. I just hope it'll work. I'll feel pretty good.

Co Trying will be good for me!

Cl I hope trying is a good idea. I just hope so. It just has to be a good idea and make me happy. I'll feel good about myself. I have a feeling that it *is* a good idea after talking with you.

Co The more I think of this good idea about trying, the more I like myself.

Cl The time is almost up, I guess. I'll feel *really* good, if it works. Then I can feel good about myself. At least there is some good . . . some good in me . . . when I try.

DISCUSSION TOPICS

1. Identify the developmental psychological needs of children and discuss the degree to which a child-centered counseling relationship meets those needs.

2. How would child counselors of different theoretical persuasions attitudinally and verbally respond to Sue and Fred?

3. Discuss the applicability of different counseling theories to children.

4. Identify those aspects of a counseling relationship which would make sense to a child.

5. Identify the developmental stages of becoming a child-centered counselor.

6. Discuss the factors which might inhibit the development of a child-centered counselor.

7. Discuss some of the weaknesses of a child-centered counseling relationship.

8. Discuss the strengths and weaknesses of a counseling program based upon voluntary participation by children.

9. Discuss the degree to which a child counselor's values influence the theory of counseling which he or she applies.

10. Discuss the long-range effect of the counseling experienced by Sue and Fred as they progress through adolescence and adulthood.

11. Discuss the degree to which Sue and Fred showed improvement in their self-concepts and behaviors.

12. Discuss the long-range effect of the counseling experienced by Sue and Fred as they progress through adolescence and adulthood.

Chapter 4

PHASE THREE ALTERNATIVES IN CHILD-CENTERED COUNSELING

When phase three is reached, the child-centered counselor is faced with a number of alternatives for continuing the counseling process. The reflective process started in phase two can be continued if it is producing results. Results can take the form of increased self-awareness on the part of the child, a release from previously repressed feelings which were negatively affecting behavior, an understanding of how feelings influence behavior, an assumption of responsibility for one's behavior rather than blaming others, the attainment of the psychological strength to endure and overcome a debilitating environment, a trusting of one's judgment regarding the positive and negative influences in one's life, and the inclination to seek life experiences which enhance rather than diminish one's psychological stability. If phase two is producing any of the preceding results, then the counselor should continue with the reflective process. It is producing the results intended and the child is acquiring more control of his or her behavior. Rather than being victimized by life's negative experiences, the child develops a control over his or her reactions. Such control comes from the psychological strength that the child has developed as an outcome of a skillfully applied phase two.

Other children, however, are not as receptive to phase two. They use it as an excellent opportunity to have a catharsis, but they never develop the psychological strength to be an active participant in overcoming a problem. Such children need the guidance of a phase three process which to them is more concrete, understandable, and supportive. A process which does not overload the child with responsibility. A process which promises improvement on a gradual basis and only with the active participation of the counselor in helping activities.

The work of child-centered counselors would be far more clear and systematic if all children had a positive response to the reflective process

95

in phase two. But this is not the case. Children, like all persons, are such individuals that one counseling process cannot meet all of the vastly different needs of such unique individuals.

When the child is not achieving the goals of phase two's reflective process, over several counseling sessions, the counselor must be prepared to give up the reflective process in phase three and identify a different process to take its place. This different process must be connected to the child's needs and provide the child with a more concrete way of understanding the cause of a problem and a clear and implementable way to overcome the problem.

Before we turn to several different counseling processes which can be utilized in phase three, we would like to reinforce the availability of common sense (the logical conclusion) for helping the child in phase three. Children are usually uncomplicated. They haven't lived long enough to learn the evasive and devious ways of behaving that characterize adult life. Sometimes all the counselor needs to do in phase three is use a common sense (the logical conclusion) approach for helping the child to solve a problem. Some counselors tend to make phase three a complicated helping process that is doomed to failure because of its complexity. Sometimes all that is needed in phase three to help the child is something simple, direct, and concrete.

When neither the reflective process nor a common sense approach is producing results for the child in phase three, the counselor can turn to approaches drawn from other major theories of counseling. These approaches can be used in whole or in part or they can be used in combination with each other. Whatever helps the child is the criterion for judging which of these approaches is most helpful. The counselor also needs to remember that what may work with one child may not be effective with another. A lot of tailoring needs to occur in phase three in order to implement an approach which fits a particular child's needs. The effort is worth it, however, because the approach utilized has the best chance to work because of its individualized quality. It evolved for use with *this* child and is unique to that child.

When using a particular phase three approach the child-centered counselor should be primarily interested in the utility of the techniques and procedures associated with a theory of counseling. The counselor does not have to have a belief in a particular theory in order to use its techniques and procedures. The use of a theory's techniques and procedures does not carry with their use a requirement to believe in the philosophical constructs which support the theory. A child-centered counselor should be able to implement techniques and procedures borrowed from the different theories of counseling.

When implementing the techniques and procedures drawn from the following counseling theories, the counselor must realize that they will not work automatically. The counselor needs to be patient with the application of a theory and not attempt to apply all of its techniques and procedures in one meeting with a child. The theory's techniques and procedures need to be gradually introduced to the child over several counseling sessions and the counselor needs to cushion his or her introduction by sandwiching them between reflections of a child's feelings. The reflective process, which characterizes phase two, is not abandoned in phase three. It is still used to soften the techniques and procedures of other theories which may be "too much too soon." The reflective process can also be used to help clarify a child's reactions to a particular technique and procedure. The child's reactions will help the counselor evaluate whether the technique or procedure has the potential to be useful in future counseling sessions with the child.

The following seven major theories of counseling and their characteristics are presented in alphabetical order and without bias. The reader needs to understand each of the theories and add its techniques and procedures to the body of knowledge that the counselor draws from for use in phase three. The authors suggest that the best way to understand each of the theories, however, is to read the original works written to support each theory, and form or attend workshops designed to improve one's understanding and application of the techniques and procedures associated with the different theories.

ADLERIAN APPROACH

Alfred Adler's thinking and work generated a theory of personality and counseling known as *Individual Psychology.* It reflects certain philosophical assumptions: the person is a social creature; wants to belong to groups—wants to find a place in society; becomes human in the group; the person's basic need is belonging; and the person must find a place in society to be happy. Leading exponents of the Adlerian approach in the United States have been Dreikurs (1950, 1967) and his protegé, Dinkmeyer (1968, 1971). They collaborated in 1963 (Dreikurs & Dinkmeyer, 1963) and Dinkmeyer went on to advance the application of Adlerian theory in the elementary school. The Adlerian view continues to have a special focus on the counseling needs of children (Dinkmeyer, Pew, & Dinkmeyer, 1979).

Basic Premises

1. The child is goal seeking. All human behavior is purposive. A child's actions and movements are directed toward specific goals. It is impossible to understand a child's behavior unless a child's goals are known. Goals explain behavior and actions.

2. The child is basically active and relatively free to determine personal behavior. Each individual has the creative power to make biased interpretations of events and experiences. Behavior reflects a Stimulus-Interpretation-Response model. The person's perceptions and interpretations of a situation are more important in developing an understanding of the person than the objective reality of the situation.

3. The child is primarily a social being and the child's behavior can best be understood if it is viewed in terms of its social setting. The social context in which behavior takes place is essential to understanding the behavior. Social striving and acceptance is a primary factor in the life of the child. The search for significance and for a place in society are basic objectives of every child and adult.

4. Emotions are social and personal tools used to serve the child's purpose and actions. They are movements that facilitate the achievement of goals.

5. Belonging is a basic human need. Everyone has a desire to belong to someone or something. Generally, the more concerned one is for others, the better adjusted one is as an individual. Much maladaptive behavior and many anxieties emanate from the child's fear of not belonging.

6. Each child expresses in actions, attitudes, and behavior a unifying theme—a characteristic pattern of life—a life style. The life-style represents offensive-defensive strategy and tactics for satisfying needs and achieving goals in life. The life-style is an important strategic-tactical pattern for controlling or reducing tensions and conflicts on psychosocial levels. It is characterized by different levels of social adaptability and involves use of mechanisms, reaction formations, and evasive behaviors.

A child's life-style takes direction after specific types of difficulties have been encountered again and again. Out of the constant repetition of the difficulties, real or imagined, which the child encounters, the child develops special ways and means which appear to be effective and serviceable in achieving goals. These special ways and means characterize the child and everything the child does like a characteristic theme in a piece of music (Dreikurs, 1950).

Some examples of life-styles are:

I have a place only if I get approved.

I have a place if I am in complete control.

I have a place if I am intelligent, superior and right.

I have a place if I am taken care of by others.

I have a place if I am morally right.

Procedures

Adlerian counseling applies an uncovering, analytical, and interpretive emphasis. Counseling is seen as a learning process in which the child learns about the self and interpersonal relationships. In the Adlerian approach the counselor focuses on acquiring certain types of information, e.g., family constellation of the client; psychological position of the individual among siblings; ages, sex roles of various siblings as viewed by the counselee; and general family atmosphere.

There are four phases in Adlerian counseling: the relationship, the investigation of dynamics, interpretation to the child, and reorientation.

1. *The relationship.* Counseling is conversation with a purpose. If counseling is to be effective it should be built around a common purpose. Counseling is a collaborative process in that counselor and the child establish a common goal and work together in close cooperation for the achievement of the goal.

2. *The investigation.* The current life situation as it is viewed by the child is explored. The counselor is interested in the subjective view of the child and seeks to determine what the child's basic assumptions are in confronting life situations. The child's complaints, problems, and symptoms are investigated. The child's relationship to the three major areas of life—work, social, and sex—is explored and discussed.

   The counselor investigates the work area by exploring the child's adjustment relative to school tasks. Does the child participate in the work of the school? Does the child seem to enjoy school? What is the child's self view as a learner? What is the child's pattern of work in the school?

The social area is investigated by exploring the quality and quantity of the child's friendships. How does the child get along with peers and adults? How many friends does the child have? How does the child behave in social situations?

Information regarding the area of sex in the child's life is obtained by determining how the child perceives members of the opposite sex and how does the child relate to and behave with the opposite sex?

The investigation focuses on "here and now" problems. Through questioning the counselor explores the child's current situation and assesses the way in which the child approaches social relationships and responsibilities. The counselor is interested in what the child says and does not say.

Family relationships and constellations are significant. The Adlerian counselor is concerned with both the ordinal position and the psychological position of the child. A study is made of the relationship between parents, and the child's relationship with the parents.

The investigation helps the counselor to understand how the child thinks, how the child came to hold assumptions, and what the child's life-style is.

3. *Interpretation to the client (insight).* In the interpretation to the child the counselor confronts the child with the child's goals. The counselor attempts to help the child understand feelings and the purposes of feelings. The child is helped to become aware of the child's private logic and interest is shown in helping the child to change behavior. Emphasis is not placed on describing feelings or reflecting them but rather is focused on the *purpose* of the feelings. The child's life-style and its basic premises are disclosed to the child. Confronting the child with the child's purposes and life-style provides the child with a mirror to see the self and stimulates change by making the child aware of why the child chooses to function in a certain manner. In the interpretation the counselor tries to find one point or place where the child may want to change. The interpretation is presented in the form of tentative hypotheses, e.g., Could it be ...? or Is it possible ...? In this way the child is not told what to think but has the opportunity to identify purposes and to explore one's private

logic. By becoming aware of a personal life-style and intentions the child can become ready for change.

4. ***Reorientation.*** In the reorientation phase the counselor and the child work together in a cooperative relationship to help the child give up mistaken concepts and beliefs in favor of more accurate evaluations. The child is helped to see the alternatives in attitude and behavior. Encouragement is given to the child so that the child will develop the courage to change, realize personal strengths and abilities, and develop a belief in one's dignity as a person. The encouragement process is essential if the child is to change and decide the way in which the child will behave. Important changes which should emerge from the reorientation phase are changes in self-concept, value systems, purposes, life-style, and interpersonal behavior (Rathvon, 1990).

Counselor's Role

In the Adlerian approach the counselor: strives to know the subjective field in which the child's behavior takes place; looks for the child's goals; records and observes all pertinent behavior; recognizes behavior as a creative act of the child; looks for recurring patterns and themes in behavior; confronts the child with the child's purposes and life-style; and encourages the child to change.

BEHAVIORAL APPROACH

A number of behavioral approaches to counseling have been developed. All reflect an emphasis on learning theory and attempt to explain counseling and behavioral change in terms of objective, observable, and quantifiable learning processes. Much of the work of Krumboltz and Thoresen (1969) and their colleagues deals with the application of behavioral counseling with children. In behavioral counseling one specific kind of behavior is dealt with at a time and is changed in direct, observable, and scientific ways (Szykula, 1987).

Basic Premises

1. There is a direct cause and effect relationship between behavior and its antecedents. Human behavior is learned and predictable. By studying the relationship between antecedent events and behavior one can discover the specific effects of prior events or occurrences in

behavior. Once it is known how the child has learned about present behavior, and what the specific antecedents to this behavior are, then behavior can be predicted, antecedents manipulated, and consequent behavior can be controlled and changed.

2. Human behavior is lawful, i.e., there are specific observable relationships between antecedents and behavior which can be expressed as statements of scientific law. Behavior can be explained in terms of stimulus-response models in each individual case. Learned behavior is maintained by external stimuli and conditions and in most situations is a function of environmental consequences.

3. Desired behavioral change comes about by manipulating the child's environment rather than in manipulating hypothetical entities (feelings, attitudes, and personality) within the individual.

Procedures

1. The counselor conceptualizes the child's problems as problems in learning. Personal, social, and educational problems are viewed as learning problems which are subject to change through relearning and unlearning. Adaptive and effective ways of behaving can be learned as a result of different educational experiences presented to the child as part of counseling.

2. The child's goals are stated in terms of specific behaviors desired by the child. Counseling goals are not imposed on the child but are mutually accepted changes in behavior. Goals are established at the request of the child, can be agreed to by the counselor, are individually tailored to the child's problems, and enable progress to be assessed. The goals of behavioral counseling can be accommodated in three categories: (1) altering maladaptive behavior, (2) learning the decision-making process, and (3) preventing problems. In learning the decision-making process, Krumboltz (1966) thinks that behavioral counseling can be effective in helping children learn how to: (1) construct alternative behaviors, (2) seek relevant information about each alternative, (3) estimate chances of success in each alternative, (4) weigh the possible outcomes and values of each alternative, and (5) formulate tentative plans of action.

3. Counseling techniques and procedures which will best accomplish the mutually agreed upon goals are used. They will vary for different children and are specifically designed for the unique problem of each child. Techniques and procedures are based on a knowledge of

the learning process and include: well timed reinforcement; imitative learning (models); cognitive learning techniques (behavior contracts and role playing); and systematic reduction of fears and anxieties. A combination of techniques and procedures can be used to effectively and efficiently treat a child's problem.

4. Behavioral counseling is not limited to the counseling interview which is often only a small part of the total helping process. Significant people and events in the child's environment are seen as important stimuli in facilitating new learning.

5. Counseling procedures are employed to modify the problem behavior presented *directly* and in the situation in which it occurs. The behavioral counselor tries to get into or as near as possible to the *actual* situation in which the problem behavior may be modified.

6. In behavioral counseling problem behavior is recorded objectively and by frequency of occurrence to determine specific relationships between antecedent and stimulus events and behavior and to measure whether the helping process is changing behavior.

7. Counseling procedures are carefully planned to change the child's behavior in small progressive steps. This strengthens small increments of the child's desired behavior in a positive manner and with little frustration and discouragement. It also enables the child to see the immediate results of the child's efforts and reinforces the child's behavior in small bits.

8. The counselor experimentally evaluates specific procedures for specific goals. The counselor attempts to determine which kinds of procedures work best to accomplish which objectives with which kind of children. Such evaluation calls for specifically defining the problem of the child, clearly stating the direction of change desired, delineating the precise counseling procedure used, and the circumstances under which counseling occurred.

EXISTENTIAL APPROACH

Because existentialism emphasizes freedom with accountability and focuses on the person as the creator of one's culture and the master of one's destiny, it has become an attractive and dynamic philosophical force in counseling. It has potential for producing an adult-like psychological strength and control in children.

Common Existential Principles

A great deal of diversity may be found among such existential writers as Sartre, Heidegger, Kierkegaard, Jaspers, and Buber (Marcel, 1963). As a philosophical movement existentialism embraces a variety of viewpoints. Running through these various viewpoints, however, are several principles which have special relevance for those who wish to include existentialism in the third phase of child-centered counseling (Moustakas, 1966; Kitano and Levine, 1987).

1. The basic philosophical principle of existentialism is that *existence precedes essence.* One chooses one's essence; the child exists first and then defines the self through the choices the child makes plus the actions taken. Thought without action is meaningless. One is what one does.

2. At every moment the child is free from external forces and free from what the child has been. A child's past is history, it no longer exists *now* in the present. A child is influenced by external agents or by the past only when the child chooses to be influenced by these forces.

3. Accompanying freedom is the burden of responsibility. Everyone is responsible for what one is and does. No child can avoid the responsibility that accompanies the freedom to act. The child cannot give away freedom and responsibility to the state, to parents, to teachers, to weaknesses, to environmental conditions, or to one's past.

4. Every truth and every action implies a human setting and a human subjectivity. There is a world of reality but it cannot be reality apart from the people who are the basic part of it. Reality lies in each child's experience and perception of an event rather than in the isolated event, e.g., two children may hear the same introduction to a new lesson by a teacher. They hear the same words. One child's reality may be that the teacher is a demagogue, for the other child the reality is that the teacher is democratic.

5. The child must be self-reliant and not depend upon others. A person's relationship to others must provide psychological nourishment and have meaning. Superficial relationships are tolerated but provide little psychological nourishment and meaning.

6. The person is not an object; the person is a subject. Each person is unique and idiosyncratic. Each person has some control over what is happening in one's life. Each person does not have to be victimized by the behavior of those in one's life.

Existential Concepts in Counseling

Rogers (1952, 1951, 1961), Moustakas (1953, 1959, 1966), Frankl (1955), May (1961), Maslow (1962), Van Kaam (1966), and Arbuckle (1975) are historically the most noted advocates of existential counseling. Their writings include several common concepts that are of relevance for counseling children.

The purposes of existential counseling with children are: (a) to foster freedom of choice, (b) improve the child's interpersonal communication, and (c) to assist the child to discover meaning for one's life and behavior (Kitano and Levine, 1987).

The existential child counselor views counseling as a "person-to-person" relationship, an encounter in which the counselor sees as the child sees, feels as the child feels, and experiences as the child experiences. The world of each child is unique, and entrance into that world is gained by a commitment to see and perceive that world from the child's eyes. The commitment also requires that each child is seen as a very special person with unique viewpoints. Knowing the child as a unique feeling and perceiving person is more important than knowing about the child. This requires the counselor to ignore externally acquired data and information about the child, as represented by test data and the information usually found in a file, and to instead trust the child's viewpoints and perceptions regarding what is occurring in the child's life.

Existential counseling operates on the principle that the child is responsible for the self and must remain so. As soon as the counselor attempts to control the child the counselor disallows the child the freedom and responsibility needed for the child to control his or her behavior.

To the degree that the counselor directs the child, gives the child advice, and fosters a dependency relationship, to that degree does the counselor diminish the child's freedom and responsibility. The movement toward free and responsible behavior is facilitated in a counseling relationship characterized by complete acceptance of the child as the child is and a deep belief in the child's potential for psychological growth. The more the counselor relies on the potentiality of the child and the child's capacity for choosing, the more the child discovers that potentiality and capacity. To the degree that the counselor enables the child to become a self-determining individual, to that degree does the counselor contribute to the child's psychological strength.

In the existential counseling relationship the child is allowed the right to be so that the child may become. This means giving the child the opportunity to express feelings and opinions without ridicule or moralization, thereby reinforcing the child's right to see things in a personalized way. Counseling provides an atmosphere of safety. The child is not required to defend feelings and opinions. The child who is free to be different in counseling is also free to look at the behaviors which nourish or diminish one's psychological stability.

Counseling for Social Individuality

In the counseling relationship the existential child counselor adopts the role of learner rather than teacher allowing and encouraging the child to do the teaching since the child's understanding of personal feelings is more accurate than that of the counselor.

The counselor uses any technique or procedure which seems appropriate, remembering that the truth the child seeks or the choices the child makes must come from the child, if individuality is to be fostered. To encourage the child to look elsewhere for personal answers is to detract from the significance of these answers. Advice is incompatible with existential counseling since it supposes the fallacy of certainty when the only thing for certain is the existence of the child. It assumes the child's ability to evaluate is equal to that of the counselor. The counselor can only provide a counseling relationship which is conducive to the process of self-exploration and self-understanding. Attempts to advise the child indicates a lack of respect for the child's ability to advise himself or herself.

An especially important dimension of existential counseling is the ability of the counselor to listen in a nonevaluative way. The existential counselor listens by merging the self with the child's flow of experience so that the counselor is emotionally and cognitively congruent with what the child is feeling and saying. The existential counselor responds to the nonverbal and subtle cues conveyed through the tone of voice, posture, bodily movement, a way of breathing, expression of the eyes—the subterranean signals that constitute the subliminal language of counseling. Such communicative sensitivity enables the counselor to experience the child directly, and to understand the child's world and its meanings.

For the existential child counselor, counseling is a unique relationship in which the counselor is concerned with the child as a total person, continually involved in the process of becoming. The child can only come to grips with the meaning of the experiences of life, and become more fully functioning, when the child feels that the counselor's primary concern is the child. This means communicating to the child that the child's needs, feelings, and opinions are of value and relevance. The counselor, in effect, says, "It is you who are important; it is your experience that counts; it is your being that is significant; it is your internal advice that is relevant."

The existential counselor believes that each child has dignity—intrinsic value—because the child exists and because the child is a free being who defines personal essence through the choices made and the actions taken. Existential counseling offers a challenge to implement one's belief in the dignity of the child and the child's right to choose. The counselor who believes in the dignity of each child will, by actions, show respect for the child. Respect requires respecting a child's individuality, complexity, uniqueness, capacity for making choices, humanness, and the right to exercise control over one's choices and actions. Respect is not based on any extrinsic value; the value of the child is not determined by what the child does, the respectability of a child's diagnostic category, what clothes the child wears, where the child lives, how the child speaks, or the language the child uses to communicate. The child's value stems from the very fact of the child's existence, the child's freedom to choose, and the child's capacity to carve out a personally meaningful life.

The following are indications of individual development by the child as a consequence of existential counseling:

1. The child shows increased comfort and acceptance of the uncertainty involved in decision making.
2. The child shows increased awareness and is able to act on the subjective understanding of objective facts.
3. The child shows more acceptance of personal limitations and becomes less involved in unrealistic coping.
4. The child invests personal energies in areas where there is a potential for success.
5. The child moves from selfish antisocial concerns to a recognition that personal growth occurs through interaction with others. The child learns there can be no individuality without others.
6. The child demonstrates increased confidence in making decisions based on a respect for the authority within oneself rather than outside authorities.

7. The child assumes responsibility for the consequences of freely made personal choices.
8. The child makes choices based upon internal satisfactions rather than external rewards.

The dialogue between an existential counselor and a child is relatively unstructured. The counselor follows the child's feelings, perceptions, and opinions and challenges them only when they are not self-determined. The counselor wants the child to discover the strength that comes with controlling one's reactions to the experiences of life. We may not be able to control those experiences but we can, according to the existential view, control how we react. The existential message is powerful. When a child absorbs the message, the child's behavior will be based on the child's values rather than those of the adult world. Interestingly, however, the child's values, when self-selected, will have a high degree of congruence with those that are fundamental to the psychological stability of others.

GESTALT APPROACH

Gestalt therapy was initiated and developed by Frederick S. Perls. Many of Perls' ideas about Gestalt therapy can be found in the book, *Ego, Hunger, and Aggression* (Perls, 1969). The title of this book conveys one of the central ideas of Gestalt therapy—that we must adopt toward psychological and emotional experiences the same active, coping attitudes that we employ in healthy eating. In healthy eating we bite the food; then we effectively chew, grind, and liquefy it. It is then swallowed, digested, metabolized, and assimilated. In this way we have truly made the food a part of ourselves (Levitsky & Perls, 1971). Gestalt therapy with its emphasis on the here and now encourages the client to undertake a similar "chewing up" and painstaking assimilation of emotional dimensions of life that have been unpleasant to the taste, difficult to swallow, and impossible to digest.

Much of the formulation of Gestalt therapy is rooted in the conceptions of Gestalt psychology with its emphasis on the wholeness of the person. The normal healthy child reacts as a whole organism, not as a disorganized, disoriented organism (Sluckin, Weller, and Highton, 1989).

The chief insights of Gestalt psychology used in Gestalt counseling are:

1. *The relation of figure and background.* The human organism has a tendency to form figures and grounds. A figure is what the child is

paying attention to—it occupies the center of attentive awareness. As new needs arise new figures are formed, i.e., a figure is any process that emerges (becomes foreground) and stands out against a background. In the normal child there is a continuous flow of figures emerging from the background, fading away, or being destroyed, and something else emerging as foreground. If a need is satisfied the Gestalt is destroyed, permitting the formation of new Gestalts.

2. ***The formation and destruction of Gestalts.*** Before the child can assimilate anything, some degree of destruction (destructuring) is necessary. This destruction enables the child to absorb selectively according to its own needs. Without this process the child is unable to pick and choose; assimilation is impossible. Three kinds of interference with the formation and destruction of Gestalts are identified as follows (Wallen, 1971):

(a) There is poor perceptual contact with the external world and with the body itself.

(b) The open expression of needs is blocked.

(c) Repression of needs prevents the formation of the good Gestalten.

These interferences have direct implications for Gestalt therapy and counseling.

3. ***Closure.*** A child tends to seek closure. A Gestalt which is incomplete or unfinished demands attention until it is unified and stabilized. A series of dots is seen as a line. The process of having a conversation is disrupted when someone asks, "Who starred in that film?" and no one can remember. Finally, someone recalls the name and the immediate Gestalt is closed and the conversation flows again.

4. ***A child will complete a Gestalt in accordance with a current need.*** Flash a circular object in front of a group of playful children and they will report it as a ball. Hungry children may perceive it as an apple or hamburger. Sexually deprived men may "see" a woman's breast.

5. ***A child's behavior is a whole which is greater than the sum of its specific components.*** Listening to a piece of music is a process which involves something more than hearing specific notes, just as a melody is more than the constellation of notes (Passons, 1975). A child's specific behavior can only be understood when we view it as part of the child's total behavior pattern.

6. *A child's behavior can be meaningfully understood only in context.* The cowering of a child when approached by an adult carrying a stick is understood in light of beatings the child has experienced. The scars carved on the bodies of some primitive tribes are seen as adornment only in that environment. A child is an integral part of an environment and cannot be understood outside this broader context (Passons, 1975).

7. *A child experiences the world in accordance to the principles of figure ground.* When looking at a painting, the colors and shapes are its figure. The frame and wall are its ground. If attention is shifted to admiring the frame, it becomes figure and the painting itself becomes ground. If a stranger rudely bumps the painting's viewer with a sharp elbow, it is likely that the pain and the stranger will emerge as figures, while the painting will become ground (Passons, 1975).

In *Gestalt Approaches in Counseling* (1975), Passons makes a significant contribution to counseling by translating the theory and work of Perls and his colleagues into understandable and usable approaches which can be used by child counselors. In developing an overview of the theoretical dimensions of Gestalt therapy, Passons identifies several pivotal assumptions about the nature of the child which underlie the approach (1975, p. 14):

1. A child is a whole who is (rather than has) a body, emotions, thoughts, sensations, perceptions, all of which function interrelatedly.
2. A child is part of an environment and cannot be understood outside of it.
3. A child can be proactive rather than reactive and can control his or her responses to external stimuli.
4. A child is capable of being aware of one's own sensations, emotions, and perceptions.
5. A child, through self-awareness, is capable of choice and is thus responsible for his or her behavior.
6. A child possesses the ability to change negative behaviors in positive directions.
7. A child can experience him/herself only in the present. The past and the future can be experienced in the now through remembering and anticipating.
8. A child is neither intrinsically good or bad.
9. Every individual, every plant, every organism has only one inborn goal—to actualize itself—to become all that it can.
10. There is no universal hierarchy of needs. Each child has an individual formula that dictates which needs will dominate in a given situation. In situations where needs are in competition, one will dominate if the move-

ment of needs, from figure to ground and back, is fluid and flexible. There are grey areas. At any moment, however, one of the needs will have a greater urge to be fulfilled (Passons, 1975, p. 16).

Goals

The goals of Gestalt counseling are to teach persons to assume responsibility and to facilitate psychological maturity. These goals are achieved only in approximation. Responsibility is never fully assumed; maturation is never completed. Both are ongoing processes. There is always something to be learned. We are always growing (Perls, 1969, p. 4).

The principal means of facilitating responsibility and maturity is the enhancement of self-awareness. Perls emphasized this point succinctly saying, "This is the great thing to understand: that awareness per se—by and of itself—can be curative."

Passons (1972, pp. 183–190) presented a number of Gestalt interventions which can be used by a child counselor in individual or group counseling.

1. *Enhancing Awareness*

   At the start of a counseling session, the counselor might say, "I'd like you to finish the sentence: 'Now I am aware of . . . ' or, in a group, 'Having heard about Mary's situation I'm wondering what the rest of you are aware of now?'."

2. *Personalizing Pronouns*

Child:	We can never please our parents.
Counselor:	Can you change the "we" to "I"?
Child:	I can never please my parents.

   or

Child:	Is it comfortable in here today?
Counselor:	What is "it?"
Child:	Me. I am comfortable in here today.

3. *Making Contact*

   The counselor might invite counselees to speak directly to a member of the group:

Child:	Nobody understands me.
Counselor:	Can you ask someone whether or not that is so?
Child:	Warren, do you understand what I'm saying?

   In the preceding:

— Speaking *to* someone enhances the speaker's awareness of own feelings by making the speaker's message a disclosure that is shared.
— Person spoken to is engaged directly and more likely to respond.
— Encourages responses from group members.

4. ***Changing Questions to Statements***

Child:	Why are we wasting so much time?
Counselor:	Tell us what you're trying to say with that question.
Child:	I don't like it that we're wasting time.

or

Child:	Don, you don't really think you'll be able to do that?
Counselor:	What are you really saying to Don?
Child:	I don't think he'll be able to do that.
Counselor:	Say that to him.

In the preceding:

— The implicit becomes more explicit.
— Questioner learns to accept responsibility for expressing self more openly and accurately.

5. ***Assuming Responsibility***

Counselor:	I would like each group member to state something he/she is doing, thinking, or feeling and complete it with "and I am responsible for it."
Parent:	I am not sure what to say, and I am responsible for that.
Parent:	I am worrying about my child, and I am responsible for that.

or

Child:	I just can't study.
Counselor:	Would you try saying "won't" instead of "can't?"
Child:	Okay, I just won't study.

or

Client:	I can't talk to her.
Counselor:	Try saying "won't" instead of "can't."
Client:	I won't talk to her.

6. ***Asking "How" and "What"***

— One of the ways to elicit pat answers, intellectualizations, and fruitless rationalizations is ask people *why* they do what they do or *why* they feel as they do. Such questions create three problems:

- They precipitate a search for a prime cause, the supreme insight, or a historical journey into the past.
- "Why" is too easily answered by "because" which places responsibility on an external or unknown locus of control— outside the client.
- "Why" leads the person into figuring things out in a cognitive, problem-solving fashion that rarely enhances the experiencing and understanding of emotions. Instead of asking, "Why?" the Gestalt counselor proceeds as follows:

  Child: I don't know why I keep getting into all this trouble.

  Counselor: Maybe you could tell us *how* you do it.

7. *Bringing the Past into the Now*

   Child: Boy, I was confused. I was running around and didn't know what to do.

   Counselor: Bill, could you try to tell us about it as though it were happening now?

   or

   Child: I felt badly when I yelled at him.

   Counselor: That was then. How do you feel about it now?

   Child: Now I don't feel so bad.

8. *Expressing Resentments and Appreciations*

   Gestalt counseling indicates that there are resentments and appreciations which need to be expressed by clients:

   Counselor: I would like to close today's session by asking those members to express what they appreciate or resent about today's meeting.

   Client #1:   I resent that it has to end.

   Client #2:   Lou, I appreciated having you try to help me.

Used at the end of the meeting, this procedure will enable children to express unfinished business that might otherwise nag and build up.

Gestalt counseling wants the child to abandon masks and to become more honest in expressing feelings about the everyday experiences of life. If the child can learn to do this there is not the build-up of unexpressed negative feelings which can take their toll over a period of time. To the Gestalt viewpoint, learning to communicate one's feelings honestly, in the moment they are felt, is a release that serves as the foundation for one's psychological maturity. The techniques and procedures of Gestalt counseling are aimed at helping the child move closer to this goal.

RATIONAL-EMOTIVE APPROACH

Rational-Emotive counseling is an approach which encourages the child to use reason and logic as a method for handling problems. Albert Ellis (1962, 1971, 1972), who developed this approach, asserts that people's problems are the result of irrational thinking and can be resolved through rational thinking. The R–E–T approach is primarily didactic and reeducational (Bernard, 1990; DiGiuseppe and Bernard, 1990).

Basic Premises

1. Emotions rarely have an independent existence in themselves. They are allied to and are the products of human thinking. We *think* something is bad and consequently we *feel* badly. We *think* something is good and we *feel* happy about it. Emotional disorders and neuroses are the results of illogical, unvalidatable sentences a person says to oneself and believes in. The R–E–T approach holds that disturbed emotions develop because the child acquires irrational thoughts, beliefs, attitudes, or philosophies about the self and one's environment. Self-defeating emotions and acts are based on illogical ideas.

2. Irrational thinking and behavior is a natural human state and all of us are more or less afflicted by it. The tendency to tell ourselves things that are irrational is an inborn characteristic in all humans. We tell ourselves many irrational things during childhood. Many of them become part of our belief system about ourselves. The repetition of illogical and unvalidatable sentences to ourselves can sustain and perpetuate a child's (and an adult's) problems.

3. The rational-emotive view believes that a simple (as simple as A–B–C) sequence of events can explain why we tell ourselves irrational things. It says that it is never stimulus A which causes us to react as we do at point C, but rather it is our interpretation of stimulus A at point B which causes the reaction at point C. Ellis often expresses this premise in the form or quotes from: Spictetus—"Men are disturbed not by things, but by the views which they take of them" and Hamlet—"There's nothing either good or bad but thinking makes it so."

4. The essence of all human disturbances is blame. Anxiety emanates from: (a) the objective sentence, "I don't like my mistaken behavior and it would be better if I changed it," and from (b) the irrational

self-blaming sentence, "Because my behavior is wrong and self-defeating, I am no good as a person and I deserve to suffer," or from the invalid statement, "Because I don't like this event that is occurring or that may occur, I, slob that I am, cannot stand it, and dire things must happen to me because I can't stand it."

5. Rational-emotive therapy posits that there are a number of main irrational ideas that humans continually repeat to themselves and that consequently keep them neurotic or psychotic. According to the rational-emotive view, many children use one or more of the following irrational ideas in making self-defeating decisions:

— It is a dire necessity to be loved or approved by virtually every significant person in our environment.

— One must be thoroughly competent, adequate, and achieving in all possible respects if one is to consider oneself worthwhile.

— It is catastrophic when things are not the way one would very much like them to be.

— It is easier to avoid than to face life difficulties and self responsibilities.

— One's past history is an all important determiner of one's present behavior; because something once strongly affected one's life, it will indefinitely have a similar effect.

— That human unhappiness is externally caused and one has little or no ability to control personal disturbances.

Procedures

In practice the rational-emotive counselor tries to determine what irrational simple sentences the child is telling the self to create disordered emotions. The counselor functions as an educator by teaching the child how to contradict these disturbing sentences. The child is taught to *act* and to *think* in counterpropagandizing ways. The counselor: (1) isolates the illogical idea, (2) proves to the child why it is illogical and the harm it does to the child, and then (3) helps the child accept a more rational view of oneself and one's world by actively encouraging and supporting the child to live more logically.

Rational-emotive counseling is perhaps the most activity-directive of the different counseling approaches. The counselor is very active and does considerably more talking than the child. By aggressively challenging the child the counselor helps the child see the illogic of disturbed thinking. The counselor actively interprets to the child and consistently tries to persuade and argue the child out of irrational tendencies and ideas. Interpretation is an important tool and is used to help the child see that a problem exists because of a fallacy in the child's thinking.

When the unvalidatable and irrational ideas of the child are isolated, the counselor encourages the child to try new behavior by assigning homework. Assignments are given so that the child will not only think but will also *act*. The child might be encouraged to complete a classroom paper no matter how poor a job the child does just to prove that doing part of a job is better than doing none at all and that improved competence in anything requires practice. The child might also be assigned the task of trying to point out to the parent that the more the child attempts to do all things well, the more difficult it might become, because of the child's self-imposed stress, to do *anything* well. The child attempts to show the parent that the child can't become a perfect student over night and possibly never will. The child might, however, by continued practice, improve.

In the rational-emotive approach the counselor does not encourage the child to change by offering the child love and respect. The counselor teaches the child to change and to improve for the child's own benefit and not for the love and respect of parents, teachers, or the counselor. The counselor strives to educate the child to understand that not everyone can possibly like us, that achieving to win the love or respect of others is many times self-defeating, and that it is important to learn to relate to life's difficult people, be they disagreeable parents or a rejecting teacher. The counselor emphasizes to the child the importance of forming productive working relationships rather than unattainable "love and respect" relationships.

Rational-emotive counseling focuses on the child's present experiences. The counselor is not interested in developing a case history of the child but rather works toward changing what the child is telling the self *now*. Self-defeating behavior changes when the child stops telling the self irrational invalidatable sentences and begins acting on the basis of new and rational sentences. The child learns that the past is the past and is not an important determiner of one's present behavior. No matter what the child has done the counselor never *blames* the child even for the child's worst errors. The counselor's goal is to help the child achieve a new outlook *now* so that the child behaves in healthy ways *now*.

Although the rational-emotive counselor aggressively challenges the child's illogical thinking, this does not mean that the counselor does not accept the child. The child is accepted—the child's behavior is not. Criticism of the child's thinking and behavior does not exclude accepting the worthiness of the child as a person.

Counselor's Role

The counselor's role in rational-emotive counseling is twofold: (1) the counselor acts as a role model for the child. The counselor is rational, behaves rationally, and has the courage to face the child's problem squarely and frankly; (2) the counselor acts as a teacher and in a highly didactic and reeducational manner instructs the child to alter thinking and consequently behavior.

Even though the counselor thinks and behaves rationally this does not mean that the counselor is a cold and unfeeling person. On the contrary, the counselor sees emotions as thoughts—the thinking person is a feeling person. According to the viewpoint, the more positive and healthy one thinks the more positive and healthy one feels.

REALITY APPROACH

Reality therapy was developed by Wiliam Glasser (1965) who views his approach as a here and now active procedure for helping children to become responsible persons. One of the basic constructs of reality therapy is that we must be involved with other people from birth to death. We cannot avoid them. Involvement with people is a necessary reality of life.

Basic needs which must realistically be filled are: (1) to be loved and to love; (2) to feel worthwhile to self and to others. To be and to feel worthwhile, we must maintain satisfactory standards of behavior.

Responsibility and responsible behavior is defined as the ability to fulfill one's needs in a way that does not deprive others of the ability to fulfill their needs. Irresponsible persons are defined as those who are incarcerated or harmless people such as recluses and eccentrics. All other people are responsible for themselves and their behavior. Glasser feels that labeling people as neurotic or psychotic removes them from assuming responsibility for their behavior.

Regarding discipline and the teaching of it, Glasser feels that parents who have no self-discipline cannot successfully discipline their children. He feels that counselors must be tough, interested, human, and sensitive. Counselors must not be frightened by aberrant behavior. Counselors must be able to become emotionally involved with the children they hope to help. Glasser notes the differences between his approach and other approaches:

Conventional Approaches	***Reality Therapy***
Believe in existence of mental illness, classification, and treatment based on diagnosis.	Will not accept the mental illness concept. Will not become involved with a child who will accept no responsibility for personal behavior.
Treatment necessitates probing of child's past. Once the child understands the influence of the past, he or she can change current behavior.	Don't accept limitations based on past. Stay away from it. Stick with present leading to future.
Child will relate on a basis of transference. Insights out of this will produce change.	We relate as ourselves.
If the child is to change, the child must have insight into the unconscious mind.	We don't look for unconscious conflicts or reasons for them. Child cannot excuse current behavior because of the influence of the unconscious.
Avoids problem of morality, i.e., right or wrong. Deviant behavior is part of a disease. Children, therefore, should not be held responsible for their behavior.	Emphasize the morality of behavior, the right or wrong of it.
Teaching children to behave better is not considered an important part of therapy. Children will learn better behavior once they understand themselves and the unconscious.	Teach children better ways of fulfilling needs. Help child to find more satisfactory ways for fulfilling needs.

Applying Reality Therapy

The counselor working under principles devised by Glasser is primarily concerned with *what* the child is doing, not *why* the child is doing it. Most counselors would testify that almost all clients who come for help have numerous reasons why they do things. Knowing "why" or gaining insight, however, is not always enough. Any person will do better, be better, or change only when the person fulfills personal needs more satisfactorily (Glasser, 1965, p. 33). This is as true for children as it is for adults. Therefore, the primary focus in counseling children must always be *what* the child is doing, not *why* the child is doing it. In Glasser's conceptual framework the child behaves in the ways that meet personal needs. If the child is behaving in the ways that are not responsible (or if the child wishes to increase personal effectiveness or "do better"), the counselor may have to help the child develop a willingness to try a new pattern of behavior.

The counselor and child jointly examine what the child is *doing.* Suggestions and alternatives may be proposed by the counselor, but the responsibility for acting on them lies with the child. The child is *never* forced into behavior that the child does not feel is appropriate. The counselor's role in this process is a very active one, but it does not seek to impose solutions, direct the child's behavior, or control the child. Rather it is a process that assists the child in discovering ways to direct and control one's behavior.

Much of what the child does outside the counseling relationship is a trial-and-error process. The child is asked numerous times to decide whether or not the child's behavior is helping the child meet personal needs. Children are asked to make a plan for changing behavior. Counselor praises them for any small progress toward their expressed goals. At the same time, the counselor withholds praise for behavior that is self-defeating or irresponsible.

Steps in Reality Therapy

1. The counselor and child engage in a completely honest, warm, human relationship. The child should in no way perceive this relationship as threatening or harmful. The counselor is an adult with a value system who has learned to meet personal needs in a responsible way, but the counselor is also an adult who does not wish to impose a personal value system on the child.

2. Together, the child and counselor explore the many factors of the child's life, especially the child's sense of values. The focus of the discussions is on the present and the future, and the counselor is primarily concerned with the *what* of the child's behavior rather than the *why.* The reality-oriented child counselor is more concerned with behavior than attitudes.

3. Decisions should be made by the child regarding better ways to meet

personal needs. If these decisions are not "responsible" the counselor may have to work with the child to show the child that the behavior is *not* responsible. Children should make commitments to all decisions, and the counselor and child should explore the progress of these commitments. All positive progress should be praised by the counselor, but the counselor should withhold praise for irresponsible behavior.

4. If the child does not live up to a commitment, steps two and three should be repeated. When the child is successful, counseling should proceed, but care should be taken to insure that the child has a reasonable chance to successfully accomplish whatever the child sets out to do.

5. Commensurate with the child's maturity level, the child is always responsible for behavior. Excuses for behavior are not acceptable nor does the counselor continually focus on the child's "problem."

6. Any topic is appropriate for counseling children except for prolonged discussions of the child's past. Counselor and child discuss interests, hobbies, school, sports, or any other topic. All discussions are linked to values, standards, and responsibility.

7. Termination gradually takes place as the child learns new and better ways to meet personal needs.

TRANSACTIONAL ANALYSIS APPROACH

Transactional analysis (TA) includes an understandable theory of personality, a specific but easily learned vocabulary, a method of analyzing interactions between persons, and techniques by which a child can learn to improve relationships. It has been used by counselors and teachers to understand themselves, to interact more effectively with children, to improve the classroom climate, and to help children learn and use transactional analysis concepts (Campos, 1986; Clarkson and Fish, 1988).

Transactional analysis had its beginnings in the teachings and writings of psychiatrist Eric Berne. Berne's concepts quickly intrigued others because they were seen to be concrete and usable.

Berne's book, *Games People Play* (1964), brought TA to the attention of a wide public. Groups of psychiatrists working with the concepts formed five institutes, one of them under the leadership of Thomas A. Harris.

Harris's work in transactional analysis, with private practice groups and in teaching courses, led him to believe that the TA process could be simply presented to all ages and people could learn to use it as a way to understand and improve their interpersonal relationships. His book, *I'm OK—You're OK* (1969), subtitled "A Practical Guide to Transactional Analysis," presented his version of TA in popularized form.

One strength of TA is the precision of its language. It uses ordinary words in a special way, a knowledge of the eight basic vocabulary terms is necessary.

The first group of terms is Parent, Adult, and Child, representing the concept that the personality of every person includes these three distinct parts. They are spelled with capital letters to distinguish them from the same words used with ordinary meanings. Collectively, these are called ego states.

From reports of experimental brain stimulation using electric probes, Harris came to believe that the brain works like a recorder to permanently "tape" every conscious experience and its accompanying emotion. He also decided that these "tapes" can be, and often are, played back in our present-day activities, and that their influence on behavior can be observed. Once recognized and understood, the tapes—although inerasable—could be turned off, or their data examined and compensated for in behavior.

"Your Parent" is thus a recording of your interactions with your parents, or those who cared for your infant and childhood needs. These recordings, made in your first five years of life, consist mostly of injunctions telling you what you should and should not do. You believed these completely and literally because your survival depended on it. Especially at first, you also had no mental tools or outside information for checking on the truth and value of what you were told. Your first and strongest opinions of yourself and your world are based on parent dictums.

"Your Child" is a recording of your emotions, made simultaneously with and as part of the data received in "Your Parent." Although positive emotions such as creativity, curiosity, discovery, and delight are recorded, so are feelings of helplessness, fear, frustration, and anger. This is true even with well-nurtured babies, and far more for the neglected ones. A child thus cannot help but conclude, "I'm not OK."

"The Adult" part of the personality is more like a computer than a recording. This is the rational part, the seemingly inborn need to make sense of the world. It uses as input, data received from the Parent, the Child, and the real world. The Adult starts its lifelong growth around ten months, when the infant begins to move around and obtain some non-Parent and non-Child data. Developing with use and practice, the growth of the Adult especially spurts with the acquisition of language.

Since the Adult identity starts after the Parent and Child, its boundaries are fragile. The Adult identity can easily be retarded by the cutting in of Parent and Child tapes. Being out of date, the tapes are often inappropriate now, and may contain contradictory and confusing data. The ideal state is to have your Adult state "uncontaminated" by Parent and Child—that is, free not to act according to their suggestions. Although most of us have such contamination, we should keep trying to minimize it.

The ego states are diagrammed by a vertical row of three equal-size circles, P at the top, A in the middle, C on the bottom. The circles are shown touching rather than overlapping or contaminated.

Another important term—the one from which transactional analysis gets its name—is transaction. This denotes any encounter between two people, in which a stimulus from the Parent, Adult, or Child of one person is responded to by the P, A, or C of the other. A transaction can be of any duration, from a single exchange to one that can last for years! Transactions are analyzed by the counselor and child so that they can be understood. Some transactions are useful, some damaging. Transactions are diagrammed using the P–A–C circles.

Persons participate in transactions to get strokes. A stroke is the physical or psychological equivalent to an act of caring that is vital to the child's survival and growth. Strokes can be verbal, visual, or tactile; they can be active or passive, positive or negative. Strokes are recognition. A positive stroke indicates approval; a negative one is disapproval, but it is better than no stroke. It shows that someone cares. Everyone needs and seeks strokes.

Understanding the games we play to manipulate others is vital to understanding our behavior. A game is a stroke which is also called a payoff. A child plays games because the child has not overcome negative feelings and hopes to feel better by playing one of the many variations of "I'm Better than You." Such a child obtains only temporary relief because no steps have been taken to overcome feelings of inadequacy.

Even though a child's helplessness and fear of abandonment make the child feel "not OK," the care the child does receive makes the child decide that the caring person (and by extension, the world) is OK. The child thus concludes that, "I'm not OK—you're OK," which the Harris version of transactional analysis calls the "first life position." Stroke-deprived youngsters, neglected or abused, may move into the second life position, "I'm not OK—you're not OK," or the third, "I'm OK—you're not OK," the first indicating a giving up and the second projecting all the child's troubles on others. Based on feelings rather than reality, these positions are settled by the age of three.

The fourth life position and the one to strive for is "I'm OK—you're OK." It is the position of trust, of respect, of communication. An understanding of the first three positions is important in working with children in order to understand their level of psychological maturity and the intention of their behavior. The fourth position is the one to work toward in order to develop OK interpersonal relationships.

A glossary of TA terms

Adult —An ego state representing the rational part of the personality which solves problems by using internal and external data.

Child —An ego state representing the emotional part of the personality, in which is recorded the emotions experiences by the child before the age of three.

Ego state —One of the three parts of the personality—Parent, Adult, Child—which at any particular time is in control of a person's behavior.

Game —A series of transactions by which a person habitually tries to manipulate others.

Life Position —A decision about the value of oneself that influences all of our thoughts and actions.

Parent —An ego state representing the directive part of the personality, in which is recorded the dictates of the actual parents as perceived by the child before age three.

Transaction —An encounter between two persons consisting of any number of interactions and which can be described and analyzed.

Transactional Analysis —A descriptive theory of personality and interpersonal relationships that furnishes a method for understanding and influencing behavior.

CONCLUSION

The child-centered counselor's understanding of other approaches to counseling is vital. All of them possess the potential for being applied during the third phase of child-centered counseling. After the child-centered counselor has developed a close and empathic relationship with the child and has assimilated the child's values, motives, and behaviors, an approach presented in this chapter can be used to meet the needs of *this* child with *this* problem.

All theories of counseling have merit. The difficulty arises when the counselor applies one theory to all children. Doing this demonstrates a lack of recognition of the unique and individual needs of children. Applying one approach to all would be much like attempting to impose one value system on all people while disregarding the individuality of their needs and rights.

The child-centered counselor can use one of the approaches presented in this chapter when it matches the needs of the child in phase three. If the child needs more than what child-centered counseling can deliver, the counselor can more easily apply one of these approaches because phases one and two have increased the possibility of its success in phase three. Of course, the child-centered counselor can continue the phase two reflective process into phase three if it is producing results. Phase three, then, can be: (1) a continuation of the reflective process, or (2) the use of techniques and procedures from other theories of counseling when they better meet the needs of the child, or (3) the implementation of a logical and natural common sense procedure because it best meets the individual needs of the child.

REFERENCES

Arbuckle, D. S. (1975). *Counseling and psychotherapy: An existential-humanistic view* (3rd ed). Boston: Allyn and Bacon.

Berne, E. (1964). *Games people play.* New York: Grove.

Bernard, M. E. (1990). Rational-emotive therapy with children and adolescents: Treatment strategies, *School Psychology Review,* 19(3), 294–303.

Campos, L. P. (1986). Empowering children: Primary prevention of script formation. *Transactional Analysis Journal,* 16(1), 18–23.

Clarkson, P. & Fish, S. (1988). Systemic assessment and treatment considerations in TA child psychotherapy. *Transactional Analysis Journal,* 18(2), 123–132.

DiGiuseppe, R. and Bernard, M. E. (1990). The application of rational-emotive theory and therapy to school-aged children. *School Psychology Review,* 19(3), 268–286.

Dinkmeyer, D., & Dreikurs, R. (1963). *Encouraging children to learn.* New York: Prentice-Hall.

Dinkmeyer, D. (1968). The counselor as consultant: Rationale and procedures. *Elementary School Guidance and Counseling,* 3, 187–194.

Dinkmeyer, D. (1971). The C-group: Focus on self as instrument. *Phi Delta Kappan,* 52, 617–619.

Dinkmeyer, D., Pew, W., & Dinkmeyer, D., Jr. (1979). *Adlerian counseling and psychopathology.* Monterey, CA: Brooks/Cole.

Dreikurs, R. (1950). *Character education and spiritual values in an anxious age.* Boston: Beacon Press.

Dreikurs, R. (1967). *Psychodynamics, psychotherapy, and counseling.* Chicago: Alfred Adler Institute.

Ellis, A. (1962). *Reason and emotion in psychotherapy.* New York: Lyle Stuart.

Ellis, A. (1971). *Growth through reason.* Palo Alto: Science and Behavior Books.

Frankl, V. E. (1955). *From death camp to existentialism.* Boston: Beacon Press.

Glasser, W. (1965). *Reality therapy: A new approach to psychiatry.* New York: Harper and Row.

Harris, R. A. (1969). *I'm OK— You're OK.* New York: Harper and Row.

Kitano, M. K., & Levine, E. B. (1987). Existential theory: Guidelines for practice in child therapy. *Psychotherapy,* 24(3), 404–413.

Krumboltz, J. D. (Ed.). (1966). *Revolution in counseling: Implications of behavioral science.* Boston: Houghton Mifflin.

Krumboltz, J. D., & Thoresen, C. E. (Eds.). (1969). *Behavioral counseling: Cases and techniques.* New York: Holt, Rinehart, & Winston.

Levitsky, A., & Perls, F. (1971). The rules and games of Gestalt therapy. In J. Fagan, & I. L. Shepherd (Eds.)., *Gestalt therapy now.* New York: Harper and Row.

Marcel, G. (1963). *The philosophy of existentialism.* New York: Citadel Press.

Maslow, A. H. (1962). *Toward a psychology of being.* Princeton: Van Nostrand.

May, R. (1961). *Existential psychology.* New York: Random House.

Moustakas, C. (1953). *Children in play therapy.* New York: McGraw-Hill.

Moustakas, C. (1959). *Psychotherapy with children.* New York: Harper.

Moustakas, C. (1966). *Existential child therapy: The child's discovery of himself.* New York: Basic Books.

Passons, W. (1972). Gestalt therapy interventions for group counseling. *Personnel and Guidance Journal,* 51, 183–189.

Passons, W. (1975). *Gestalt approaches in counseling.* New York: Holt, Rinehart, & Winston.

Perls, F. (1969). *Ego, hunger, and aggression.* New York: Random House.

Rathvon, N. (1990). The effects of encouragement on off-task behavior and academic productivity. *Elementary School Guidance and Counseling,* 24, 189–199.

Rogers, C. R. (1942). *Counseling and psychotherapy.* Boston: Houghton Mifflin.

Rogers, C. R. (1951). *Client-centered therapy.* Boston: Houghton Mifflin.

Rogers, C. R. (1961). *On becoming a person.* Boston: Houghton Mifflin.

Sluckin, A., Weller, A., & Highton, J. (1989). Recovering from trauma: Gestalt therapy with abused child. *Maladjustment and Therapeutic Education,* 7(3), 147–157.

Szykula, S. A. (1987). Child-focused strategic and behavioral therapy process. *Psychotherapy,* 24(2), 202–211.

Van Kaam, A. (1966). *Existential foundations of psychology.* Pittsburgh: Duquesne University Press.

Wallen, R. (1971). Gestalt therapy and Gestalt psychology. In J. Fagan, & I. L. Shepherd (Eds.), *Gestalt therapy now.* New York: Harper and Row.

Willis, A. (1972). *Emotional education.* New York: Julian.

Chapter 5

CHILD–CENTERED COUNSELING THROUGH PLAY

Caplan and Caplan (1973) offer a historically enduring perspective on the extraordinary power of play in the child's psychological development. They cite some exceptional and unique features of play which we paraphrase as follows:

Play is a voluntary activity. It is intensely personal. Self-powered, it embodies a high degree of motivation and achievement. Play is an autonomous pursuit through which one assimilates the outside world to support one's ego.

Play offers freedom of action. Play is always free in the sense that each act can be performed for its own sake and for its immediate results. During play, one can carry on trial and error activities without fear of ridicule or failing.

Play provides an imaginary world one can master. Play is a voluntary system that admits both reality and fantasy. The one who plays is in full control. In the world of play one can reduce one's world to a manageable size so that it can be manipulated to suit personal whims.

Play has elements of adventure in it. It has uncertainty and challenge which can prompt one to be exploratory. In play, the ordinary laws of life do not count since play is larger than life.

Play provides a base for language building. The earliest years are nonverbal. Words come from a foundation of play experiences, from encounters with people, objects, and events which make up our world. Play nourishes reflective thinking, associative memory, and the naming and labeling necessary for the eventual mastery of reading.

Play has unique powers for building interpersonal relations. Play provides contacts with others while letting us engage in natural behaviors. Much of play aids our psychosocial development by helping us to define ourselves and fit that definition into a social context.

Play offers opportunities for mastery of the physical self. One can learn body control through active physical play. Physical play helps us to improve our laterality, directionality, and coordination.

Play furthers concentration. One's power of concentration in the here-and-now world is improved through play. That improved ability to concentrate can be generalized to activities outside of play.

Play is a way to learn about ourselves. Play helps us to learn how we'll respond to a certain set of circumstances. Connections are made between stimuli and responses during play and we can see equivalent stimuli outside of play which generate similar responses. We begin to see a unity to how we respond to certain stimuli both in play and outside of play.

Play is a way of learning about roles. In early play, children imitate the behavior, attitudes, and language of the important adults in their lives. Play may be considered a rehearsal for adult roles and anticipatory to adult life. Adults learn about the similarities and differences in role expectations in play and outside of play.

Play is always a dynamic way of learning. The layers of meaning implanted by play often include conscious organization of the environment, explorations of physical and social relationships, and deep levels of fantasy. One's perceptions of reality often evolve out of play requiring fantasy.

Play refines one's judgments. Play is often an accepted vehicle for expressing one's feelings and thoughts. Through play one analyzes which feelings and thoughts can be expressed and accepted by others and which cannot.

Play is vitalizing. Play has important neurophysiological effects on us. Play is a diversion from routines, demands, and pursuits. For a period of time, play permits one to reverse one's behavior and do the opposite of what one has been doing. Play is essential in order to bring renewed vigor to the formal and required activities of our lives. Play enables us to engage in natural and spontaneous behaviors so necessary to freeing us from the pressures of life.

PLAY AND COGNITIVE DEVELOPMENT

According to Piaget (1951), play is an indispensable step in the child's cognitive development. Play is the bridge between sensory-motor experience and the emergence of representative or symbolic thought. In his study of play, Piaget concluded that there are three main categories of play: practice games, symbolic games, and games with rules.

Practice games appear first and are an outgrowth of the imitative activities which are characteristic of the sensory-motor period of development. Such games may lead to improved motor performance or to destructive performance (e.g., knocking over blocks). They may develop into constructive games like building or weaving which are viewed by Piaget as a bridge between play and work.

Symbolic games imply representation of an absent object and are both initiative and imaginative (Piaget, 1951). Insofar as these games symbolize the child's own feelings, interest, and activities, they help the child to express the self creatively and to develop a rich and satisfying fantasy life. Between the ages of two and four symbolic play is at its peak. One type of symbolic play identified by Piaget is compensatory play which involves doing in make-believe what is forbidden in reality. Closely related to compensatory play is play in which emotion is acted out in gradual degrees, so that it becomes bearable. Often children will use play to act out unpleasant scenes of actions. In reliving them by transposing them symbolically, they reduce some of the unpleasantness and make the situations more tolerable. The function of symbolic play is seen in the "make-believe" games of children from two to four. According to Piaget (1951), symbolic play frees "the ego from the demands of accommodation" (p. 134).

Games with rules. After the age of four or five, symbolic play becomes increasingly social, according to Piaget. Symbolic games lessen as socialization progresses. Around the age of seven or eight there is a definite decline in symbolic play coinciding with increased interest in school and in socialized activities. The child becomes involved in games with rules which are essentially social, leading to increased adaptation. Piaget believes that since these games persist even among adults, they may provide the explanation of what happens to children's play; that it dies out in later years in favor of socialized games through which the child develops social skills and attitudes (Pulaski, 1971). The child is required to share, to cooperate, and to assume different rules and consequently learns the first lessons of mutuality in social relations and begins to build more complex relationship skills.

THE PSYCHOSOCIAL VALUE OF PLAY

Play is the child's natural medium of expression (Axline, 1969). "In his talk and his toys are his words" (Ginott, 1961) and this form of communication gives the adult a tool with which to understand and relate to the child with confidence and warmth (Schiffer, 1969; Moustakas,

1973; Jernberg, 1979; Orlick, 1983; Rubin and Tregay, 1986). Indeed, Allen (1942) was one of the first to observe that it would be difficult to establish a relationship with a child without play activity. Axline's (1964) book, *Dibs: In search of self,* provides a historically respected example of play as an accepting, reflecting, clarifying, and communicating relationship with a child.

Amster (1943) was one of the first to identify the enduring values and benefits coming from play:

1. Play can be used for diagnostic understanding of the child. . . . We can observe the child's capacity to relate to the self and others, the child's distractibility, rigidity, areas of preoccupation, areas of inhibition, aggression, perception of people, wishes, and the child's self-perception. In the child's play, the child's behavior, ideas, feelings, and expressions help our understanding of the child's problem and how the child sees it.
2. Play can be used to establish a working relationship. This use of play is helpful with the young child who lacks the adult's facility for verbal self-expression and with the older child who shows resistance or inability to articulate.
3. Play can be used to break through a child's way of playing and the child's defenses against anxiety. This is helpful as an additional way of treating distortions in a child's way of playing.
4. Play can be used to help a child verbalize certain conscious material and associated feelings. This use is helpful when a child hesitates to discuss certain material.
5. Play can be used to help a child act out unconscious material and to relieve the accompanying tension. This cathartic use of play deals with symbolic material which may have deep significance to the child. The child counselor must be aware of how much release in play the particular child can tolerate.
6. Play can be used to develop a child's play interests which the child can carry over into daily life and which will strengthen the child for the future. This use of play has particular importance because of the correlation between the play and work capacities of an individual (pp. 63–67).

Erickson (1964) indicates the psychological value of play when he says that "the child's play is the infantile form of the human ability to deal with experiences by creating model situations and to master reality by experiment and planning. . . . To 'play it out' in play is the most natural self-healing measure childhood affords" (pp. 10–11).

Nelson (1968) indicates that many of the elements and principles of play therapy are appropriate to helping all children with their psychosocial development. He cites the work of Moustakas (1959) and Axline (1969) on play therapy with "normal" children as supporting the concept of helping all children through play activities.

Meeks (1968) indicates that any process of helping through play should not be diagnostic but should be compatible with child-centered goals since child-centered play therapy offers: (1) a most favorable condition for children to experience growth, (2) allows the child to face feelings through a natural medium of expression, and (3) by facing feelings, it assists the child to control them or abandon them. Through play the child is able to realize the power possessed by the self, can be an individual, think, make decisions, and become more mature. In presenting a theoretical basis for the use of play to help children, Nelson (1968) points out that play provides a vehicle for the individual to explore thoughts and feelings and evoke self-enhancing courses of action, behavior patterns, or attitudes. This process may take place on a nonverbal as well as on a verbal level. The historically established function of play is to facilitate psychosocial self-exploration and clarification and is consistent with the contemporary goals of child-centered counseling.

GENERAL CHARACTERISTICS OF PLAY THERAPY

Although there is a variety of approaches used in play therapy, there are certain general basic characteristics (Ellis, 1973). First, play therapy involves the use of play media ranging from unstructured materials such as sand and clay to more structured toys such as dolls and play houses. Second, through the use of play materials, and through talking, the child expresses feelings and experiences. Third, as a result, the child experiences a solution to a problem, a reduction in tension, or a release of emotion (pp. 120–127).

What magic function does play possess that enables it to work so well as a therapeutic tool? Through play, the child expresses forbidden physical impulses in a symbolic way, releases anxiety and hostility, tells stories about traumatic situations thus relieving tension, and symbolically manipulates toys in such a way as to test out possible solutions to problems. And finally, through play the child externalizes or projects painful feelings of shame and inferiority, bridges the gap between dreams and reality, and even assumes a role different from the child's normal life role (Landreth & Verhalen, 1982; Thompson and Rudolph, 1992).

BRIEF HISTORY OF PLAY THERAPY

The beginnings of play therapy have emanated from a Freudian or psychoanalytical attempt to deal with children and their emotional concerns. One of the primary goals of Freudian therapy was to bring repressed and denied experiences into conscious awareness. This was usually accomplished through free association which worked well with adults but not as well with children who would refuse to free associate. Viewing this as a significant problem, Anna Freud modified the classical psychoanalytic approach by indicating that children do not generally have transference problems and could therefore interact with an adult therapist. To reach a child, she would often play with the child. Such play, however, was considered preliminary to the real work of psychoanalysis and not central to it.

Independently of Anna Freud, Melanie Klein began developing her own techniques with children, which also evolved from the theories of Freud. She assumed that a child's play activities were as motivationally determined as free association in adults, and could thus be interpreted to the child. The term used to describe this process was "play analysis" and it became one of the first approaches which provided interpretations of children's behavior.

Soon after Klein and Freud, Jessie Taft began applying Otto Rank's theories to play therapy, bringing about some important changes in the goals and procedures of therapy with children. Rank's focus was on "relationship therapy"—the relationship between therapist and client was seen as growth producing in its own right, and the emotional problem, as they existed in the immediate present, were more important than the past experiences of the client. From these influences emerged "nondirective" play therapy which reflects the Freudian concepts of: permissiveness and catharsis, repression, play as natural language of the child, the meaningfulness of apparently unmotivated behavior, the Rankian emphases on unexpressed feelings rather than content, and on the diminution of the authoritative position of the therapist.

These were the early thoughts and ideas of play therapy. These thoughts and ideas began to take on more breadth and depth, research regarding their effectiveness was started, and the following formal approaches to play therapy emerged.

APPROACHES TO PLAY THERAPY

Psychoanalytic

The psychoanalytic approach uses interpretations of the child's behavior in the play therapy sessions. Interpretation consists of making connections for the child where the child sees none. Sometimes these connections are between a defense and a feeling or between a fantasy and a feeling (Ellis, 1973). The psychoanalyst hopes, through interpretation, to help the child achieve some insights into the child's behavior and problems. In the process of achieving this the therapist tries to make the unconscious conscious to the child for the purpose of enabling the child to recognize personal feelings and defenses and deal with them directly (Levy, 1978). Psychoanalysts work on the child's past in order to provide a cleared and improved ground for future development (Kessler, 1966). Psychoanalysts are convinced that their treatment process is essential for alleviating certain kinds of symptoms, such as acute anxiety, and a sense of helplessness and inadequacy.

Release Therapy

Release therapy is an approach developed by Levy (1939) as a particularly useful way of relieving severe anxiety, fear reactions, or night terrors precipitated by traumatic experiences (surgical operations, accidents, divorce of parents). In this approach, the therapist supplies the child with dolls and other play media and depicts a ploy concerned with what the therapist feels is the child's major problem, e.g., separation from mother. This approach is advocated by Levy as most appropriate for children under 10 who present a recently acquired symptom generated by a specific event in the form of a frightening experience. Levy (1939) indicated that it is important for the appropriate use of this approach "that the child is suffering from something that happened in the past and not from a difficult situation going on at the time of treatment" (p. 916).

Existential Approach

Moustakas (1959, 1973) borrows a phrase from Otto Rank and entitles his form of play therapy, "relationship therapy." Moustakas characterizes play therapy as a unique growth experience created by one person seeking and needing help and another person who accepts the responsibility of offering it.

A sense of relatedness of one person to another is an essential requirement of individual growth. For children, as well as adults, this involves an internal struggle. But the struggle must take place within a relationship where the child eventually feels free to face the self, where the child's human capacity is recognized and respected, and where the child is accepted and loved. The child will then be able to become more and more individualized. The focus lies in the present living experience— the existential moment. The child is able to see the therapist as a new reality in the *present* world, and from this relationship, the child reclaims the powers of the child's individual nature and affirms the real self. The helping relationship is one in which the adult maintains a deep concern for the psychological growth of the child, is sensitive to the child's individuality, and possesses the ability to explore the child's psychosocial experiences with the child.

Moustakas has found that the best setting for relationship therapy with children is a playroom. Toys and materials form a part of the setting and, to some extent, influence the nature of the child's play.

Three basic attitudes which Moustakas feels should be conveyed to the child are faith, acceptance, and respect.

Moustakas feels that a child who has *faith* knows:

1. Personal growth
2. What can be done, when an adult says to the child, "That's up to you," or "You're the best judge of that."
3. What will be done in the future, when an adult says to the child, "It is important that you do what you want."

In the matter of *acceptance,* there must be a commitment on the part of the counselor to accept the child's feelings, the child's personal meanings and perceptions. A statement on the part of the counselor such as: "Mmm," "I see," "That's the way you feel," "You're really afraid of him," "It can be anything you want it to be" conveys acceptance of the child's viewpoint.

In the matter of *respect,* the counselor has concern for the individual child as a person and wants the child to be self helping. One does not probe or otherwise violate the child's privacy. One empathically follows the child in play.

Moustakas outlines stages of the play therapy process as follows:

1. The child starts with undifferentiated behavior that is hostile, anxious, and/or regressive.
2. The clarification stage in which the child's actions become more specific.
3. Stages of ambivalence by the child about the child's traditional or characteristic actions.
4. Undifferential positiveness on the part of the child (anger mixed with positiveness).
5. Modified and moderated reactions by the child.

Client-Centered Approach

According to Axline (1969) there is a powerful force within each individual which constantly strives for complete self-realization. This may be characterized as a drive toward maturity, independence, or self-direction; and it needs good "growing ground" to develop. For the child, Axline views the "growing ground" to be the playroom.

The playroom atmosphere grants the child permission to be open and honest in the process of play. The child is accepted completely, without diagnosis, evaluation, or pressure to change. The counselor recognizes and clarifies the expressed emotions or feelings of the child through a reflection of the feelings behind the child's words. This offers the child an opportunity to learn to know the self, and to chart a course for attitudinal and behavioral change. All suggestions, restraints, and criticisms are absent from the counselor's behavior, and are replaced by a complete acceptance of the child and a permissiveness for the child to feel, think, behave, and play in a personally honest manner.

In a child's playing out of feelings—tension, anxiety, etc.—the child brings these to the surface, gets them into the open, faces them, and learns to control them or abandon them. When the child has finally achieved an emotional catharsis, the child begins to realize that one can be an individual—to think, make decisions, become psychosocially more mature, and in so doing, to realize "selfhood."

Group Play Therapy

Ginott's (1961) main emphasis is on group psychotherapy with children—working with children in groups within the playroom setting. Ginott indicates that in group play therapy the presence of other children seems to diminish tension and stimulate activity and participation. The group induces spontaneity in children. They begin to relate to the group's therapist and trust that person more readily than in individual relationships outside the group. This observation is confirmed by Schiffer (1969).

Ginott feels that the medium which is best suited for the psychological growth of children is play. In therapy, this "is equivalent to freedom to act and react, suppress and express, suspect and respect." The *group* setting further provides a tangible *social* setting for the discovery of new and more satisfying ways of relating to peers. For the aim of play therapy is to help children develop behaviors which are consistent with society's standards (Bleck & Bleck, 1982).

GROUP PLAY THERAPY

Group play therapy is generally accepted as a better method to use when the child's problems are primarily social (Schiffer, 1969; Bleck and Bleck, 1982). On the other hand, individual therapy is deemed more useful for individualized emotional problems. The only difficulty with this approach may be the fact that individualized emotional problems are often expressed socially. There are times when a combination of individual and group therapy is useful. For example, individual therapy may be given for the first session and group therapy for subsequent sessions. Some therapists will have individual therapy with a child and then encourage the child to invite friends to a group therapy session. Such a group may be even more valuable for therapy than a group chosen by the therapist because often the child will invite withdrawn youngsters who are not particularly troublesome and hence unlikely to be referred for therapy by adults.

There are a number of other distinct advantages in the group approach. For one thing, *there is the sharing of a problem* and the realization that a particular problem is not unique. This factor makes the problem seem less "earth-shaking" to the child. Also, *there is the interplay of personalities* which adds a new dimension to therapy. In a group play session one may find significant emotional fluctuation from person to person ranging all the way from smiles to tears. In addition, as a result of the rapt attention which members show toward the activities of their peers, the group may notice one child forging ahead at a particular task and try doing the same. This results in a positive reinforcement for certain activities. Sometimes in group play it is not even necessary for other group members to "try out" a particular behavior because they can vicariously experience it by watching it being expressed by one of their play therapy peers (Bleck & Bleck, 1982).

INDIVIDUAL PLAY THERAPY

Individual play therapy becomes enhanced when it includes the following eight principles derived from Axline's (1969) historic work.

1. The helper must develop a warm, friendly relationship with the child, in which good rapport is established as soon as possible.
2. The helper accepts the child as the child is.
3. The helper establishes a feeling of permissiveness in the relationship so that the child feels free to express feelings.
4. The helper is alert to recognize the *feelings* the child is expressing and reflects those feelings back to the child so that the child gains insight into the meaning of such feelings and their relationship to behavior.
5. The helper maintains a deep respect for the child's ability to solve problems. The responsibility to make choices and to institute change is the child's.
6. The helper does not attempt to direct the child's actions or conversations. The child leads the way; the helper follows.
7. The helper does not attempt to hurry the play process along. It is a gradual process and is recognized as such.
8. The helper establishes only those limitations that are necessary to anchor the helping process to the world of reality and to help the child develop a sense of responsibility in the relationship.

When using individual play, the helper must become sensitive to the pitfall of functioning as a "playmate." Helping children through play requires empathic personal and professional qualities. It is not meant to be a maudlin, sugar-coated, or sentimental approach to working with children. Play is used to facilitate communication, self-awareness, and to put the child in contact with the reality of the child's behavior. To help the child move in these directions the helper must be genuine, empathically understanding, warm in a nonpossessive way, concrete, and possess skills in reflecting and clarifying feelings (Moustakas, 1973; Trostle, 1988).

In the play therapy relationship, the child learns that one can do anything that one likes in the room—that it is a time in which there is an absence of pressure—that this is the child's room and the child's hour. The helper accepts the child as the child is at the moment and does not try to mold the child toward socially approved behavior. The child is not forced or manipulated to play with certain toys and is freely permitted to remain silent and inactive if the child chooses. The helper accepts the meaning of the child's symbols at the child's level and works at the child's level of communication even when the meaning appears obvious. The helper, by being accepting, observing, and understanding, learns something of how life is going for the child—from the way the child handles materials we learn something about the child's level of maturity—from verbalizations made while the child is at play we learn something about the child's feelings about the self and others.

The helper makes no interpretation of the child's behavior or selection of play materials. The child is not reduced to an object to be analyzed. In using play media the helper works with the child's current behavior. There is no reliance on historical or case history information about the child. This here-and-now view stresses the importance of seeing the child's world in the present. The child in play shows personalized ways of seeing, choosing, and acting at this moment in time. No matter what the child has endured in the past, a positive, facilitating, *present* experience contributes to the child's psychosocial stability. Providing positive, present experience does not depend on knowing the child's past experiences or on the subjective and sometimes biased interpretations of the meanings of those experiences contained in a case history.

Catharsis and insight, which occur for the child during the process of play, are not by themselves, therapeutically curative. Catharsis in children usually involves mobility and acting out. Acting out has no curative effect beyond pleasure and release and it does not usually lead to self-evaluation, awareness of motivation, and attempts to change behavior. This is particularly true in young children for whom acting out becomes just fun. Insight also has its limitations. For children, there is no direct relationship between insight and behavioral change. Often insight is a result rather than a cause, attained by children who have grown emotionally ready through the play process to become acquainted with denied elements of their experiences.

Beyond catharsis and insight the use of play gives the child an opportunity to try out new behavior in the safety of an accepting and permissive atmosphere created by the counselor. By providing the child with the opportunity to be, the child is encouraged to experiment with new roles and behaviors and to vicariously experience the kind of psychosocial behaviors that the child would like to move toward and own.

SELECTION OF PLAY MATERIALS

Nearly any toy, as Nelson (1968) points out, has expressive possibilities in the eyes of the child, but he suggests three key criteria for selection of play materials for use with children: (1) select materials that may be used in a variety of ways such as clay, paints, and pipe cleaners; (2) select materials that promote communication such as toy telephones; and (3) select materials (punching bag, hand puppets) that encourage the expression and release of aggressive feelings. Generally, the more unstructured and flexible the toys the more readily the child can express his or her imagination and feelings through them.

Ginott (1961) indicates that there are five major criteria for selecting and rejecting materials for play therapy, stating that a play therapy toy should: (1) facilitate the establishment of contact with the child by the helper, (2) evoke and encourage catharsis; (3) aid in developing insight; (4) furnish opportunities for reality testing; and (5) provide a vehicle for sublimation.

The toys used with children should be within each child's realm of play. If exposed to toys that are too old for the child, the child won't be able to express true emotions through them. By using toys the child is used to playing with, the child will feel free to be imaginative and reveal psychosocial needs and feelings (Moustakas, 1973).

Beiser (1955) studied the free choice of a selected group of toys of 100 children, 79 boys and 21 girls, ranging from 2 to 12 years of age, who had been referred to the Chicago Institute for Juvenile Research. Each toy was tabulated according to the total number of children who played with it (Popularity), a ratio of popularity and total dynamic interpretations stemming from play with a toy (Communication Value), frequency with which the toy stimulated fantasy on the child's part (Fantasy Stimulation), the breadth or number of dynamic interpretations that could be made from a child's play with an individual toy (Dynamic Spread) and a Combined Total ranking of toys. In terms of highest Combined Total rankings toys were listed in the following order: (1) doll family; (2) soldiers; (3) guns; (4) clay; (5) paper and crayons; (6) animals; (7) planes; (8) Nok-Out Bench; and (9) trucks. The lowest Combined Total ranking toys were: (1) pencil; (2) paste; (3) scissors; and (4) ball.

The particular toy used by a child should not be an issue. It is more important that it is something which will motivate the child to see the toy as having meaning, see it as something which can be incorporated into play, and see it as a vehicle through which feelings can be expressed. Helping the child to select facilitative toys is an important early step in the play therapy process.

PLAY MATERIALS

The following play materials have been used with varying degrees of success by Dorfman (1951), Ginott (1961), Axline (1969), and Moustakas (1959, 1973).

Doll Family/Doll House — A spacious doll house appropriately furnished and peopled with dolls depicting male and female, children and babies. The treatment accorded by the child to a parent and sibling dolls can give the counselor an understanding of the child's perceptions of self and others within the family context. The sleeping patterns in the doll house may be of some interest (Ginott, 1961) as well as the targets of anger and affection. In some studies it has been found that the child most often selects the doll family as play material. There are some who feel that through the use of dolls the child is best able to express feelings. It should be borne in mind that all acting-out with dolls or puppets is not significant. It is only significant when the child uses these media to express a variety of feelings or to work through feelings that are troublesome.

Toy Animals — Some children find it difficult to express aggressive feelings against people even though the make-believe world of dolls. They do, however, find they can express aggressive feelings in safety against "bad" animals. It should also be pointed out that toy animals can elicit feelings of affection and love.

Blocks — Blocks satisfy children's need for risk and adventure and may also serve as a substitute object for hostility. Blocks enable children to build and destroy without dire consequences and are very amenable to a rapid rebuilding. The child can destroy a block building over and over again and learn in the process that one's aggression is not catastrophic.

Water — Water play can involve pouring water, blowing bubbles, squeezing sponges, washing, soaking, and rinsing anything that can be immersed. Water, according to Ginott (1961), is perhaps the most effective of all playroom materials. It does not require any special skills so every child can play with it with success. It enables even the meekest of children to experience a sense of accomplishment. The materials make too little demand and offer so little resistance that every child can manipulate them. It allows for cleansing or it can become, in the child's imagination, an agent for messing. Water play is limited only by the child's imagination. Materials for water play are inexpensive, readily available, and a delight for children.

Sand Box — Sand is another excellent medium for the child's aggressive play. It can be thrown about with comparative safety — dolls and other toys can be buried in it — it can be "snow," "water," or a "burying ground." It can also elicit creative impulses and provide excellent opportunities for the use of the child's imagination.

Easel and Finger Paints — These offer a suitable outlet for the satisfaction of the child's need to mess. They are nonthreatening media which allow children to translate feelings into color and movement. Even for the over controlled and inhibited child the contact with soft, colorful, mercurial like substances encourages spontaneity and a free flow of fantasy.

Clay — Clay allows for success at any level of a child's development and skill. It provides an outlet for both creative and destructive urges. It lends itself to random manipulation; it requires no intermediary; it can be used by aggressive children to punch and pound; it gives a sense of accomplishment in the child's mastery of pliable material.

Aggressive Toys — These should be chosen with care to avoid physical harm to the child. Punching bags and pounding boards provide harmless outlets for expressing hostility. Noise making toys such as drums and xylophones can also be used by children for a nondestructive expression of hostility.

Puppets — Many children find that they can use the anonymity of puppets to express their feelings in safety. Puppets are a delight to work with and can be manipulated by the child to express a wide range of psychosocial needs and feelings.

Many other toys can be used to enhance the psychosocial development of the child (Caney, 1972). It should be noted that almost every toy which can evoke a destructive response can also produce a positive response. This was brought about in a graduate course when students who were experientially learning about play began to talk about their personal reactions to the spring back punching bag. During the time the graduate students played with the materials nearly all of them had a chance at the punching bag and expressed delight in hitting the bag as hard as they could. However, a few students stated that when they approached the punching bag, rather than hit it, they hugged it. What emerged in the ensuing discussion was that toys and other play materials are neutral objects and whatever feeling is expressed with a toy is a reflection of the person using it rather than the toy itself. It is not surprising then, when a child picks up a toy gun, looks at it momentarily, and then puts it aside saying, "I wish people would stop hurting each other." For the child the toy gun may bring forth a feeling of sadness rather than aggression. It is wise to put aside stereotyped images about the emotional valences of toys and to encourage the child to share perceptions and feelings as these are evoked by the toy or medium used in play.

THE PLAYROOM

The necessity of having a special room set aside and furnished for helping children through play is questioned by Axline (1969) who believes there are many possibilities for using the medium of play within limited budget and space appropriations. A small rug, an easel, and a toy box located in a corner of a room would constitute an adequate play media environment. In the toy box would be a doll family, a few pieces of furniture, nursing bottle, telephone, puppets, crayons, drawing paper, water colors, finger paints, and some transportation toys such as cars and trucks. These materials would be sufficient for play therapy and could fit a space as small as a suitcase.

If a special room is to be put aside for play, it should have the following features. The playroom should be kept simple. Other than basic furniture the only things which should be there are toys. The floor and walls should be washable and easily cleaned. The room should have acoustical ceiling tile and wall materials which will absorb and reduce sound. It would be useful to protect the windows with screening. The room should be bright and attractive, well lighted, well ventilated, and play materials should be visible and available. There should be a sink with running hot and cold water, a sand box, and a wooden bench for use as a table or work area. Materials should be kept on shelves which are easily accessible. Regardless of the mess made in previous play sessions, the room should be put in order so that it is always neutral and free from the suggestive indicators regarding which play materials were used by a previous individual or group using the playroom.

It would greatly enhance the child's sense of freedom if the child were provided with a smock, an old shirt, or some sort of coverall to protect clothing. The child will then have the freedom to be messy.

ESTABLISHING LIMITS

Rationale for Limits

In his discussion of play therapy, Ginott (1961) offers five reasons for establishing limits:

1. Limits direct catharsis into symbolic channels.
2. Limits enable the helper to maintain attitudes of acceptance, empathy, and regard for the child and not be distracted from those attitudes.
3. Limits assure the physical safety of the child.
4. Limits strengthen ego controls.
5. Limits are set for reasons of law, ethics, and social acceptability (pp. 103–105).

Landreth, Strother, and Barlow (1986) indicate that limits consistently anchor the play experience to the world of reality, give the child a sense of responsibility in the relationship, and safeguard the helping process from possible misconceptions, confusion, guilt feelings, and insecurity.

The use of durable and inexpensive media in a playroom which is easily cleaned will obviate the need for limits relating to materials (with a few exceptions). It is evident that some limits bearing on the relationship are required if the child is to learn how to deal with the real world and if the purposes of the play experience are to be met. There appears to be general agreement (Dorfman, 1951; Ginott, 1961; Axline, 1969; and Moustakas, 1973) that the following limits serve to improve the psychosocial quality and effectiveness of play experiences.

Time Limit —A time limit is determined and held to. The helper tells the child of the time limit and toward the end of the session reminds the child that there are only a few minutes left to play. Extending time at the request of the child is not wise. When the child learns that time limits are part of everyone's reality, the child will begin to make profitable use of the time available for play.

Taking Toys from the Playroom — Toys should remain in the playroom. Broken toys should also remain in the playroom, otherwise some toys would be broken for the purpose of taking them home. If a child wants to show a toy to a parent, then the child may ask the parent or teacher to the playroom to see it. Children should be allowed to take home paintings and clay work that they themselves create.

Breakage of Toys/Destruction to Room — Children's destructive urges and feelings should be recognized, reflected, and respected, but limits on action should be invoked and implemented. It is more of a help to the child to let the child face the limits that human relationships require than to let the child give rein to destructive *actions.* There is little self enhancing value in permitting a child to break play room equipment or toys. The child's negative actions should be channeled toward materials in the play room designated for the purpose.

Physical Assault — There is no benefit in letting a child physically assault another child or the helper. It is generally agreed that this is a limit which should not be modified under any circumstances. It is more helpful for the child to channel aggressive feelings through symbolic actions against play materials which are there for that purpose. Permitting a child to attack another person can cause harm not only to that person but also to the child who needs to learn that mutual respect requires some control of feelings and that the unbridled expression of anger through physical assault is no solution for the child's problems.

Limits should not be mentioned before the need for them arise. If limits are kept to a minimum and are introduced only when the need emerges, then the play experience progresses more naturally. There appears to be little advantage in beginning the play experience by prescribing limitations on actions that may never occur. Children's everyday experiences usually prepare them for some prohibitions upon their actions and it is better to wait until the need for limits comes up, before identifying them.

PARENTS AND PLAY

As a consultant to parents, the play therapist can help parents to use play to facilitate the psychosocial development of the child. The value of play as a vehicle for fostering the psychosocial development of the child cannot be underestimated. The play therapist and parents can work together to use the extraordinary power of play to enhance the psychosocial maturity of children (Moustakas, 1973). One vehicle for doing this is a toy lending program for parents and children.

The toy lending program is based on two basic ideas: that play activities should be self-rewarding so that a child participates because of the enjoyment the child receives, not because the child is coerced or coaxed; and that psychosocial development cannot take place without free expression. The goal of a toy lending program is to create psychosocially helpful play environments in the home and to encourage play between parents and children as a medium for getting to know each other and learning about each other's psychosocial needs. In play at home the child should also be free to give vent to feelings of anger and frustration and be able to talk to the parent(s) about the experiences and circumstances which cause these feelings.

Initiating a toy lending program is not difficult. The components are simple: a meeting place, a group of interested parents, a presentation on the psychosocial purposes of play, demonstrations on how play elicits feelings, an identification of the play materials which evoke feelings, role playing opportunities to engage in play, and the formation of a support group atmosphere in which parents can be encouraged in their play efforts to contribute to the psychosocial development of their children.

In conclusion, the psychosocial benefits of play cannot be underestimated. Play is the child's natural language for expressing a wide range of feelings. When the counselor attempts to assist a child to express feelings only through verbal interactions, the experience can be frustrating for the child who typically does not possess the language to express those feelings. But when the counselor establishes a play relationship with the child, the child is able to express feelings which are more accurate, honest, natural, and spontaneous. The feelings which previously could not be expressed now emerge because of the stimulus provided by play materials.

USING PLAY MEDIA TO FACILITATE
A CHILD'S SELF–AWARENESS

by
Lucy Weeks

Rationale for the Use of Play

The child's response to life, in the form of continual striving, growing, and changing as the child observes and experiences the world and the people in the child's life, can be supported and nourished by the child's self-awareness as a valued human being. If the child knows love and acceptance from others the child will more readily accept the self. If the child is continually unsure of the self as a person of worth much of the child's energy for growth is spent in defending the self against the hurt of not being completely acceptable. Through play the child expresses the self and feelings; the child experiments and tries out behavior; the child comes to know the self more fully and vicariously experiences what the child would like to become.

A child's play in the presence of, or with, an adult frequently represents the child's self-concept and how the child perceives an environment, and the child often implicitly assumes that the adult is able to understand both. The more acceptance, warmth, and understanding the child receives from an adult the more the child is able to reveal the self. As the child sees the self through childhood's natural medium of play, the child comes to a greater self-awareness and self-understanding.

A Child's Problem and Attitudes

I would like to describe one elementary school child as I have seen him through the medium of play and with the aid of audiotapes and my notes, to trace a developing self-awareness as he struggles to understand and express himself. All names and references are changed and with this agreement I have the generous permission of the child's parents to use the material collected for professional writings and understandings. The boy himself was happy to use the tape recorded, and often would play back, for his own listening, the tape of the previous session.

I came to know Gid initially as a boy who was constantly in difficulties with his teachers and playmates. In the fourth grade, in public school and in church school, he was alternately disruptive and inattentive, rude or in tears, and at times destructive. His elementary school teacher was concerned at what seemed evidence of deep anger when he gouged and mutilated his desk. Efforts to play with others usually ended in tears followed by solitary activity. The same behavior was observed in church school and he caused exasperation in all who were in contact with him. A difficult and unhappy classroom pattern seemed to have been firmly established and was continuing when I first came into contact with Gid. He was brought to me, trembling and scared, by an exasperated teacher. I asked him to sit down and talk things over and tried to assure him that I was not there to punish, but that perhaps together we could find some way to help him. He said:

Well—well—those—they—the others won't let me simmer down.
Counselor:

They won't let you simmer down.
Gid: No—they—they—they—they're always after me.

I suggested he might like to meet with me once a week for a while, to which he agreed eagerly. Later, at a conference with his mother, to make arrangements, he was very silent and agreed to meet with me with a very matter-of-fact, "Yeah, I'd like to." He remained across the room and aloof and I confirmed the appointment with Gid and ended the interview by avoiding his mother's tendency to discuss Gid in his presence.

Place: Playroom and Materials

The play room is a large basement with a blackboard, piano, building blocks, books and puzzles. There is a sand box full of toys—trucks, shovels, etc. Nearby is a doll house with furniture and dolls of all sizes and kinds. Near the sand box is a table and bench where I leave out clay, colored Play-Doh®, and finger paints and paper. There is an adjoining lavatory with toilet and wash bowl, and paper towels. The two doors to the room are closed when the room is used, but there are glass panes through which an adult can see.

Counselor Attitudes and Atmosphere for Play

Other than his acting-out behavior in the classroom, Gid seemed to be a very self-controlled child. At times he was impassive and detached. I felt that a child-centered play climate could provide Gid with a completely accepting, permissive, and relaxed atmosphere where he could play out his feelings and perhaps come to discover himself more easily and more fully than he had yet been able to do. He needed to find an adult who could respect him entirely, uncritically, with all his tension and confusion.

The time was set for one hour each week. At times we went on a little longer, but an hour and a half was the maximum. The room itself and the closed doors limited the play area quite clearly. If Gid decided to leave early this ended the session for that day. With Axline's (1969) discussion of limits in mind I was prepared to channel aggressive play, or to stop destructiveness, if necessary. The occasion never arose.

STAGES IN SELF AWARENESS

Testing Out the Situation — In our first session in the play room I told Gid the hour was his to do as he pleased, that he could use any of the toys or equipment he found there. He stood still and surveyed the room, then wandered from one thing to another, picking up, inspecting, and then dropping a toy. His constant glances in my direction indicated his doubt as to how much freedom I would allow. His whole body gradually relaxed, no words were exchanged until he found the tape recorder which delighted him. I showed him how to use it and then suggested that we tape our sessions together and that at any time he could turn it back and listen to himself or that he could turn it off. He proceeded to try it out, and handled it in a competent manner. I sensed in him a pride in his ability. He discovered the piano and played a few notes, looked over his shoulder several times, and played a few more notes before inspecting more of the toys.

Gid: Who uses this room anyway, the nursery?
Co: Yes, on Sundays it's for the little people.
Gid: Ha, sand box, doll houses, dolls, — house — doll house — dolls — I don't play with dolls.
Co: Lots to play with but you don't play with dolls.
Gid: I want to hear my voice again.
Co: You want to hear it.
Gid: Yeah.

Tension and Catharsis — Earlier in the session Gid had run the tape back and played it again without hesitation. This time he seemed confused and looked at me. I showed him how again.

At this point I felt that permissiveness and support was better than the assumption he could do it and perhaps the pressure to succeed which might have been implied.

He had been testing the situation, checking out the use of the room, and watching me for reactions. Gid's rejection of the doll house, his repeating (almost stammering) the words of rejection, seemed to say he was not ready to look at a family situation. It was a brief look at himself and his subsequent confusion at the tape recorder indicated that the doll house had produced some tension. He returned to talking about family when he compared my age and his father's. He then tried to speak of his grandfather, who had died recently, but could not complete what he wanted to say.

Gid: When were you born, Mrs. W.? What year?
Co: You are wondering how old I am?
Gid: My father, he is 47 and you're older.

He went to the piano, played a simple tune, using both hands, banged one hand on the keys, then stopped. A long silence . . . then, "You know what, Mrs. W.?"

Co: What, Gid?
Gid: My—my—my—gran—my—no, my father—

He turned to the piano again and banged the keys as hard as he could with both hands. Then he said again, "My father, he's 47." Then he turned to the piano again and banged the low notes one by one moving up the keyboard a little way, then back to the low notes harder and faster. Was the question of death his real concern here in speaking of age?

Gid then repeated the same piano banging very hard and loud. He once looked at me as if expecting to be stopped. Then he began again, went to the tape recorder and replayed the tape, listening intently. He repeated this behavior four times. Then:

Gid: OK, I'm going to get a drink.

There was a change in the tension and tempo of his movements. He went to the bathroom, carefully adjusting the door so that it was not quite closed. This pattern was typical of Gid's playroom behavior for several months. Tension seemed to build up in him; he found release in some intense activity such as pounding clay, banging the piano, or hammering wooden blocks, with little or no verbalization even when feelings and actions were reflected to him. Then he would suddenly depart to the bathroom and return to use paints or the sand table. I later began to wonder if this amounted to catharsis followed by flight from the disturbing thoughts and feelings inside him. It was certainly catharsis, and each time I waited for signs of self-awareness, meanwhile letting him set the pace.

At another point Gid indicated something of his inner feelings by drawing on the blackboard. He had been very silent and very restless, picking up and dropping one thing after another. At the blackboard he fiddled with chalk, asked if we had colored chalk, then drew up a chair, stood on it and moved one piece of chalk from top to bottom of the board in great peaks and valleys.

> **Gid:**   You know what this is, Mrs. W.? Mountains and
>   glaciers—gl—glaciers, glaciers. And nobody on them,
>   nobody around—now *one* person. Not—not—not—Do
>   you like ice cream, Mrs. W.? You know the best ice cream
>   cone there is? It's at Andy's. I'd like a big cone each
>   Friday. Can we get one?

And so we arranged to get ice cream at the end of each session. Gid seemed to be picturing something for me—either loneliness, or a desire for solitude, and he moved away from it so quickly I accepted it without words. Later I questioned my lack of response to his blackboard drawing. Would a reflection have helped him become more aware of what he was picturing?

During the first months another clue to Gid's feelings came regularly on arrival at his house at the end of the afternoon. He would sit a moment in the car and survey the yard, the number of bicycles in the driveway, etc.

> **Gid:**   Do I have to go home now?
> **Co:**   You'd like to stay.
> **Gid:**   I like it there by myself, but you'll get some colored
>   chalk next time?
> **Co:**   Mm. I'll see if I can get some good colors.
> **Gid:**   OK—that brother of mine is home.

He got out of the car slowly. Often he would say, "I wonder who is home?"

Blaming Others—In the subsequent weeks, Gid referred to his own behavior in school and blamed others. He could speak of himself, but could not acknowledge responsibility.

> **Gid:**   You know what, Mrs. W.? I couldn't think of anything to
>   write until I stood out in the hall for a while. The teacher
>   made me.

Co: At school.

Gid: Yeah. I stood there and thought of a story I could write, but the others had theirs all done when I got back in the room.

Co: It was hard to write when you were in the room with everyone else.

Gid: It was hard to think.

Co: But you could think when you were by yourself.

Gid: Yeah. They make me do things.

Co: The other kids make you do things.

Gid: Well, I get all excited, all simmered up.

And later:

Comments on self —

Gid: I forgot what I got a D in, maybe it was writing. I got an A in math.

Co: A D is discouraging but you like math.

Gid: Yeah. It's good; I can do it. You know I like rocks — I'll tell you about them. (He gave me a long description of various rock samples he had at home.)

Co: It feels good to know about some things like math and rocks.

Gid: You know — I — I — I like to forget some things.

Co: You like to forget; you feel better.

Gid: Mmm — some — sometimes. (A long silence while he carefully screwed lids on paint jars.) Then: I could eat some ice cream now.

At times like this I feel strongly the need to accept *his* pacing as he grows more aware of himself.

Fantasy — Gid often mentions distant places and large sums of money in his conversations. As he was painting, he said:

Gid: Purple. (He began to hum to himself.) Purple and black, or dark green — that's what it makes. (Still humming.) I'll make a map of the U.S. — try anyway — they never let me — they make me laugh. Florida — ha-ha-*thing*, ha-ping-thing-ping. Know what? Oh, that's wrong. (He went to wash his hands, returned to the table. He reached for the clay.) I'm going — going to, to — to — I'm going to Germany to college.

Co: To Germany.

Gid: Did you ever go far away, Mrs. W.?

Co: To far away places.

Gid: Yes, all on your own, just away. You know how much money baseball players make? A million — no, a trillion dollars.

Co: A lot of money. (He dropped the clay abruptly and went to the blackboard, picked up chalk and then dropped it back in the tray. He was restless.)

Self and Reality — About two months later he was talking about going to New York City, "on his own — all by himself." But a week later he said:

Gid: You know last time I said I wanted to go to New York by myself. Well — I like baseball and I like to sort of dream — dream about going away but I'd really want my family. I guess I just think things but — well — I know — I really know — well —.

Co: You know that you're dreaming and you know what's real, too.

Gid: Yeah, yeah. There's dreams and there's real things.

In early sessions Gid seemed to use play materials as a means for catharsis. He was often restless, endlessly picking up, then dropping, whatever he came upon as he drifted around the room, silent until he suddenly settled to piano, play or paint, and finally, one day, the sand table. At two different times he pulled out the doll house, then shoved it back against the wall vigorously. He never seemed to notice two puppets lying on the shelf, one white and one black skinned.

I began to see real changes in Gid after one particularly rough day at the playroom. He had arrived extremely tense and silent. This appointment was the result of a very incoherent telephone call from Gid the day before. Less than a week had elapsed since I had last seen him and I was aware of family stresses in the background. In the playroom Gid was soon throwing paint on papers and the floor, with no words at all. Suddenly he stopped and looked at what he had done, and then with tears running down his face, he squatted down and started to pry up the clay.

Co: You feel very angry, and then very sad.

Gid just nodded his head and put his head down and sobbed. I put my arm around him and in a few minutes he was quiet. I handed him a tissue and he said tearfully, "Can we get some ice cream?"

Co: Yes, it's time for it.

Carefully Gid began to put things in order, papers and clay in the box and tops on paint jars.

Gid: I'll turn out the lights and you close the door.

He seemed to be closing the door on those moments. He avoided the playroom the next Friday and asked to stay in my office. It was soon after that I realized he was playing with more purpose.

During his third month of play therapy, he entered the playroom one day and went straight to the puppets, picked up the white one, and began talking, at first in a whisper.

Gid: See that—he is a goop—he is a dumbhead, always in
            trouble—a mess.
Co: Always in trouble—a mess.
Gid: We could bury him in the sand so he couldn't get up.
            But he'd do it—he would—he—he'd kick his way out—
            and he, he'd—maybe he'd hurt someone, too.
Co: He'd get out, he would, but it might hurt.
Gid: Here—now—ah—oh—oh.

Gid dug a hole, put the puppet in very gently, and swiftly covered him up. He piled trucks and shovels on top of the pile of sand, and then just stood looking at the pile. Suddenly he spoke in a very tender voice:

Gid: He's got sand up his nose—he—he can't breathe. Come
            on—we'll help him out. He'll be OK. Come on, you
            help me.

So I helped him uncover the puppet. He held it up high and looked at it.

Gid: Boy, you've got friends. You didn't need to kick—you
            might have broke your leg.
Co: Friends can help. He didn't break a leg.
Gid: Well—yeah—sand's like—like—well—it's easy if it's a
            lot. I could eat a huge ice cream cone.

Gid continued his play with the puppet for several sessions, talking to it, alternately giving it a rough time and treating it with warmth and tenderness.

Erickson (1964) has said that "to 'play it out' is the most natural self-healing measure childhood affords." To Gid the puppet was himself, and through it I listened, and reflected as he played out some of his own hurt, anger, and doubts. He made the puppet call Sam names and kick him (Sam is Gid's older brother) and finally:

Gid: (with puppet, using high voice) Plonk— dead he got it— a bat, no, a ball right in the face. Ah—ah—oh—oh—no, not quite—he'll go to the hospital—they'll fix him—he— he'll *think* —I guess—we'll—we-ee'll see.

And yet three weeks later he returned to a direct reference to his brother and how they called each other names.

Gid: He calls me *'weekend,'* get it? And I call him the 'bonk.'
Co: And how do you feel when he does?
Gid: Oh, I go after him and make him say—he's a dope (laughing).
Co: And does Sam feel hurt?
Gid: Sometimes. But when he tells me I never do it. Sometimes it's fun having a brother around. Sometimes it's lousy.

By now Gid could accept his feelings about his brother.

Reflection about Self —After eleven months of weekly sessions, Gid could talk directly about himself. Now he preferred to stay upstairs in my office and talk. He would fling himself in the armchair and swing his legs across the arm.

Gid: You know what, Mrs. W.? I've sort of got used to things. I—we—I got Mrs. R's dying out of my system (a neighbor) and Midget's dying (his puppy)—and my grandfather. I don't know if we'll go to Seattle. —But it's OK somehow.
Co: You sort of find it easier to take what comes, even if Seattle leaves you feeling uncertain.
Gid: It isn't Seattle. That might be OK—except I'd have to leave Billy and Jack (friends). Maybe—well—I-uh—I don't have to forget things so—you know.
Co: You feel more comfortable—more—
Gid: Yeah. I'm feeling—huh? Funny, that's good—*I'm feeling*—

> that's it. Oh, boy—you know, I'm gonna make that team—
> and I got *good* marks—an—an—well—I guess I'm gonna
> go on wanting ice cream, though (chuckling).

The following week Gid said:

> Mrs. W., I used to think about what you were like and
> now I think about what I'm like.

After that I saw Gid less frequently. He telephoned if he wanted to talk, and his last phone call was a jubilant one to tell me he'd made the baseball team. His parents and teachers reported that he improved in his grades and behavior. He gained in self-confidence, stability, and self-understanding.

CONCLUSION

Any elementary school could profitably use a "play center." A small room would serve quite adequately if provided with clay, paints, and puppets. Small doll figures would aid the child in expressing concerns with the child's world. The immaturity of the child may limit verbalization, but the child's ability to speak through clay can demonstrate to the child and to the counselor the child's feelings and perceptions. As Gid began to express himself, he used puppets, clay, and the truck in the sand with purpose and meaning, but as he became more sensitive to himself and his environment, he used materials less, and became more verbal.

Erickson (1964) speaks of play as the infantile way of mastering experience by meditating, experimenting, and planning. These are three steps which the child counselor would desire to facilitate in a child. The stages of play first observed and classified by Lowenfeld (1935) are still accurate. I believe they were illustrated by Gid's use of play materials and his subsequent ability to speak more realistically and insightfully about himself. In early play sessions Gid showed great tension and restlessness. He tested out the counselor's acceptance at first, then found release from tension through *bodily activity*. He talked very little, and when he did it was to a great extent about interests other than self and family. When he mentioned his own behavior it was to blame others, a refusal of responsibility for his actions, and he would move away very rapidly from any subject that was uncomfortable. A counselor needs great patience at these times and a conviction that the child can and will grow in awareness and toward a more positive concept of self. At the child's own pace. The counselor's trust in the child's own pacing will give the child the freedom to grow when the child is ready.

Gid soon began to use play media with more purpose. He found a means to express what he had experienced (*repetition of experience*), and what he dreamed (*demonstration of fantasy*). He expressed himself, often with great feeling, and seemed to move to a greater realization of himself and his environment. His next steps were toward a more realistic assessment of himself and a greater acceptance of his family and peers (*realization of environment*).

Erickson (1964) also speaks of the ego's capacity to find a self-cure in play, but he also says this about the child's play: "Such peace gained by play must, however, be sustained by new insight on the part of the parents."

While insight and cooperation on the part of the parents is highly desirable, I believe Gid has made significant gains in spite of continuing parental turmoil in the background, and the burden of his mother's fluctuating emotional distress.

Within the elementary school the counselor may profitably serve as consultant to teachers and parents, but my experience with Gid confirms Rogers' (1951) belief that the child's capacity for self-help and growth can occur without planned change in the child's environment.

REFERENCES

Allen, F. H. (1942). *Psychotherapy with children.* New York: Norton.

Amster, F. (1943). Differential uses of play in treatment of young children. *American Journal of Orthopsychiatry, 13*, 62–68.

Axline, V. (1964). *Dibs: In search of self.* Boston: Houghton Mifflin.

Axline, V. (1969). *Play therapy.* New York: Ballantine Books.

Beiser, H. R. (1955). Therapeutic play techniques: Play equipment for diagnosis and therapy. *American Journal of Orthopsychiatry, 25*, 761–770.

Bleck, R. T., & Bleck, B. L. (1982). The disruptive child's play group. *Elementary School Counseling and Guidance, 17*, 137–141.

Caney, S. (1972). *Toy books.* New York: Workman.

Caplan, R., & Caplan, T. (1973). *The power of play.* New York: Anchor Books.

Dorfman, E. (1951). Play therapy. Chapter 6 in C. R. Rogers, *Client-centered therapy.* Boston: Houghton Mifflin.

Ellis, M. J. (1973). *Why people play.* Englewood Cliffs, NJ: Prentice-Hall.

Erickson, E. H. (1964). Toys and reasons. In M. R. Haworth (Ed.), *Child psychotherapy: Practice and theory.* New York: Basic Books.

Ginott, H. G. (1961). *Group psychotherapy with children.* New York: McGraw-Hill.

Kessler, J. W. (1966). *Psychopathology of childhood.* Englewood Cliffs, NJ: Prentice-Hall.

Landreth, G., Strother, J., & Barlow, K. (1986). A reaction to objections to play therapy. *School Counselor,* 33, 164–166.

Landreth, G., & Verhalen, M. (1982). Who is this person they call a counselor? *School Counselor,* 29, 359–361.

Levy, D. M. (1939). Release therapy. *American Journal of Orthopsychiatry,* 9, 113–136.

Levy, J. (1978). *Play behavior.* New York: John Wiley.

Lowenfeld, M. (1935). *Play in childhood.* London: Gollancz.

Meeks, A. R. (1968). *Guidance in elementary education.* New York: Ronald Press.

Moustakas, C. C. (1959). *Play therapy with children.* New York: Harper.

Moustakas, C. C. (1973). *Children in play therapy.* New York: McGraw-Hill.

Nelson, R. C. (1968). Play media and the elementary school counselor. In D. C. Dinkmeyer (Ed.), *Guidance and counseling in the elementary school.* New York: Holt, Rinehart and Winston, pp. 267–270.

Orlick, R. (1983). Enhancing love and life mostly through play and games. *Humanistic Education,* 21, 153–164.

Piaget, J. (1951). *Play, dreams, and imitation in children.* New York: Norton.

Pulaski, M. A. (1971). *Understanding Piaget.* New York: Harper and Row.

Rogers, C. R. (1951). *Client-centered therapy.* Boston: Houghton Mifflin.

Rubin, P. B. and Tregay, J. (1989). Play with them: *Theraplay groups in the classroom: Techniques for professionals who work with children.* Springfield, IL: Charles C Thomas.

Schiffer, M. (1969). *The therapeutic play group.* New York: Grune and Stratton.

Chapter 6

COUNSELING: A CHILD-CENTERED PERSPECTIVE

The counselor's role is that set of activities which constitute the counselor's work day. In some settings, this person called "counselor" does little counseling. Instead this person performs a range of administrative, evaluative, and clerical activities while carrying the title counselor.

This chapter will emphasize that the counselor's primary and most important function is counseling; and professional counselors should not be deflected from that function by special interest groups which insist that the counselor attend to their special interests rather than counsel. Those who make policies for organizations are often insensitive to the importance of counseling. They instead create policies which involve the counselor in everything but counseling.

Child-centered counselors are more deeply committed to the importance of counseling than counselors representing other theories. While other theories identify an increasing number of activities for the counselor (Thompson & Rudolph, 1983), the client-centered tradition is to emphasize counseling as the core of the counselor's role. This emphasis is due to the fact that client-centered counselors have seen their process produce results. They have experienced their human and empathic attitudes, when expressed through the power of the reflective process, get at those feelings which affect behavior. They have experienced clients move those feelings and behaviors in positive directions. The foundation for this change has been the steady application of the counseling process over a period of time.

Child-centered counselors know that positive outcomes take time. They are willing to give it. They know that behavioral change occurs after a series of counseling sessions. They are willing to provide them. They know that positive outcomes will occur in proportion to the counselor's patience and skill. And, finally, they know that it is the power of the counseling relationship which encourages the client to perceive more deeply and accurately; and they know that the only way

157

that these counseling relationships will take place is when their importance is emphasized in the counselor's work (Boy & Pine, 1979).

FACTORS INFLUENCING THE COUNSELOR'S ROLE

There are several factors which influence the counselor's role or
responsibilities. Some of these factors exert a positive influence and help
the counselor develop a role description which is truly aimed at meeting
the needs of children. Other factors exert a negative influence. They
produce a role description which involves the child counselor in a
potpourri of activities which often circumvent the true needs of children.
These factors affect how the counselor conceives and executes a role
description. This section will identify these factors and point out the
degree to which they influence the child counselor's inclusion of counseling as the top priority in a role.

Community Expectations

Some community expectations can have a positive influence on the
child counselor's role. In communities where the counselor is perceived
as someone whose primary responsibility is to be with children in helping relationships, the counselor is encouraged to develop a role which
emphasizes the counselor's commitment to counseling.

When a community senses the importance of counseling in the lives of
children, it furnishes the counselor with the needed support to move
toward a role in which counseling is the core of a counselor's responsibility.

When the community expectation is that the child counselor will
counsel, then the counselor feels comfortable in fulfilling community
expectations by devoting the major portion of each working day to
counseling children; and the community's recognition of the importance
of counseling becomes spelled-out in the child counselor's role description.

Some other communities expect the child counselor to function as a
super clerk who pays careful and detailed attention to tabulating the
behavior of children. Such an expectation will prompt the child counselor
to develop a role in which the counselor's clerical activities are given
prominence. Counseling children is given a low level priority in such a
counselor's role because the community's concept emphasizes the child
counselor's clerical responsibilities.

Institutional Policies

Some institutional policies have a positive influence upon the role of a child counselor, especially in those institutions which recognize the need and importance of counseling. When the counselor is bolstered by such an institutional policy, the counselor is encouraged to feature the importance of counseling in a role description.

When an elementary school's policy is sensitive to the psychological needs of children, the child counselor is encouraged to give counseling the highest priority in a role description. The child counselor is motivated to engage in counseling because school policy encourages such an involvement.

Other institutional policies have a negative influence upon the counseling dimensions of a child counselor's role. Some elementary schools desire that the counselor administer institutional policy and want the counselor to function as an administrator of that policy rather than allowing the counselor to engage in counseling. Faced with the need to administer policies as a primary function, the counselor features such administrative activities in a role description while relegating counseling to a secondary level of importance.

Other institutions require that the counselor function as a gatekeeper of institutional policy, making judgments regarding which children will and which will not, receive certain services. When child counselors perceive themselves as such, counseling receives low priority in the counselor's role.

Administrative Behavior

Some administrators can have a positive influence upon the child counselor's commitment to the importance of counseling. Such administrators perceive counseling as the most important thing that a counselor does for children. They acknowledge that counseling will best serve children and give the counselor the administrative support needed to build the counseling dimension of the counselor's role.

Some administrators desire an environment which encourages staff utilization of their specialized skills. These administrators realize that services will be more efficiently delivered by the staff if the administrative atmosphere is supportive and encouraging (Bogue & Saunders, 1976; Flowers & Hughes, 1978; Boy & Pine, 1990). In such a reinforcing administrative environment, the child counselor is encouraged to feature counseling in his or her role.

Other administrative behavior can deflect the child counselor away from counseling. Some administrators desire to make use of the counselor as a loose ends coordinator or junior executive. They are so overwhelmed by their administrative responsibilities that they seek relief from these responsibilities and enlist the aid of the counselor in their performance. Once committed to administrative functions, the child counselor has difficulty in finding the time for counseling.

Counselor's Formal Preparation

Some child counselors are graduates of programs which emphasize the need and importance of counseling. Such counselors commit themselves to providing children with counseling. They identify counseling as the primary responsibility within their roles.

Such counselors realize that the activity which has the greatest impact on the child's attitude and behavior is counseling. Being with the child shows the child that someone cares. When the child knows this, he or she cooperates with the helping process. Since counseling has the best chance to penetrate a child's attitude and behavior, such counselors want to give it more time than the other responsibilities of a counselor's role.

Other child counselors are products of preparational programs which have prepared the counselor to do everything but counsel. Such programs have constructed courses and learning experiences in which prospective counselors learn how to assess, count, diagnose, manage, evaluate, measure, administer, and manipulate. Products of such programs do not identify with the importance of counseling. They instead identify with activities and functions which are more characteristic of the behavior of psychometricians, diagnosticians, or administrators.

Attitudes of Colleague Counselors

Some colleague counselors give the child counselor the support necessary to give counseling major consideration in a role description. They are counselors who have seen the depths of turmoil among children and have come to the conclusion that an important way to alleviate that turmoil is to assist children through counseling. They understand how counseling can influence attitudinal and behavior changes. They develop a role description which emphasizes the counselor's counseling responsibility. Such colleague counselors compose the support system which encourages the counselor to list counseling at the top of a list of role priorities.

Other colleague counselors function as obstructionists. Such counselors have developed a comfortable work pattern for themselves and they don't want that pattern disturbed (Sweeney & Witmer, 1977). They identify more with paperwork that counseling and always manage to create a mountain of paperwork to hide behind. To them, looking busy is more important than being busy.

Such counselors resent the child counselor who is committed to counseling. Counselors interested in counseling will make them look badly. Someone might get the idea that they too should counsel children instead of using paperwork as an excuse to avoid counseling. It is much easier for them to shuffle paper than to attend to the counseling needs of children. The existence of such colleagues makes it difficult, but not impossible, for the child counselor to give role priority to counseling.

Priorities of Professional Associations

Sometimes professional associations for child counselors do not emphasize the importance of counseling in the counselor's role because they themselves are not committed to its importance. Such associations often become immersed in issues which tend to primarily perpetuate the association's administrative, political, and public relations functions. Sometimes it appears that they are more interested in preserving and strengthening the association's financial and political base rather than attending to vital professional goals. When a professional association for child counselors engages in a wide range of miscellaneous activities (Wubbolding, 1977) without featuring the importance of counseling, counselors respond by not featuring the importance themselves. Counseling becomes lost in a maze of activities which perpetuate the well-being of the association.

The Counselor's Self Concept

The child counselor's self concept often influences the degree to which the counselor includes counseling in a role description. The counselor who conceives the self to be a giving self, a person-centered self, a self that desires to be in service to children, gives high priority to counseling. Such a counselor realizes that the more willing the counselor is to affectively extend the self toward the child, the more positive will be the outcomes of counseling (Hulnick, 1977). The giving aspect of the child counselor's self concept will directly influence the featuring of counseling in a role description. The selfless counselor, the giving counselor, the counselor who exists for the child's improvement and development, desires to translate this part of a self concept into counseling relationships.

Other counselors possess self concepts in which the need to see themselves as dominant and better able to provide answers for children than the children themselves. Such counselors do not see children as able to develop answers for themselves. Action for these child counselors centers around themselves and the best action evolves from the counselor's ability to analyze a problem and plan the child's behavior for dealing with the problem. Such child counselors give low priority to the counselor's time consuming involvement in counseling. Closing a case often becomes more important for these counselors than helping a child.

The Counselor's Theoretical Inclinations

A child counselor's theory of counseling is essentially an expression of the counselor's self concept. The child counselor who knows the self also recognizes certain personal needs which must be met. Such a counselor will be inclined toward a theory of counseling which fulfills the self and those needs. Certain theories of counseling focus on the psychological needs of the child and feature the importance of counseling. Child-centered counseling is explicitly one of these theories. It conceives the child counselor primarily as a counselor. Counseling is central to the theory of child-centered counseling. Child-centered counselors see counseling as the most effective way for assisting children and they express this commitment in their role descriptions.

The Counselor's Career Goals

Some counselors see themselves as child counselors for the lifetime of their careers. In their early professional development, they make an intellectual and visceral commitment to serving the needs of children by being a counselor. They stay with that commitment throughout their professional careers because they realize that counseling gives them a unique and meaningful mode for helping children. They desire to serve and assist children through the process of therapeutic counseling. They become professionally fulfilled when they make a contribution to improving the lives of children. They desire to serve children and they express that desire through the counseling dimension of the counselor's role. They see counseling as a continuing professional commitment.

The Needs of Children

Child counselors who primarily engage in counseling do so because the psychological needs of children are best met through this process. They realize that behavioral change will take place within a child only when the child is exposed to a series of steady, sustained, and continual counseling sessions with a therapeutic child counselor. A child basically needs to be attended to as a person, to be in an association with a counselor who possesses and expresses attitudes of caring, understanding, empathy, acceptance, positive regard, authenticity, and concreteness. It is this kind of relationship which best meets the needs of the child and induces behavioral change. A child exposed to such counselor attitudes is able to move toward behavioral change. Such a child counselor features counseling as a priority in a role description because it best meets the human and behavioral needs of children.

Other counselors conceive the needs of children in a far more superficial way and, therefore, are not inclined to give counseling a high priority when developing a role description. Such counselors appear to want to isolate themselves from the counseling process. Since such counselors perceive the psychological needs of children superficially, they perceive the role of the counselor superficially.

Many current child counselors are much like Shakespeare's *Hamlet.* They have reached a point where they must decide whether they are "To be . . . or not to be" when considering the issue of giving emphasis to counseling in their role descriptions. But unlike the procrastinating Hamlet, child counselors cannot mull over the question for too long. If they do procrastinate, they will find that pervasive and negative influences have gained in strength and the future of the child counseling profession will be a shell of what it might have been.

RATIONALE FOR THE CHILD–CENTERED COUNSELOR'S COMMITMENT TO COUNSELING

Child-centered counselors emphasize the importance of counseling as the core of the helping process. They see counseling as the deepest form of interaction. They feel that only the deep interactions which characterize counseling will have an effect on the client's feelings and behavior. Other forms of helping do make a contribution to the child's psychological stability (DeCarvalho, 1991). Counseling, however, affects that stability at the deepest level, at the level of the child's self concept. At this level, the depth and degree of attitudinal and behavioral change is more real and permanent. It is at this level that the child-centered counselor sees the need to invest time and energy. At this level, the counselor's work has the potential to produce its deepest and most permanent results. It is at this level that the child-centered counselor sees the value of his or her work and reinforces the contribution of counseling to that satisfaction. Counseling is needed. It makes a difference.

Counseling contributes to the child's psychological stability as a process which deals directly with children and their problems, which is ultimately preventive, and which helps children understand how feelings influence thinking and behavior.

Counseling deals directly with children and their problems. There is a tendency to look upon the child's world as being filled with lollipops, games, tree houses, lovely family portraits, and first walking shoes bronzed into bookends. In our American culture we have fictionized childhood as a time of joy and merriment in which children skip and play in a perpetual rose garden. The fantasy of childhood has been conceived and promulgated by an adult world which writes the storybooks, takes the pictures, showers the gifts, and constructs the commercial playlands. Certainly, these attempts to idolize childhood are often well-intended and will continue as long as there are adults who commercially or aesthetically attached to the child's world.

Whether the child lives in the inner city or affluent suburb, the child possesses the problems of living; of finding some meaning to life, in attempting to glean understanding, acceptance, and empathy from parents, in the child's desire to be perceived as able by peers, brothers, and sisters. The child's world is filled with a desire to understand the self, how the child relates to others, and what this mysterious and wondrous experience called "life" is all about. The child wants to know the self and this knowledge is far more relevant to the security of the child than the superficialities which surround the child's world.

Since adults are emotionally many years removed from the experiences of childhood, they tend to forget the difficult and painful aspects of being a child. Many adults put on rose-colored glasses when they look back on their childhood and are only able to recall the pleasant experiences. They have been able to repress many of the experiences which caused them psychological stress and which, in many cases, still affect their behavior as adults.

Many adults have a "they'll grow out of it" attitude toward the typical problems of children. Fortunately, some children do outgrow some of their problems. But for the majority, these problems carry over into the adolescent and adult years. They show themselves in various forms of delinquent behavior, underachievement, self-centeredness, destructive tendencies, rebelliousness, personal irresponsibility, strained relations between husband and wife, personality clashes at work, lack of commitment to anything, and an inability to love or find meaning in life.

Anyone who reads a daily newspaper realizes that many troubled adolescents and adults exist within our American society. Spectacular stories concerning our inhumanity toward each other make the reader wonder where our civilization is headed and if we, as a country, can become psychologically mature when we have so much difficulty overcoming problems within our communities, our homes, and ourselves. The behaviors reported in our newspapers tell us that, individually and collectively, we are a troubled people.

The child's psychological and social development is more critically important today than at any time in history. Today's children are faced with problems which are unprecedented in their severity. The world has changed and that change has produced deeper and more debilitating problems than those faced by any previous generation. The availability and use of alcohol and drugs is common and those who sell both find an eager market among young people. The physical and psychological abuse of children startles our standards of decency. The sexploitation of young people is increasingly shocking. Children run away from home in growing numbers. Divorce is now commonplace but the children of divorce are still not able to accept it as easily as their parents. Children are terrified about the possibility of being shot in their neighborhoods and although some adults are comfortable about discussing death, many children remain frightened about its meaning and certainty.

In the past, youngsters lived in a world which had its problems, but they were not subjected to the magnitude and kinds of problems being experienced by today's youth. The major problems being identified today revolve around alcohol and substance abuse (Capuzzi & LeCoq, 1983), psychological stress (Stensrud & Stensrud, 1983), depression (Ribner & Ginn, 1975), separation and divorce (Goldman & King, 1985), anger (Alschuler & Alschuler, 1984), loss through death (Berg, 1978), adolescent pregnancy (Foster & Miller, 1980), child abuse (Courtois & Leehan, 1982), suicide (Lee, 1978), delinquency (Lee & Klopfer, 1978), human sexuality (Kirkpatrick, 1975), various physical, emotional, and learning handicaps (Fagan & Wallace, 1979), minority group membership (Woods, 1977), the deterioration of the family (Lifton, Tavantis, & Mooney, 1979), racism and sexism (Jeghelian, 1976; Woody, 1976), extramarital relations of parents (Thompson, 1982), foster care (Norton, 1981), school violence and vandalism (Mayer & Butterworth, 1979), learning problems (Charlton, 1985), and AIDS (Manning & Balson, 1987).

In commenting about the problems of young people, Conley (1983), a teacher, says:

> They are scared to death about things that they see in the world. One out of three is from a broken family and they are worried about getting sucked into the same mistakes as so many of the adults they see. Decisions are pushed on them and they are forced to grow up early; they are pushed into the pool before they are ready to swim (p. 8).

Child counseling is ultimately preventive. The psychological problems of adulthood are not easily overcome. These problems have had the time to deepen during the passage of time between childhood and adulthood. Anyone who has ever attempted to assist a troubled adult realizes that much time, energy, and professional skill is needed to help such a person. Time is working against the attempt to help. Today's behavior is but a manifestation of the experiences which took place during the early and formative years of a person's life. Because a child's life is just beginning and is relatively uncomplicated, the child absorbs and internalizes, in an indelible way, each and every experience. Childhood is a period in which experiences find easy entry into a child's self-concept because the child is psychologically open and nondefensive. The psychologically stable adult is one who was exposed to many more self-enhancing than self-destructive experiences during childhood; and after those self-destructive experiences, felt the warmth and understanding of a significant adult who intuitively offered some form of counseling.

A concentrated effort must emerge to assist children in dealing with those problems that hamper their effective functioning today, and if not resolved, will have an effect upon their values and behavior during their adolescent and adult years. We've often heard that an ounce of prevention is worth a pound of cure. It's a simple statement that has been with us for centuries and is still loaded with meaning today. If we wish to develop an adult population which acts and reacts at a higher level of psychological maturity, we must assist them while they are children.

Today's childhood becomes tomorrow's society just as today's society was yesterday's childhood.

ESTABLISHING THE RELATIONSHIP BETWEEN FEELINGS AND BEHAVIOR THROUGH COUNSELING

We like to think of ourselves as being very rational and, indeed, our ability to learn anything is dependent on our rationality. Very often, however, we do not use our rationality. Intellectually, we know how we should respond, but somehow we don't end up responding the way that we should. We know that excessive speed on our highways is an invitation to death, but we insist on exceeding speed limits. We know that children should be emotionally nourished and physically protected, but the statistics tell us of the increasing rate that children are being abused. We know what constitutes proper schooling, but we insist on providing children with second-rate learning experiences.

Regarding our behavior, one clear and fundamental answer to why we behave as we do lies in the covert world of our feelings. We do not behave in a vacuum. We often behave as a response to feelings that have developed over a period of time. Feelings that have been nurtured and influenced by an entire range of life's experiences and events. An employer may insist on badgering an employee not because the worker is inefficient but because the employer has unresolved feelings of inadequacy. A pupil may act out in class not because the learning experience is inadequate but because of unresolved and angry feelings about the death of a parent. A male child may engage in abusive sexist language because he has unresolved feelings about his own sexuality.

We are not the rational persons that we think we are. Yes, the rationality exists, but it is often unused and hampered because our feelings get in the way. These feelings interfere with the use of our intellect and prompt us to behave in ways that are not good for ourselves or the well-being of others. Life would be good, simple, and clear if our thinking were based upon rational analysis. We'd have a world free from the threat of war, child abuse, murder, and rape. Our rationality would clearly indicate the inhumanity of these acts. But the reality of our world indicates that we do have these crimes and their cause is often due to unresolved feelings which were never expressed or dealt with. Each perpetrator of a crime has a rational grasp of the difference between right and wrong, but strong negative feelings overwhelm and block out that rationality. We all have the potential to use our minds well and reach logical conclusions, conclusions based upon the evidence of objective facts. But our ability to reach logical conclusions is influenced by feelings which interfere with the mind's ability to function logically. A teacher may logically explain the importance of studying mathematics to a child, but the child's feelings of intellectual inadequacy will prevent the teacher's message from being received. The child's feelings of inadequacy prevent the assimilation of the logical message that mathematics is a necessary life skill.

Counseling helps children understand how feelings affect thinking. We all want to think well. To gather the facts, analyze those facts, and reach logical conclusions. But the thinking process is influenced by feelings. Clear thinking emanates from a person whose feelings are known and under control. Faulty thinking emanates from a person who is unaware of how feelings influence our ability to reason well.

If the logic of a work situation dictates that an employee should have an open and frank discussion with an employer, a subconscious fear of authority figures will result in that discussion never taking place. If logic dictates that one should not smoke cigarettes, the feelings which nourish the desire to smoke overpower the logic of not smoking.

We are not what we appear to be. As persons, we are supposed to be logical and rational. But leaf through the pages of any daily newspaper. There you will read stories that serve as prime evidence that we do not think well. When these stories are examined in detail, we find persons who engaged in illogical behavior not because they lost the ability to think but because their unexpressed and unresolved feelings obstructed the clarity of that thinking.

Counseling helps children understand how feelings affect behavior. Feelings affect thinking and thinking affects behavior. One's behavior is not random. It is caused by something. We often look at negative behavior and conclude that it's due to poor thinking. "If he had only used his head he wouldn't be in this mess!" This statement is true, but we often fail to identify what caused the person to think as he did.

Feelings lead to good or faulty thinking and the quality of that thinking leads to good or faulty behavior. Simply stated, *feelings influence thinking and thinking influences behavior.* Good behavior is preceded by good thinking which is influenced by good feelings; poor behavior is preceded by faulty thinking which is influenced by negative feelings.

Our ability to think is buffeted from two sides: our feelings on one side and our behavior on the other. The quality of our feelings, however, influences the quality of our thinking and the subsequent behavior. This chain reaction is put in motion by our feelings. When our feelings are positive then the thinking and behavior will be positive. When our feelings are negative then our thinking and behavior will be negative.

When examining any behavior and attempting to determine the cause of that behavior, we must avoid examining superficial causes (i.e., home conditions, physical handicap, family income, etc.). The person may be a product of these conditions but the deeper cause for the behavior is the person's unexpressed and unresolved feelings about these conditions. It is these feelings which caused the thinking which caused the behavior.

Counseling helps children understand that repressing feelings leads to interpersonal conflict. Many of us keep our feelings bottled up. We smile, do our daily work, and try to come across as friendly and reasonable people. But too many persons have unexpressed, antagonistic feelings toward others. We often tolerate an insensitive employer, spouse, parent, or politician. We do that by putting on a front. But if these negative feelings persist, they must eventually find expression. When they are expressed, they often come out in a torrent of bitterness, anger, and resentment. In some cases these repressed feelings eventually find their expression through some act of violence.

Some people attempt to deal with their repressed feelings through physical activity or fantasy. Runners and joggers are often able to release a build-up of negative and angry feelings. Other people find solace in their fantasies or daydreams of a better life. In both cases these persons may develop an ability to cope with life. But they may not. In far too many cases, when repressed feelings have built up over a period of time, they must be expressed more directly. This direct expression is most often toward another person and usually takes the form of "clearing the air." The benefit of doing this is enormous. But far too many people fear this exchange and prefer to hide behind a mask. They prefer to keep negative feelings to themselves. They fear coming out into the open because of a fear of the consequences. The problem with doing this is that there is a corresponding build-up of tension. And eventually that tension may reach a point where it has to be expressed. It sometimes becomes expressed in dehumanizing and harmful ways.

Counseling helps children understand that repressing feelings leads to negative physical consequences. When feelings are continually repressed the result can be nagging backaches, stomach disorders, migraine head-aches, or low levels of energy. These are the less severe consequences.

Medical research has now produced evidence which links one's psychological behavior to heart attacks and various forms of cancer (Levy, 1985). This is a logical outcome for the person whose life is filled with repressed feelings. Feelings were repressed in childhood, during adolescence, during marriage, and on the job. This build-up of unexpressed feelings, over the years, can only result in the eventual deterioration of the body and its normal functioning.

Medical research also indicates that a large percentage of patients who appear in a physician's office do not have physical problems which can be medically treated. They have psychological problems which produce pseudophysical symptoms that have no medically discernible basis.

We pay little attention to our feelings since we cannot see or touch them. We do pay attention to the swollen breast, the limp, and the back pain because they are obvious. Feelings, however, are hidden from sight and touch. They're there but we often label them as moods and figure that what we can't see or touch can't harm us. The consequences of negative feelings, however, are far more incapacitating than a broken leg. The leg can fully mend in a short period of time. Negative feelings, however, are not that easily mended. They linger, grow, cause us anxiety and tension, and affect not only our interpersonal behavior but our physical well-being.

Counseling helps children understand that expressing feelings involves risk. Repressed feelings often cause us to feel isolated, lonely, angry, and not understood. We'd like to turn to people in our lives in an effort to get help but we often feel that they're too busy with their own problems to give us the time and understanding we need. Furthermore, getting help from them requires an enormous risk that we're often not willing to take. If we do express our feelings to relatives, coworkers, and friends, there is the possibility that our human frailties will not be understood or accepted. So instead of risking the expression of how we feel, we turn inward. We keep those feelings inside since there is less apparent risk involved. The risk, however, of keeping those feelings inside is far greater than the risk of expressing them. Bottling up feelings can lead to psychosocial and physical consequences that can be far more painful and long-lasting than the risk involved in expressing those feelings. The decision, however, for most of us is not to say anything. To survive each day. To protect those feelings from being expressed and exposed to others.

Counseling helps children understand that expressing feelings enables us to examine motives. As a person becomes comfortable in expressing feelings, a desire also occurs to examine the motives which prompted the development of these feelings. The person is asking, "Why do I do these things? Why do I feel this way? Where did all of this come from?"

This self-examination of motives usually leads one to examine situations and events which influenced the development of certain feelings. Such an examination enables one to recall past experiences that influenced the development of current feelings. The person often says, "Now I know *why* I feel as I do." By recalling the situations and events which caused current feelings, one is able to determine the rhyme and reason for those feelings. Current feelings are understood more deeply, especially the motives which prompt those feelings to exist.

There are motives for feeling as we do and these motives are usually linked to situations and events in which we felt either enhanced or diminished as persons. Debilitating experiences, whether they occurred yesterday or many years ago, leave us with psychosocial scars—repressions of feelings about what transpired and how we emotionally responded. We want to know what happened and why we responded as we did. We want to identify the motives which undergird our feelings.

Counseling helps children understand that expressing feelings serves as a release. If all of the negative feelings we have accumulated do not have an opportunity to be released, we create a reservoir that will eventually overflow its banks. The victim in such an overflow is often ourselves and those around us. We cannot expect to repress negative feelings and live a life that is free from tension, anxiety, and physical consequences. The bottling up of negative feelings, for too long, can only lead to personally harmful psychological and physical consequences. The price that one pays for inhibiting feelings is too high.

When negative feelings are siphoned off as they begin to form, they are released. They no longer have the power to build up and incapacitate us. They no longer have the power to make us uncertain and insecure. When released, negative feelings have an opportunity to evaporate. Their expression releases us from the tension, anxiety, and anguish that retaining them requires. Keeping feelings inside requires an enormous effort. We have to carefully plan what we say, to whom, and the circumstances in which we'll say anything. Just saying how we feel does not require the same planning. We merely say it, feel better about having said it, and cleanse ourselves of negative feelings that have no opportunity to build up inside.

Counseling helps children understand that expressing feelings requires

responsibility. A person who has learned to express negative feelings gains in self-responsibility. There is an enormous responsibility involved in expressing feelings. It is the dual responsibility toward self and others. It is obvious that the expression of feelings is beneficial. The person will feel released from the necessity of harboring certain negative feelings as well as the psychological and physical tensions that accompany such a repression. But the person will also develop a responsibility to examine feelings. To determine whether these feelings are legitimate and emanate from an objective situation or event or whether they are more related to an egocentric need to feel angry, misunderstood, lonely, or unloved. Often we express feelings toward a person today that are totally unrelated to what that person is saying or doing. The feeling expressed often doesn't feel "right" and we know it. It is often more related to a past experience with *another* person, but we wait until today to express that feeling to an innocent bystander.

Being in touch with our feelings gives us an opportunity to examine their accuracy. The more practice we have with expressing our feelings, the better able we are to monitor their expression so that they'll be expressed to the right person in the right situation. We become less random in expressing feelings. We know more accurately how we feel and the persons to whom those feelings should be expressed. We become more responsible because we have a more accurate understanding of how we feel, why we feel that way, and identify the most appropriate person who needs to hear our feelings.

Counseling helps children understand that expressing feelings leads to personal freedom. Persons who have learned how to express their feelings are in contact with an important ingredient of personal freedom. They feel alive, liberated, and whole. They feel connected to what it means to lead a life which is psychologically and socially stable. They have freed themselves from the negative consequences of unexpressed feelings. They can make free choices and decisions based upon the logic of what should be done rather than having those choices and decisions connected to unknown and unexpressed feelings.

Clearly, an important outcome for the person who has expressed feelings is the movement toward increased psychosocial freedom. The motives for certain choices become unrelated to unexpressed feelings. A house or car is purchased because of its intrinsic value rather than being an item whereby one can impress others. A special cause is supported because of the importance of the cause rather than being a symbol of ego needs contained in unexpressed feelings. Choices are made because they are logically the best rather than being symbols of certain feelings which have not been expressed.

Psychological stability is not a luxury. It is available to anyone who has learned to understand feelings, express them, and identify the relationship of this expression to one's psychological stability.

The feelings of children affect them. When these feelings diminish the child's self concept, then the child will behave in ways that do not contribute to the child's psychological stability. Child-centered counseling is aimed at helping children express those feelings which make a negative contribution to the child's self concept; and to replace those with positive feelings which make a positive contribution to the child's self concept and psychological development. The child-centered counselor is committed to counseling because it has more potential than any other intervention to have a positive influence on the child's feelings, self concept, and behavior.

REFERENCES

Alschuler, C. F., & Alschuler, A. S. (1984). Developing healthy responses to anger: The counselor's role. *Journal of Counseling and Development, 63,* 26–29.

Berg, C. D. (1978). Helping children to accept death and dying through group counseling. *Personnel and Guidance Journal, 56,* 169–172.

Bosue, E. G., & Saunders, R. L. (1976). *Educational manager: Artist and practitioner.* New York: Worthington Jones.

Boy, A. V., & Pine, G. J. (1979). Needed: A rededication to the counselor's primary commitment. *Personnel and Guidance Journal, 57,* 527–528.

Boy, A. V., & Pine, G. J. (1990). *A person-centered foundation for counseling and psychotherapy.* Springfield, IL: Charles C Thomas.

Capuzzi, D., & LeCoq, L. L. (1983). Social and personal determinants of adolescent use and abuse of alcohol and marijuana. *Personnel and Guidance Journal, 61,* 199–205.

Charlton, T. (1985). Locus of control as a therapeutic strategy for helping children with behavior and learning problems. *Maladjustment and Therapeutic Education, 3,* 26–32.

Conley, J. E. (1983). Many paths, one call. *At home with Holy Cross.* Notre Dame, IN: University of Notre Dame.

Courtois, C. A., & Leehan, J. (1982). Group treatment for grown-up abused children. *Personnel and Guidance Journal, 60,* 564–567.

DeCarvalho, R. J. (1991). The humanistic paradigm in education. *Humanistic Psychologist, 19*(1), 88–104.

Fagan, T., & Wallace, A. (1979). Who are the handicapped? *Personnel and Guidance Journal, 57,* 215–220.

Flowers, V. S., & Hughes, C. L. (1978). Choosing a leadership style. *Personnel and Guidance Journal,* 55, 151–159.

Foster, C. D., & Miller, G. M. (1980). Adolescent pregnancy: A challenge for counselors. *Personnel and Guidance Journal, 58,* 236–245.

Goldman, R. K., & King, M. J. (1985). Counseling children of divorce. *School Psychology Review,* 14, 280–290.

Hulnick, H. R. (1977). Counselor: Know thyself. *Counselor Education and Supervision,* 17, 69–72.

Jeghelian, A. (1976). Surviving sexism: Strategies and consequences. *Personnel and Guidance Journal,* 54, 307–311.

Kirkpatrick, J. S. (1975). Guidelines for counseling young people with sexual concerns. *Personnel and Guidance Journal,* 53, 144–148.

Lee, E. E. (1978). Suicide and youth. *Personnel and Guidance Journal,* 56, 200–204.

Lee, R. E., & Klopfer, C. (1978). Counselors and juvenile delinquents: Toward a comprehensive treatment approach. *Personnel and Guidance Journal,* 56, 194–197.

Lifton, W. M., Tavantis, R. N., & Mooney, W. T. (1979). The disappearing family. *Personnel and Guidance Journal,* 57, 161–165.

Manning, D. T., & Balson, P. M. (1987). Policy issues surrounding children with AIDS in school. *Clearing House,* 61, 101–104.

Mayer, G. R., & Butterworth, A. (1979). A preventive approach to school violence and vandalism: An experimental study. *Personnel and Guidance Journal,* 57, 436–441.

Norton, F. H. (1981). Foster care and the helping professions. *Personnel and Guidance Journal,* 59, 156–159.

Ribner, N., & Ginn, R. (1975). Overcoming and managing depression. *Personnel and Guidance Journal,* 53, 222–224.

Stensrud, R., & Stensrud, K. (1983). Coping skills training: A systematic approach to stress management counseling. *Personnel and Guidance Journal,* 61, 214–218.

Sweeney, T. J., & Witmer, J. M. (1977). Who says you're a counselor? *Personnel and Guidance Journal,* 55, 594.

Thompson, A. P. (1982). Extramarital relations: Gaining greater awareness. *Personnel and Guidance Journal,* 60, 101–105.

Thompson, C. L., & Rudolph, L. B. (1983). *Counseling children.* Monterey, CA: Brooks/Cole.

Woods, E. (1977). Counseling minority students. *Personnel and Guidance Journal,* 55, 416–418.

Wubbolding, R. E. (1978). The counselor educator and local professional associations. *Counselor Education and Supervision,* 18, 87–92.

Chapter 7

CONSULTATION:
A CHILD-CENTERED PERSPECTIVE

Next to counseling, the second most powerful intervention for the child-centered counselor is consultation. Although consultation deals with those persons in the child's environment rather than the child, it can make an important contribution to improving the child's psychological maturity. Since consultation is able to serve the psychological needs of children in indirect ways which can have direct effects, the child-centered counselor includes it as an important role responsibility (Boy & Pine, 1990).

The child-centered view has been represented in the thought and action of consultation, but the involvement has been marginal when compared to the total effort of other viewpoints regarding the rationale and process of consultation. The major client-centered contributions have come from Gordon (1955) in his book, *Group-Centered Leadership*, especially Chapter 6, "The Plan of the Workshop Experiment;" Chapter 11, "Some Outcomes of an Experience in a Self-Directing Group;" and Chapter 13, "An Evaluation of an Industrial Leader." Rogers (1969) addresses the issue of consultation in Chapter 15 of the book, *Freedom to Learn*, which is entitled "A Plan for Self-Directed Change in an Educational System" and in the Epilogue to the book, "Self-Directed Educational Change in Action." In his book about the basic encounter group process, Rogers (1970) presents his concept of consultation in Chapter 8, "Areas of Application" and in Chapter 9, "Building Facilitative Skills." Pierce and Drasgow (1969), Vitalo (1971), and Orlando (1974) have used the process dimensions of client-centered counseling in psychiatric settings to teach patients facilitative interpersonal functioning. On balance, however, the interest of child-centered counselors has been more in the areas of therapeutic individual and group counseling rather than in consultation.

Our experience and observations indicate that child-centered counselors have not generally emphasized consultation for the following reasons:

1. The belief that the problems of children are essentially interpersonal and intrapersonal rather than environmental.
2. The phenomenological influence has prompted child-centered counselors to concentrate more on the perceptions of children rather than examining the environments which contribute to these perceptions.
3. The existential influence which promulgates that the individual can insulate the self against the negative influences of institutions, or situations; and further, if the individual is psychologically strong enough, the individual can influence the environment to change or can transcend the negative influences of an environment.
4. The lack of sensitivity to the fact that changes can occur within an organization as a result of structural changes or work role changes as well as changes in attitudes and interpersonal communications.
5. The process of consultation has been perceived as having manipulative connotations.
6. Many of today's clients are upset with institutions which are insensitive to their needs. Some institutions must become more receptive to client needs. Consultation is a process which can contribute to that receptivity. Client-centered counseling has focused on helping the person rather than those institutions which serve the person.
7. The client-centered theory has been generally interpreted as being a reactive process rather than proactive.

The importance of consultation as part of the counselor's role emerges from the writings of Schein (1969), Caplan (1970), Havelock (1973), Dinkmeyer and Carlson (1973), Dwyer (1974), Kurpius and Brubaker (1976), and Dinkmeyer and Dinkmeyer (1984). Lewin (1951) pioneered the interest in his landmark contribution which called attention to the process of improving the human condition through consultation.

The counselor's role as a consultant engendered so much professional interest that both the February and March, 1978 issues of the *Personnel and Guidance Journal* were devoted to consultation. Twenty-one articles were presented in the two issues and dealt with consultation in: elementary schools (Aubrey, 1978); secondary schools (Carrington, Cleveland, & Ketterman, 1978); university environments (Westbrook, Leonard, Johnson,

Boyd, Hunt, & McDermott, 1978); community mental health (Werner, 1978); career development and sex role stereotyping (Hansen & Keierleber, 1978); interpersonal conflict management (Roark, 1978); organizational development (Huse, 1978); learning environments (Wigtil & Kelsey, 1978); community agencies (Heller, 1978); college faculty groups (Parker & Lawson, 1978); and with groups planning for the future (Brubaker, 1978). As part of the concept of consultation, there has also been a growing interest in the counselor functioning as a teacher. That is, the counselor becomes involved in teaching facilitative skills to others so that they can use these skills for personal behavioral management and in improving the behavior of institutions toward people. This teaching approach to consultation has been evidenced in the work of Carkhuff (1971); Guerney, Stollak, and Guerney (1971); Alschuler and Ivey (1973); Ivey (1974); Authier, Gustafson, Guerney, and Kasdorf (1975); and Kurpius (1985).

During our nation's cultural revolution of the 1960s and 1970s, minority group members did not see themselves as problems which needed to be adjusted in order to meet the needs of institutions. They instead saw institutions as the problem and protested that institutions should meet the needs of people. Ordinary people stopped being placid about the behavior of institutions and became assertive in insisting that institutions serve human needs. During this period some child counselors became involved in a proactive role by serving as advocates for those children whose needs were being neglected. Child counselors realized that society needed to change its attitude and behavior toward children. It needed to become more committed to the needs of children. Child counselors became involved in the issue through the process of consultation. Consultation began to take form as a legitimate and necessary part of the child counselor's responsibility (Dougherty, 1990).

RATIONALE FOR CONSULTATION

Gunnings (1971) indicates that the counselor must be willing to confront systems that have been dehumanizing. Osipow (1971) states that counselors are obligated to foster institutional changes so that these institutions will more accurately meet human needs. Morrill and Hurst (1971) show that counselors can best meet human needs by becoming involved in preventive and developmental outreach programs. Ivey

(1973) indicates that unless the child counselor gives greater priority to consultation, the behavioral problems of children will never be significantly improved. While child counselors counsel, some organizations are engaging in behaviors which tend to produce negative psychological consequences for children.

Lewis and Lewis (1977) emphasize that social action should be part of *every* counselor's role because:

1. Negative aspects of the community environment may be detrimental to the growth and development of individuals.
2. Positive aspects of the community environment can support individual growth and development.
3. Counselors are helpless in their attempts to serve individuals if environmental factors do not change to keep pace with individual change.
4. Self-determination itself is not only a political goal, but a mental health goal.
5. Counselors, working alone, and individual citizens, working alone, are both powerless to make the community responsive to the needs of community members (pp. 156–157).

Brubaker (1978) writes about providing consultation for organizations interested in designing desirable futures rather than responding to momentary needs in a haphazard manner. He indicates that the future's consulting process is:

. . . a consultation process for involving individuals, groups, or organizations in the creation of their own future. The purpose of this process is not to predict what a future of the future will be, but rather to explore various future images that remain open to change, are a result of our individual or collective actions, and are accessible to human decision making (p. 431).

Kurpius (1978b) points out the following in his rationale for consultation:

Persons functioning as consultants do not model authority and control. Rather, their newly developing image and related functions are quite the opposite— they model helping behaviors that are nonjudgmental and noncompetitive. Such behaviors reinforce openness and collaboration that create mutually beneficial work situations and work outcomes. These persons are being recognized as the long needed "new professional" in the work force (p. 335).

Some consulting comes from counselors who are already employed within an institutional setting. Walz and Benjamin (1978) indicate that being an "insider" has an inherent advantage:

Counselors usually have freedom of movement: They can move around, see people and interact with them. Counselors usually know and are known by the system; they speak the language, know the norms, and can relate to the system's needs and interests. In many ways, counselors are in an excellent position to assess the impact of the system on its members; what the system does to people in its efforts to do something for people, what is going well, and what may be causing unhappiness or dissatisfaction (p. 331).

Werner (1978) emphasizes a preventive rationale for consultation when he states that the process of consultation:

> ... kindled our imaginations to the possibilities of preventing emotional and behavioral problems (p. 368).

Regarding the choice faced by counselors to affect behavioral changes within individuals or institutions, Heller (1978) indicates that:

> Ultimately, of course, we need a balanced view; both social change and personal change are important. Environments influence behavior, but persons also have the capacity to shape environments. What this means is that psychological professionals should recognize the need for both individual and social change skills and should understand the conditions under which each approach might be optimal (p. 420).

For the child-centered counselor, the counselor's consultative contributions are essentially an extension of the human attitudes which characterize the relationship and process dimensions of child-centered counseling. That is, the child-centered counselor perceives the consultative aspect of the counselor's role as an extension of the fundamental attitudes and processes of child-centered counseling (Drapela, 1985).

Child-centered counselors have traditionally emphasized the primacy of counseling as the most essential and effective intervention for helping children. The authors support the critical importance of the child counselor's commitment to counseling but they also recognize that child-centered counseling is remiss if it fails to explicitly conceive the counselor as also being a consultant, social activist, advocate, and change agent. It is logical that the child counselor's role also emphasize the importance of the counselor's involvement in consultative activities which serve to improve the lives of children. As Kurpius (1978a) has noted:

> Consultation is one process for synthesizing environmental and human adjustments, and although consultation is not a panacea for all ills, it does provide an alternate form for influencing change (p. 320).

The child-centered counselor's role more accurately serves the needs of children when it gives priority to *both* counseling and consultation. The impact of the child-centered counselor's role becomes enlarged when it includes both counseling *and* consultation.

COUNSELING AND CONSULTATION: A RECIPROCAL RELATIONSHIP

Although the functions of counselor and consultant are different, we see reciprocal elements in the counseling and consulting processes (Cowen, 1984). We assume that:

(1) Cognitive and affective aspects of personality cannot be separated— they mutually and reciprocally influence each other and should not be dichotomized in the way we look at or treat behavior. An individual's basic assumptions, mutually cognitive and emotional, form a person's personal theory from which the person views the world and responds.
(2) An accomplished counselor is one who practices the attitudinal aspects of counseling in all aspects of life. The roles of counselor and consultant can be seen in terms of interpersonal relationships where counseling philosophy and practice can be applied.
(3) The communication process of equal to equal exists both in counseling and consulting and it is through the communication process that counseling and consulting fuse and synthesize in reciprocity.

Emanating from these assumptions counseling and consultation can be viewed as incorporating several generic features.

The counselor attempts to initiate a good interpersonal relationship with a client through acceptance and respect. The counselor attempts to communicate to the client as an equal. In order to be effective, the consultant must also initiate the same good interpersonal relationship, communicating as an equal (Hawes, 1989).

In group counseling the counselor assumes group membership with an equal to equal communication system and further relies on group members as therapeutic agents in collaboration. In the same manner, the consultant must collaborate with consultees to determine pertinent information, achieve workable hypotheses for action, and to help consultees become more facilitative and therapeutic in their relationships with children (Shaw & Goodyear, 1984).

The counselor counsels for the purpose of facilitating personal growth. The consultant provides resources, information and support, in order to facilitate personal growth. Though the means may be different the goal is essentially the same: the facilitation of behavior through a change in feelings and attitude.

The counselor working with a child may find all of the counselor's accomplishments deflected by the child's parents or teachers. Consultation may bring about a change in the attitude or approach of significant others to the child which could enhance what the child accomplishes in improved feelings and behaviors. Through a release of feelings many parents can begin looking at themselves more objectively and see the relationship between child and parent behavior.

In discussions with parents, the counselor is in an excellent position to clarify parental misunderstandings regarding the typical behavior of children and to contribute new understandings of child growth and development.

Sometimes parents express negative and hostile feelings, but by accepting these and not assuming a judgmental role, the counselor can help parents to deal with these feelings in a constructive manner.

Parents may misunderstand the role of the counselor. Many occasions arise which allow the counselor to define and clarify a professional role and interpret the counseling program. By developing the image of the counselor as a professional person, trained and competent, the counselor helps to build a positive attitude toward counseling and related services (Humes, 1986; Spitzer, Webster-Stratton, and Hollinsworth, 1991).

A GUIDING PRINCIPLE

The ability to foster healthy interpersonal relationships with consultees is necessary for effective consultation to occur. In forming relationships with others, it is well for the counselor to remember the following principle: Even when the counselor sets up a personal ethical code and value system, even when the counselor carefully defines a working relationship in advance, it is naive to assume that the counselor's interpersonal problems with consultees will be eliminated. The counselor's consultation often involves working with people in emotionally loaded circumstances. To work effectively in such situations requires a great deal of perceptiveness, calm judgment and stamina. In many instances no matter what the counselor does, hostility and dissatisfaction are experienced. The counselor will often have to absorb hostility which should be rationally directed toward others. In many situations it is necessary for individuals to vent their hostilities upon someone before they are able to view situations more objectively. The counselor will have to recognize early that it is impossible to win the approval of everyone. If such universal approval is important, the counselor will have to find it outside of the consulting process.

In the process of consultation, the counselor, in all likelihood, will never be appreciated or even liked by some consultees. The counselor can, however, win the respect of consultees and the even more satisfying sense of self-worth which comes from courageously following the dictates of professionalism during the consultative process (Crego, 1985).

CONSULTEE GAMES

The consultee analogue to the "yes—but" game is *"Tell us what to do."* This game, of course, must be differentiated from sincere requests for direct consultation. In the game situation a demand for direct advice is made for the purpose of avoiding more important issues or to release the consultee from responsibility. This places the burden of responsibility on the shoulders of the consultant. If the consultant attempts to "tell" or "advise," the consultant is reinforcing the client's dependency and encouraging the game. On the other hand, if the consultant attempts to avoid the issue, the consultant's behavior may serve to alienate the client.

Another game observed, most notably in group consultation with teachers, is *"join us in our misery."* This game typically takes the following form: As a consultant you are asked to meet with several teachers. A case or several cases are presented, followed by anecdotes relating to the symptoms of the defined problem child or children. The unpleasant behavioral descriptions soon become contagious with each teacher discussing the difficulties of different situations. Other examples are documented as the "gripe session" grows. Although this typically has an abreactive effect on the teachers, it serves also to get away from the real issue: How can we mutually work as consultant and consultee to help this child or these children?

Frequently encountered from the consultee, especially in a school setting, is *"but doesn't it really all go back to the parents,"* which is a variation of *"I'm so busy focusing on my class that I can't take time for the individual child."* This game is usually entered as the consultant and the consultee discuss the dynamics of a case and move to formulate a program of classroom procedures that the teacher will execute. The teacher becomes uncertain and attempts to relieve uncertainty by saying that nothing can be done because, "as we all know, parents are the real problem." This serves, of course, to relieve any feelings of guilt the teacher or consultee might have and places the problem itself in the "impossible" range, thereby absolving the consultee from any responsibility.

A final game is entitled *"But you don't really understand the situation."* This game, of course, must be distinguished from honest feedback. All too often it is a defensive maneuver on the part of the consultee following a series of recommendations made by the consultant. The intent, of course, is to elicit guilt and cause the consultant to withdraw some of the consultant's "demanding" recommendations. An alternative intent is to have the consultant take over part or all of the problem, thereby relieving the consultee of responsibility.

These are some of the more obvious and frequently encountered games in consultation. Essentially, the games of consultation result from communication failures on the part of both parties. On the part of the consultant it is easy to fall into a variety of traps which involve assuming: (a) that the requested help is really wanted, (b) that the intellectual and emotional elements of the problem are consonant, and (c) that a problem once defined is clarified. On the part of the consultee, impediments to developing a working relationship are assuming: (a) that the consultant will immediately grasp the essentials of the problem, (b) that the consultant might provide a simple and ready solution to the problem, and (c) that the consultant might magically cause the problem to disappear. These assumptions later create anxiety and provide the groundwork for games to be enacted.

Games destroy the consultation process. When encountered, it is vital that they be recognized and worked through. Curative steps can be taken before (prevention) or as games occur.

Preventing consultee games. Not all consultees will be adept at or motivated toward involving themselves in a consultation relationship. However, the following are offered as tentative criteria for predicting a good consultation risk: (a) consultees are initially willing to take responsibility for *their* clients; (b) they have a history of being able to establish good working relationships with others; and (c) they avoid projection and dependency seeking behaviors.

A second major means of preventing consultation games from developing is to educate the consultee about the consultation relationship and the consultant should clearly define the consultant's intent and, if possible, identify the clear obligations on both sides. This gives the consultant a chance to dispel anticipations that the consultant might provide a single ready-made solution to the problem (the magic phenomenon). It also gives the consultant the opportunity to specify the intent to work together with the consultee in a mutual sharing process, thus emphasizing the consultant's need for the consultee's involvement.

Process correction. Even with the best of preventive efforts, games are likely to occur during the process of consultation. These can be dealt with through process correction techniques. They include the following.

Intent cross-checking. If the consultant and the consultee have agreed beforehand to work mutually on behalf of the problem presented, this technique can be employed most effectively. It involves a reexamination and clarification of the defined relationship. Thus, if the consultant feels that the consultee is not carrying part of the load, the consultant can ask that they review their purpose in working together.

Support. A major means of relieving anxiety and thus reducing the development of consultation relationship defenses is to provide support, notably when the consultee is experiencing a high degree of stress and frustration.

Self-disclosure. Self-disclosure or the use of "I-messages" may also be employed. This technique simply involves an acknowledgement of the consultant's confusion, frustration, or other feelings. This is especially useful in response to consultee games such as "yes—but," "ain't it awful?" and "you're the expert." Through the use of "I-messages" the consultant is able to confront the consultee with how the consultee's behavior is affecting the consultant.

CONSULTING WITH PARENTS

The rationale for the counselor functioning as a consultant to parents is derived from what we know about the impact of parental influence on child development. We know that the mental health of any individual is directly proportionate to the quality of the early relationship which existed between the child and the child's parents. There is a positive relationship between a child's self-esteem and perceived level of communication with parents (Dinkmeyer & Dinkmeyer, 1984).

We know that many parents are overwhelmed by contemporary life and its swift changes in values, mores, expectations, and behaviors which are often difficult to integrate into or reconcile with family life. Family life has become less intimate, less organized, less bound by the precepts, standards, and iron command of parents over the child. In all too many families there is an on-going power struggle between parents and children which is debilitating and which reduces human growth and development. And finally we know that while for some effective parenting can be instinctive, we also know that for others it is learned and can be taught (Gordon, 1970; Krueger, 1972; Strother and Jacobs, 1986).

The problems parents have in relation to their children may range from social problems to learning problems to family problems to individual problems. Parents may also bring in their own personal and marital problems. The consultant may engage in the various roles of collaborator, educator, and counselor, in the process of parental consulting (Taylor, 1986).

Through orientation the counselor should make explicit the counselor's role as a consultant to parents. Orientation regarding parent consultation should include consideration of time available for parents. It is important that the desired nature of parent contacts be made explicit. The most effective modes of communication need to be considered and developed by the counselor so that consultative orientation will be an on-going process. There should also be built into the orientation process a statement of policy regarding what information can be shared about a child during a consulting session.

Consultation involves sharing ideas, comparing information, providing a sounding board, developing plans for action, and learning new skills. Emphasis is placed on joint planning and collaboration. The purpose is to develop tentative recommendations for action which fit the individual child and family. Parent consultation is all the above with an emphasis on specific parent-child relationships (Dinkmeyer & Dinkmeyer, 1984).

The immediate goals of parent consultation are increased parent effectiveness and facilitation of the growth and development of the child.

Operationally, the immediate goals of parent consultation are to communicate with parents about their specific problems of child rearing and effect necessary changes in attitudes and behaviors. Establishing a cooperative effort, exchanging information, setting up mutually acceptable goals, formulating tentative hypotheses for action, and follow-up are the operational means to the goals.

The long-range goal of parent consultation is increased parent effectiveness for all parents in the community. The means to this long-range goal are parent education centers and training groups with the consultant serving as a resource for child development information and materials and human relations training.

Consultation should result in increased relationship competencies for parents. As parents develop an understanding of their problems and further understanding of human behavior and acquire relationship skills, they may use these in interaction with the total family. Hopefully they will be better able to get along with marriage partners and with their children.

Through consultation a counselor can come to better understand and help the child. From the parents the counselor learns what expectations the parents hold for the child, the concept they have of the child, and the ways they interact with the child. As the counselor consults with parents, the counselor can begin to understand their contribution to the child's self-concept.

It is most important for the consultant to follow effective counseling practices in consulting rather than mere advising devoid of involvement. Establishing a positive relationship and promoting communication is the art of the counselor and the critical determinant for effectiveness in consulting. The effectiveness of parent consultation can be most significant in motivating some parents to seek out counseling. Using the art of counseling through consulting could well be what sells counseling to the community (Gallessich, 1985).

THE COUNSELOR AS CHILD ADVOCATE AND CHANGE AGENT

Some counselors have done more harm than good in an attempt to be child advocates and change agents. In attempts to represent children to an institution and to initiate change, they have often generated more heat than light and many institutions have responded by becoming threatened and more resistant to change. This is unfortunate because the human contributions which the child counselor could make as an advocate-change agent have become blunted, and in some cases, irrevocably lost.

> The problem is well defined by Loughary (1971): It is apparent that in many attempts to bring about social change, self-appointed social change agents display bungling, poorly thought out, and frequently self-defeating behavior which results at best in no change and at worst in less desirable conditions than before they began (p. 332).

The concluding section of this chapter will address this problem by identifying and developing concrete principles of advocacy and planned change which will enable the counselor to function effectively in the role of advocate-change agent. The role of the counselor as an advocate for children and the role of the counselor as an agent of institutional change have been clearly articulated and dealt with by others (Baker & Cramer, 1972; Cook, 1972; Banks & Martens, 1973; Claverella & Doolittle, 1970; Warnath, 1973; and Dinkmeyer & Dinkmeyer, 1984). A review of their work suggests that advocacy on behalf of children often involves issues of institutional change. Accordingly, this section discusses principles of advocacy and planned change which are interdependent.

Principles of Counselor Advocacy

In presenting your case to an institution, base that case upon concrete evidence. Counselors who merely make visceral attacks upon an institution have no hope of being heard. They come across as reactionaries and the institution's response is to become further hardened in its insensitivity to the child. Too many well-intended counselors have defeated themselves and their advocacy by merely engaging in diatribes against an institution. Their message was not heard because it was blatantly delivered. Emotionally charged assertions by counselors against institutions have fallen upon deaf ears. Well-intended counselors who have desired to function as change agents have left the counseling profession out of emotional exhaustion and disgust because institutions have not responded.

Evidence moves institutions. Counselors who desire to have a positive impact upon the behavior of an institution must spend many hours developing the concrete evidence which supports their demand that the institution must change its behavior toward children. Developing the evidence is not easy. It requires a recognition of the difference between hearsay and substantial evidence.

Present the evidence in a clear, concise, and well-organized manner. Some counselors possess the substantive evidence needed to turn an organization around, but they are poorly organized in presenting the evidence. Twenty pages of evidence in the form of charts and graphs will perhaps never be read and absorbed by those in charge of policies and procedures. Evidence, if it is to be accepted, must be simplified so that it can be easily read and absorbed. Presenting complicated evidence will only result in the evidence being ignored by those whom it is intended to influence. Presenting data in a clear manner calls for the ability to develop written communication for a variety of audiences and purposes; a reasonable knowledge of the different forms of communication; the ability to represent procedures, information flow, and decision points using visual techniques; and the ability to summarize and draw conclusions from nonstatistical data (Loughary, 1971, p. 333).

Evidence must be documented. Evidence must not be based upon gratuitous assertions since such assertions can be gratuitously denied. Evidence must be documented and supported by facts, figures, case histories, or a tabulation of events which serve to bolster the credibility of the evidence being presented.

Evidence is not how the counselor feels but what the counselor knows from the documentation which supports the evidence. The counselor who asserts that a drug education program is needed locally must not only back up the assertion with facts but show how these facts were gathered.

Devote a significant portion of your working day counseling and consulting in order to develop the evidence. Evidence which comes from the source, the child, and is accurately represented by the counselor to the institution, can only be developed by the counselor who spends a significant portion of the working day in counseling and consulting relationships with children and others. Such evidence, transmitted from the child to the institution by the counselor, is far more acceptable than the counselor merely asserting that an institution must change its policies and procedures.

Select the proper audience for the presentation of your evidence. Some counselors, who have developed the evidence and documentation necessary for change, don't know to whom the evidence should be presented. They often present the evidence to an audience (individual or group) which has little or no power in affecting change. Such a procedure might be acceptable if the counselor wants to test out the credibility of evidence in order to sharpen its acceptance; but ultimately the counselor must objectively know which individual or group holds the *real power* and must be prepared to present the evidence to *that* group.

Some counselors have become discouraged because although they possess the evidence which clearly indicates a necessity for change, there has been no response. Often this occurs because the evidence has not been presented to the proper audience. Ultimately, the proper audience is the one which possesses the most power for initiating change within a setting.

Develop your credibility as a person. Organizations make changes as a response to the credibility of the person recommending such changes. At one level the organization responds to the credibility of the evidence; at a deeper level the response is to the presenter as a person. There are some counselors who possess natural credibility. They can accomplish much. There are other counselors who need to study the process of change in order to initiate it.

Counselors who possess credibility have only to do their job in order to initiate change. Personal credibility comes from observable competence, effective communication skills, and integrity. Counselors who do not possess credibility must become involved in its development for, in the last analysis, any change which occurs often takes place because the change agent is well-liked and respected.

Principles of Planned Change

Study and know your institution and develop a strategy of planned change. In every institution there are forces working in favor of change and forces working against it. An awareness of these forces is imperative if advocacy and planning for change are to have any payoff for children. Perhaps the most useful conceptual model for looking at institutional change potential and for developing viable change strategies is the "force field analysis." It postulates that institutional behavior consists of a dynamic balance of situational forces working in opposite directions within the social-psychological space of the institution. For example, suppose the counselor, on the basis of data collected from contacts with children, decides there is a need for widening the range of persons acceptable as foster parents. One can see that the issues will be caught between two forces, some driving for change—some resisting change. Change will occur when an imbalance is created between the sum of the restraining forces and the sum of the driving forces. Such imbalance unfreezes the existing equilibrium and the situation then changes until the opposing forces are again brought into a new equilibrium. After identifying the various forces and estimating their significance, the counselor can choose among several possible solutions:

1. Increase old driving forces.
2. Reduce the number and strength of old restraining forces.
3. Add new driving forces.
4. Convert previous restraining forces into driving forces.
5. Employ various combinations of preceding four approaches.

If advocacy on behalf of a group of clients is to be effective then it must be well thought out and accompanied by a plan of change based upon a careful consideration of the forces impinging on the problem. This entails a careful study of the institution and its conflicting forces.

Identify the problem and decide on the kind of intervention needed. As an advocate and change agent the counselor may intervene in a number of major ways, not all of which are appropriate for a specific problem. Blake and Moulton (1965) list nine major kinds of interventions which can be made at different structural points in an organization and which will facilitate its development.

1. *Discrepancy,* by calling attention to contradictions in or between policy, attitudes, and behavior.
2. *Theory,* by presenting research findings or concepts that enlarge the perspective.
3. *Procedure,* by critiquing existing methods.
4. *Relationships,* by focusing attention on tension between individuals and groups.
5. *Experimentation,* by encouraging comparisons of several alternative approaches before a decision is made.
6. *Dilemmas,* by pointing up significant choice points or dilemmas in problem-solving, with attention to testing assumptions and seeking alternatives.
7. *Perspective,* by providing situational or historical understanding.
8. *Culture,* by focusing on traditions or norms.

Change is difficult to effect in any organization. It behooves the child counselor to develop the appropriate conceptual skills necessary to identify problems and design interventions which can address the needs of children. Being an advocate-change agent calls for more than being emotionally committed. It involves converting those emotions into influential thinking and behavior.

Know, understand, and be prepared to work through the informal system of the institution. Every organization has informal groups and cliques which can have a great bearing on the way formal procedures are carried out. The informal aspects of an organization involve the manner in which each member relates to other members as persons. Informal relationships and communications systems should be considered in planning change. Many informal features of an organization, such as the amount of liking members have for one another or their willingness to help and support one another, may be thought of as positive and facilitating qualities which can be tapped in planning and implementing change.

On the other hand, these same processes can also constitute powerful restraining influences that can effectively block change. Whether in a factory, mental health clinic, or hospital, membership in these informal groups may be more important to individuals than the approval of their supervisors. It is essential that the child counselor know the informal structure of an organization and work with that structure in advocating and planning change.

Be aware of your own motivation and needs and place them in proper perspective. In every organization and group there are three general elements which should be considered in planning change:

Forces in the change agent. My motives and needs; my assumptions about people in general and about my colleagues, subordinates, superiors, peers in particular; my value system; my confidence in an organization; my leadership inclinations; my feelings of security and my tolerance for ambiguity; my own motives as related to the personal needs I am satisfying.

Forces in the group or organization. The members' needs for independence/dependence; their readiness to assume responsibilities; their tolerance for ambiguity; their interest in the problem; their understanding of goals and their role in formulating them; their knowledge, experience, and skill; their expectations; the effect on them of my own assumptions about them, their motives and needs.

Forces in the situation. Type of organization; pressures of time; consequences of actions; space, material and supporting resources; restraining and driving forces for change.

Dealing with these elements requires that child counselors be honest with themselves. To some degree, we all are involved in viewing the various aspects of life from our own window. We tend to hold fast to neatly-conceived concepts of what is acceptable and unacceptable in our own private worlds. We have opinions which sometimes are well-founded and other opinions which are perhaps not so well-founded, but instead reflect our own biases. Sometimes we tend to judge without having a valid foundation for judgment. Our feelings about ourselves and others often are based on past interpersonal experiences which are unrelated to a problem which exists right now. We tend to see what we want to see and hear what we want to hear. Because of these very human tendencies, advocacy and change agentry can be attractive, seductive, and comfortable means for fulfilling personal needs. It is too easy to see ourselves sweeping away all the forces of evil before us. Advocacy and change require more than the ability to scream injustice. That behavior may offer you a catharsis but effectively advocating the needs of children requires patience, tenacity, and effective communication skills. Above all, counselors must be willing to involve themselves in a self examination of the motives (feelings) which influence their interest in being advocates and consultants for change.

The most basic principle of change is that the people who will be affected by change should be involved in planning and carrying out change. The effectiveness of child counselors as advocates and change agents will largely be determined by the degree to which they can involve members of institutions in examining needed change and in formulating and testing goals and programs of change. Unless those who will be affected by the change participate in its planning and implementation, then the prospects for effecting change will be minimal.

There are several phases to the process of change requiring different levels of relationship and communications skills on the part of the counselor and varying levels of involvement on the part of members of an organization. These phases are:

1. Identifying a need for change.
2. Establishing consulting relationships.
3. Clarifying the problem.
4. Examining alternative solutions.
5. Transforming intentions to change into concrete efforts.
6. Stabilizing a new level of functioning for change.
7. Examining the consequences of this new level of functioning for change.

In all these phases of change, it is important that individuals have the opportunity to share in the process of change—from the beginning to the end. When people feel they own "a piece of the action" the goals of change will be more readily accepted, internalized, and implemented. The broader the base of involvement and support, the better will be the chances of successful change.

As a consultant, change agent, and advocate, use your counseling skills. Advocacy, consultation, and planned change necessitate that the counselor function as a vigorous spokesperson; as a skilled resource person who can help consultees identify their problems and formulate a plan of action; as a facilitator who can help an organization learn the processes and skills needed to move forward toward the accomplishment of democratically-conceived goals; and as a counselor who can listen and communicate with people. Counseling skills are at the heart and core of any successful advocacy and planned change process.

REFERENCES

Alschuler, A., & Ivey, A. (1973). Getting into psychological education. *Personnel and Guidance Journal,* 51, 682–691.

Aubrey, R. F. (1978). Consultation, school interventions, and the elementary counselor. *Personnel and Guidance Journal,* 56, 351–354.

Authier, J., Gustafson, K., Guerney, B., & Kasdorf, B. (1975). The psychological practitioner: A theoretical-historical and practical review. *Counseling Psychologist,* 5, 31–50.

Baker, S. B., & Cramer, S. H. (1972). Counselor or change agent: Support from the profession. *Personnel and Guidance Journal,* 50, 661–665.

Banks, N., & Martens, K. (1973). Counseling: The reactionary profession. *Personnel and Guidance Journal,* 51, 457–462.

Blake, R. B., & Moulton, J. S. (1965). An approach to organization and development. In D. Zana (Ed.). *Organizational development: Theory and practice.* Chicago: Rand McNally.

Boy, A. V., & Pine, G. J. (1990). *A person-centered foundation for counseling and psychotherapy.* Springfield, IL: Charles C Thomas.

Brubaker, J. C. (1978). Futures consultation: Designing desirable futures. *Personnel and Guidance Journal,* 56, 428–431.

Caplan, G. (1970). *The theory and practice of mental health consultation.* New York: Basic Books.

Carkhuff, R. R. (1971). Training as a mode of treatment. *Journal of Counseling Psychology,* 18, 123–131.

Carrington, D., Cleveland, A., & Ketterman, C. (1978). Collaborative consultation in the secondary schools. *Personnel and Guidance Journal,* 56, 355–358.

Ciavarella, M., & Doolittle, L. W. (1970). The ombudsman: Relevant role model for the counselor. *School Counselor,* 17, 331–336.

Cook, D. R. (1972). The change agent counselor: A conceptual context. *School Counselor,* 17, 331–336.

Cowen, E. L. (1984). A general structural model for primary prevention program development in mental health. *Personnel and Guidance Journal,* 62, 485–490.

Crego, C. A. (1985). Ethics: The need for improved consultation training. *Counseling Psychologist,* 13, 396–402.

Dinkmeyer, D. C. (1973). The parent "C" group. *Personnel and Guidance Journal,* 52, 252–256.

Dinkmeyer, D., & Carlson, J. (1973). *Consulting: Facilitating human potential and change processes.* Columbus, OH: Charles E. Merrill.

Dinkmeyer, D., Sr., & Dinkmeyer, D., Jr. (1984). School counselors as consultants in primary prevention programs. *Personnel and Guidance Journal,* 62, 464–466.

Dougherty, A. (1990). *Consultation: Practice and perspectives.* Belmont, CA: Brooks/Cole.

Drapela, V. J. (1985). An integrative approach to teaching consultation and supervision. *Counselor Education and Supervision,* 24, 341–348.

Dwyer, C. E. (1974). Training for change agents: A guide to design of training programs in education and other fields. *Industrial and Labor Relations Review,* 27, 658–659.

Gallessich, J. (1985). Toward a meta theory of consultation. *Counseling Psychologist,* 13, 336–354.

Gordon, T. (1955). *Group-centered leadership.* Boston: Houghton Mifflin.

Gordon, T. (1970). *Parent effectiveness training.* New York: Wyden.

Guerney, B., Jr., Stollak, G., & Guerney, L. (1971). The practicing psychologist as educator—an alternative to the medical practitioner model. *Professional Psychology,* 2, 271–282.

Gunnings, T. S. (1971). Preparing the new counselor. *Counseling Psychologist,* 2.

Hansen, L. S., & Keierieber, D. L. (1978). Born free: A collaborative consultation model for career development and sex-role stereotyping. *Personnel and Guidance Journal,* 56, 395–399.

Havelock, R. G. (1973). *The change agent's guide to innovation in education.* Englewood Cliffs, NJ: Educational Technology.

Hawes, D. J. (1989). Communication between teachers and children: A counselor/consultant/trainer model. *Elementary School Guidance and Counseling,* 24(1), 58–67.

Heller, K. (1978). Facilitative conditions for consultation with community agencies. *Personnel and Guidance Journal,* 56, 419–423.

Humes, C. W. (1986). Parent counseling in special education: Case description of a novel approach. *School Counselor,* 33(5), 345–349.

Huse, E. F. (1978). Organizational development. *Personnel and Guidance Journal,* 56, 403–406.

Ivey, A. E. (1973). Counseling—Innocent profession of fiddling while Rome burns? *Counseling Psychologist,* 4, 111–115.

Ivey, A. (1974). The clinician as a teacher of interpersonal skills: Let's give away what we've got. *Clinical Psychologist,* 27, 6–9.

Kincaid, J. (1973). The challenge of change and dissent. *School Counselor,* 20, 169–175.

Kruger, W. S. (1972). Teaching parenthood. *American Education,* 8, 25–28.

Kurpius, D. J., & Brubaker, J. C. (1976). *Psychoeducational consultation: Definition, functions, preparation.* Bloomington: Indiana University.

(a) Kurpius, D. (1978). Introduction to the special issue. *Personnel and Guidance Journal,* 56, 320.

(b) Kurpius, D. (1978). Consultation theory and process: An integrated model. *Personnel and Guidance Journal,* 56, 335–338.

Kurpius, D. (1985). Consultation interventions: Successes, failures, and proposals. *Counseling Psychologist,* 13, 368–389.

Lewin, K. (1951). *Field theory in social science.* New York: Harper.

Lewis, M., & Lewis, J. (1977). *Community counseling: A human services approach.* New York: Wiley, 156–157.

Lipsman, C. K. (1969). Revolution and prophecy: Community involvement for counselors. *Personnel and Guidance Journal*, 48, 97–100.

Loughary, J. W. (1971). To grow or not to grow. *School Counselor*, 18, 332, 333.

Morrill, W. H., & Hurst, J. C. (1971). A preventive and developmental role for the college counselor. *Counseling Psychologist*, 2.

Orlando, N. (1974). The mental patient as therapeutic agent: Self change, power and caring. *Psychotherapy: Theory, Research and Practice*, 11, 58–62.

Osipow, S. H. (1971). Challenges to counseling psychology for the 1970s and 80s. *Counseling Psychology*, 2.

Parker, C. A., & Lawson, J. (1978). From theory to practice to theory: Consulting with college faculty. *Personnel and Guidance Journal*, 56, 424–427.

Pierce, R., & Drasgow, J. (1969). Teaching facilitative interpersonal functioning to psychiatric patients. *Journal of Counseling Psychology*, 16, 295–298.

Roark, A. E. (1978). Interpersonal conflict management. *Personnel and Guidance Journal*, 56, 400–402.

Rogers, C. R. (1970). *Carl Rogers on encounter groups*. New York: Harper and Row.

Rogers, C. R. (1969). *Freedom to learn*. Columbus: Merrill.

Schein, E. (1969). *Process consultation*. Reading, MA: Addison-Wesley.

Schein, E. H. (1978). The role of the consultant: Content expert or process facilitator. *Personnel and Guidance Journal*, 56, 339–343.

Shaw, M. C., & Goodyear, R. K. (1984). Prologue to primary prevention in schools. *Personnel and Guidance Journal*, 62, 446–447.

Simon, L. J. (1970). The political unconsciousness of psychology: Clinical psychology and social change. *Professional Psychology*, 1, 331–341.

Spitzer, A., Webster-Stratton, C., & Hollinsworth, T. (1991). Coping with conduct-problem children: Parents gaining knowledge and control. *Journal of Clinical and Child Psychology*, 20(4), 413–427.

Strother, J., & Jacobs, E. (1986). Parent consultation: A practical approach. *School Counselor*, 33(4), 292–296.

Szasz, R. S. (1970). *The manufacturing of madness*. New York: Dell.

Taylor, D. (1986). The child go-between: Consulting with parents and teachers. *Journal of Family Therapy*, 8(1), 79–89.

Vitalo, R. (1971). Teaching improved interpersonal functioning as a preferred mode of treatment. *Journal of Counseling and Clinical Psychology*, 35, 166–171.

Walz, G., & Benjamin, L. (1978). A change agent strategy for counselors functioning as consultants. *Personnel and Guidance Journal*, 56, 331–334.

Warnath, C. F. (1973). The school counselor as institutional agent. *School Counselor*, 20, 202–208.

Werner, J. L. (1978). Community mental health consultation with agencies. *Personnel and Guidance Journal*, 56, 364–368.

Westbrook, F. D., Leonard, M. M., Johnson, F., Boyd, V. S., Hunt, S. M., & McDermott, M. T. (1978). University campus consultation through the formation of collaborative dyads. *Personnel and Guidance Journal*, 56, 359–363.

Wigtil, J. V., & Kelsey, R. C. (1978). Team building as a consulting intervention for influencing learning environments. *Personnel and Guidance Journal*, 56, 412–416.

Chapter 8

PROFESSIONAL ISSUES:
A CHILD–CENTERED PERSPECTIVE

The eight issues addressed in this chapter draw strong reactions from child-centered counselors. They are issues which should draw reactions from all counselors. At the moment, however, they seem to only attract the attention of child-centered counselors. Perhaps in the years ahead these issues will prompt a reaction from the entire profession. Let's hope so. The issues are: (1) accountability, (2) evaluating counseling, (3) the rights of children in counseling, (4) the rights of the counselor, (5) the use of information in counseling, (6) cognitive therapies, (7) counseling and testing, and (8) psychodiagnosis.

They are issues of justice, fairness, objectivity, judgment, equal treatment, and respect for the person, especially the child with problems. These issues would be addressed differently by other theories of counseling because of the differences in their values regarding the person and the counseling process used to help that person.

To child-centered counselors, counseling's response to these issues represents the future of the profession. If these issues aren't addressed, there is the danger, in the years ahead, that counseling can become a manipulative and impersonal process performed by bureaucratic counselors who work exclusively with referred clients. The trend seems to be in that direction. We hope that this chapter is a contribution to reversing that trend.

ACCOUNTABILITY

Pressures for the counseling profession to demonstrate concrete and tangible results for the dollars it spends is being transmitted through federal and state agencies. Human engineering, performance contracting, systems analysis, cost effectiveness, behavioral objectives, and technological procedures characterize the efforts to establish accountability in counseling. Accountability requirements have been included in union contracts and are embodied in human services legislation in a number of states. The pressure of accountability has resulted in some fundamental shifts in the ways counselors view their work. There is an increased emphasis upon behavioral objectives and the need to specifically define the desired results of counseling.

Current criticism of counseling and the related demands for accountability come from a variety of factors: the escalating cost of human services; developments in management techniques which have spurred the sharpening of goals, specificity of planning, and the establishment of cost effectiveness measures; the politicalization of human services agencies; and the rising expectations among minority groups for access to counseling and related human services. The accountability movement also reflects the American obsession with making every human activity, intellectual, physical, moral, social, and even sexual, accountable in terms of dollar expenditures. Behavioral objectives, systems analysis, and performance contracting fit the American philosophy. They are logical, ordered, objective, pragmatic, precise, and lend themselves to mechanized, computerized, and business-like ways of measuring outcomes.

The supporters and advocates of accountability are not all of one mind. Some view accountability as a process inspired primarily by a desire that worthwhile goals be regularly attained. For others, accountability may be motivated solely by the wish to economize on costs. Accountability has so many meanings, and has been used in so many different ways for so many different ends that the net result has been professional and public confusion; a rush to easy answers, plans of action, and methods of evaluation; and a developing mythology of accountability. Since it is obvious that we will be seeing more and more efforts at accountability, and that many of these attempts will not be successful, it becomes necessary to examine the mythology, confusion, and fundamental questions of accountability in order to keep it in perspective.

MYTH 1: The management and business practices introduced through accountability will increase the efficiency and effectiveness of counseling and provide insurance against deficient practices.

It is argued that counselors should incorporate the precise accountability methods that produced aerospace systems that were "zero fault." It can be questioned, however, whether accountability methods alone produced aerospace systems that were zero fault or whether zero fault occurred because of a national commitment, legislative and executive support, and billions of support dollars. Would that counselors have the same commitment, the same executive and legislative support, and the billions of support dollars. And what of the business world's accountability methods which led to such fiascoes as the Edsel, the F-111, and the Lockheed and Grummon aircraft debacles? What about the costly overruns of 200 percent in the Pentagon amounting to billions of dollars each year? Management techniques have always been available to business and government, but they have not prevented poor performance, inefficiency, costly expenditures, and some magnificent and colossal failures.

Lakes are dying; rivers are polluted; food companies are selling their cyclamate reserves overseas; major car companies recall thousands of defective cars each year; aerospray products have to be removed from the market; dangerous toys and highly flammable clothing maim and injure children; and obsolescence is part and parcel of consumer products. This is the record corporations have compiled in their race to make America productive. Although a wholesale indictment of industry and business would be unfair, it is a fact that the industrial mind set (profit first/persons second) has led to some appalling behavior which should be totally unacceptable when applied to devising accountability systems for counseling.

Indeed, the application of corporate management and accountability practices to counseling could lead to some bizarre results as revealed in the following satirical analysis conducted by a management consultant on the efficiency of a symphony orchestra. If we view the music and musicians of a symphony orchestra as analogous to counseling and counselors, then a telling point can be made about the myth of management techniques. The consultant, after carefully studying the orchestra, had several observations and recommendations:

> *Observation:* For considerable periods, the four oboe players have nothing to do. *Recommendation:* Their numbers should be reduced and the work spread more evenly over the whole of the concert, thus eliminating peaks of activity.

> *Observation:* All the violins were playing identical notes. This seems unnecessary duplication. *Recommendation:* The staff of this section should be drastically cut. If a large volume of sound is required, it could be obtained by means of electronic amplifiers.

Observation: There seems to be too much repetition of some musical passages. Scores should be drastically pruned. No useful purpose is served by the horns repeating a passage which has already been played by the strings. *Recommendation:* It is estimated that if all redundant passages were eliminated, the whole concert time of two hours could be reduced to 20 minutes and there would be no need for an intermission.

The conductor isn't too happy with these recommendations and expresses the opinion that there might be some falling off in attendance. In that unlikely event, it should be possible to close sections of the auditorium entirely with a consequential saving of overhead expenses, lighting, salaries for ushers, etc.

This satire speaks for itself and for a substantial number of counselors concerned about the intricacies, complexities, and subtlties involved in attempts to make the counseling process more efficient.

MYTH 2: All professionals are accountable—why shouldn't counselors be?

If accountability is the mark of the true professional, then we can expect that all professionals will be held accountable according to the same standards. In applying strict accountability standards to other professions some interesting outcomes might occur. For example, in medicine, a behavioral objective for the recipient of an appendectomy might read, in clearly stated terms, something like this:

> At the end of 120 hours following the removal of the appendix, the patient will, without aid, rise from bed, walk to the window and open the shade without pain; furthermore, the length of the scar will be within 7 to 11 centimeters long, the top of which will not be visible with a patient clothed in a bikini covering the anterior of the lower body from the mons pubis to 24–30 centimeters below the umbilical scar.

If the patient performs as outlined in the clearly stated objective, then the surgeon gets the fee. If the patient does better, then the surgeon gets a bonus. If the performance does not meet the objectives set up in the contract, then the surgeon forfeits the fee.

Let's turn to another profession, say, law. Imagine that you've been practically wiped out in an auto accident. Lost your car, your confidence, and time on your job. You attempt to recoup your losses through the courts. A clearly stated objective is set up:

> The claimant will leave the courtroom with a check for damages; said check will amount to no less than $100,000.

Again, being professional, your attorney will accept a fee on the basis of the performance contract.

If we look further in American life, we would find that we have certain expectations in other areas as well. Let's look at the role of a member of the clergy. We have long-range expectations here which, when expressed in terms of clearly stated objectives, would probably come out something like this:

> The soul will leave the body within 5 seconds of death and will be welcomed into the Kingdom of God as evidenced by the playing of soft music by Handel and rays of sunshine emanating through the narthex on an overcast day.

MYTH 3: There are no existing procedures and practices of accountability for counselors.

There are a variety of procedures and practices currently available which could be used by supervisors to evaluate counselors and hold them accountable. These include such devices and approaches as videotaping, interaction analysis, observations, counselor logs, surveys of clients, probationary periods, in-service training, and other efforts to improve results. The relationship between what exists now and what is proposed in the way of new accountability procedures should be spelled out and examined. Maybe our efforts should be turned not only toward the design of new accountability systems but also to making what we already have work.

Many counselors have not been disposed to assess themselves because they have been employed in organizations that have: (1) developed arbitrary evaluative criteria and imposed these criteria on professional staff without the staff's involvement in the evaluation process; (2) employed criteria developed in other settings without recognizing and accommodating the essential differences between these settings and those in which counseling takes place; (3) utilized haphazard approaches to evaluation, thus not inviting the confidence and respect of professional staff; and (4) have not established the goals and process of accountability in a manner consistent with the principles of participatory democracy.

The accountability procedures now available will work when counselors have a voice in carrying them out. Counselors need the opportunity to work with administrators, community representatives, and others in developing a philosophy and workable approach to evaluation which is based on constructive feedback which will promote the counselor's professional development. Without the counselor's involvement from the beginning, new approaches will work no better than what is currently available.

The history of accountability in controlling human behavior has not been positive. Human behavior cannot be controlled with the same precision that we can control a machine. The machine's behavior is predictable. Human behavior is not. Human behavior cannot be programmed and thus, cannot be held to the same accountability standards used in other fields.

Accountability: Under What conditions?

It is imperative that whoever is to be held accountable for accomplishing a task be given a significant measure of control over the definition of the task, the manner in which the task is to be undertaken, the resources required, and the means and methods of evaluation. It is unfair to expect a counselor to be accountable for goals which the counselor had no role in setting, with no control over the methods used to accomplish tasks, and without the resources necessary to do the job. It is equally inappropriate to expect a client to work toward goals not determined by the client. For these reasons, whoever is to be held accountable must participate in goal setting and in the selection of methods and materials to be used. Unless these selection opportunities are present, it is doubtful that any concept of accountability will ever be successfully implemented.

Accountability: The Philosophical Question

One of the clear messages coming from performance contracting is that we concern ourselves only with those objectives which can be stated precisely in simple and overt behavioral terms and which are readily measurable by some method. What happens when our goals are complex, extensive, and long-term is another matter.

An accountability model must define quite specifically, and perhaps often arbitrarily, the behaviors which are to be achieved by counselors and clients. The necessity for defining any behavior in terms of a list of specific objectives may result in a rather narrow version of human behavior, and may exclude other quite legitimate objectives that reflect other important concepts of human behavior. This brings us to the philosophical question of *who* determines the goals of counseling and the behaviors to be attained by clients. The search for accountability must be accompanied by an understanding of the philosophical, and controversial, aspects of behavioral goals and a determination not to permit testers, contractors, and objective writers to determine the goals of counseling.

Recommendations regarding accountability

To develop accountability programs that will improve counseling and facilitate psychological growth for clients, it would seem that the following would constitute minimal and necessary humanistic conditions:

1. A plan of accountability which has been developed by counselors, supervisors, and clients working together in a free and open discussion of the philosophical, theoretical, and empirical considerations that influence the counseling process and its outcomes.
2. A clearly stated philosophy and rationale for accountability developed by counselors, supervisors, and clients.
3. A continuous, on-going process of accountability characterized by continuous feedback and established monitoring points so that the counselor and appropriate supervisory personnel have specific time referents for gauging and discussing the individual performance of the counselor.
4. A clear statement of performance standards, and criteria understandable and acceptable to counselors, supervisors, and clients.
5. A plan of accountability which accommodates judgments and observations from both the internal (counselor) and external (supervisor) frames of reference.
6. A plan of accountability that includes an annual review of evaluative processes, performance criteria and standards, roles, and responsibilities.
7. A plan of accountability that takes into consideration local conditions, needs, and resources.
8. Clearly defined but flexible procedures for collecting data to test performance criteria for evaluating and supervising each counselor, such as:

   (a) Counselor and supervisor analyze and critique video tapes of the individual counselor's performance.
   (b) Colleague counselors analyze and critique video tapes of counseling performance.
   (c) Counselor conducts personal research regarding effectiveness and shares the results for critique with supervisor and/or colleagues.

This might be accomplished through the use of questionnaires or surveys of clients and former clients.

(d) Periodically, the counselor prepares a self-evaluation and the supervisor writes an evaluation of the counselor. Together they share the results and discuss areas of agreement and disagreement.

9. A plan of accountability which can be refined and modified on the basis of periodic feedback from all who are affected.

10. A plan of accountability in which all participants would accept some accountability. For each goal the parties involved (counselors, supervisors, and clients) would decide not only what is to be accomplished but what they are to be responsible for.

11. A plan of accountability based on needs assessments, philosophical considerations and goal formulations, resulting from the collaborative efforts of counselors, supervisors, and clients.

A sensible plan of accountability calls for the establishment of new relationships and the reshaping of traditional roles. Many more individuals will need to be involved in the governance of counseling and human services. When organizations and counselors collaborate in a real partnership, the issues of accountability will not be viewed within a framework of superior-subordinate relationships. Shared responsibility is the key to successful accountability which obviates the need for myths and simplistic answers. When applied to accountability, as well as other areas, democratic procedures insure the best outcomes.

EVALUATING COUNSELING

Problems in Evaluating Counseling

The obstacles one might encounter when evaluating counseling fall into three problem areas: problems in connection with the selection of evaluation devices; problems in connection with the interpretation and use of data secured through the employment of evaluative devices; and problems surrounding the organization and administration of counseling. There have always been obstacles inherent in the counseling function which hamper its easy evaluation. These historic obstacles are:

1. The specific objectives of counseling are stated in generalities rather than in specific behavioral outcomes.

2. Counseling terminology requires strict adherence to precise definitions. These are lacking.

3. Many variables outside of counseling may influence the behavior believed to be resultant from counseling.
4. There is confusion over process evaluation and product evaluation. Too often the latter is neglected.
5. Lack of a clear, acceptable statement of objectives in terms of observable client characteristics and behavior.
6. Failure to relate client objectives to an organization's objectives.
7. The use of immediate and easily available criteria accompanied by failure to validate the immediate criteria against long-term goals.
8. The tendency to regard certain goals as equally desirable for all individuals, thereby ignoring individual differences.
9. Confusion of means with ends or of process with outcomes.
10. Excessive use of subjective reactions.
11. Little or no attention to determining a satisfactory experimental design.

Such problems can be dealt with if child counselors make a commitment to engage in simple forms of evaluative research for the purpose of improving counseling programs and validating their worth. Sound evaluation depends upon sufficient counselor time and energy and a sense of obligation to evaluate counseling.

The Objectives of Evaluation

What are the purposes and objectives of evaluation? The following represent the appropriate objectives of evaluation:

1. To increase the growth of those being evaluated.
2. To help the counselor gain new insights into counseling.
3. To improve counseling theories and their application.
4. To provide a basis for a staff development program.
5. To clarify and validate hypotheses underlying counseling.
6. To provide data upon which a sound program of public information can be built.
7. To increase the competence of professional staff by providing data so staff can assess the results of their efforts.
8. To provide evidence to convince critics that counseling is valuable.
9. To facilitate smoother intra- and interinstitutional relationships.
10. To educate directors and trustees about the value of counseling services.
11. To help programs gain public support.
12. To help effect larger institutional contributions to social progress.

Most of the stated objectives of evaluation fundamentally revolve around two pivotal concerns: Are we helping children? How can we improve counselor effectiveness to be of greater assistance to children? These are not only the concerns of counselors but also of parents and the community at large. It is well for child counselors to bear in mind that such people are not unreasonable in the quest for data that demonstrates the value of counseling. Altogether too many counselors feel it is impossible to evaluate counseling and have avoided planning any procedures to verify its worth. Counselors, through the use of tape recordings, case studies, and client surveys, can gather the kinds of information needed to answer their own questions and those of the community. Although such evaluation techniques have their limitations, this does not mean that they are of little value. On the contrary, they provide reasonable evidence, which can be used to improve counseling and to inform the public and professionals of the benefits of child counseling programs.

Criteria for Evaluating Counseling

Measuring the outcomes of counseling is basically a question of measuring human behavior, for, if counseling has been successful, positive behavioral changes involves first selecting appropriate evaluative criteria. What are the criteria we use to establish that a change in behavior has occurred through counseling?

The following criteria have been used in evaluating the effectiveness of child counseling: improvements in academic achievement, family relations, peer relations, behavioral goals, self concept, school attendance, social attitudes, acceptance of authority, school adjustment, reading ability, self-esteem, self-understanding, teacher/pupil relationships, and reductions in stress, anxiety, and acting-out delinquent behavior.

Whatever criteria the counselor selects will be related to subjective judgments regarding successful and appropriate outcomes (Rogers, 1951, pp. 179–180). This means that one person can perceive that counseling has brought about positive changes in a particular child, while another believes that the changes are inappropriate. For example, let's look at the criterion of educational adjustment in terms of the suitability of educational goals: a sixth-grade child who has been withdrawn and extremely docile but a high achiever may, as a result of counseling, become more assertive and active in the classroom and less compulsive about achieving high grades. Satisfied with B's and an occasional C instead of all A's, and more strident and outgoing in behavior, the child represents a counseling outcome which could be viewed very differently by the counselor, the teacher, and the child's parents.

The criterion problem is perhaps the single most vital issue affecting the process of evaluation. Generally speaking, the application of most criteria that have been identified in counseling research have not yielded data to validate conclusively that counseling is helpful. Perhaps this is because criteria have not been derived from the child and the child's unique situation. Each child has different needs and goals. What is needed in evaluating the effectiveness of counseling is sufficiently flexible criteria that can encompass the diversity and complexity of individual behavior. The uniqueness of each individual and the distinctiveness of each counseling relationship suggest that the case study or individual longitudinal approach may represent the best approach for measuring the outcomes and value of counseling.

THE RIGHTS OF CHILDREN IN COUNSELING

The literature of counseling does not typically deal with the rights of children. Most of the literature dealing with rights violations have come from members of disadvantaged groups. In a loud and clear voice they have said to all counselors, everywhere, "Give us back our rights!" (Aragon & Ulibarri, 1971; Gardner, 1971; Killinger, 1971, 1971; Russell, 1970; Spang, 1971; Sue & Sue, 1973).

What should these criticisms coming from disadvantaged persons mean to the counselor who has always possessed rights? Simply that the counselor must realize that while the counselor was enjoying his or her personal rights, children, particularly those children in minority groups, were having their rights overtly or covertly denied.

The overt denial of a disadvantaged child's rights is easily observed and many Americans are abhorred by such behavior. The covert denial of a disadvantaged child's rights is, however, far more subtle, far more hidden from view, and in some cases can be far more malicious and psychologically damaging (Cohen and Naimark, 1991).

Counseling, if done properly, can help a child to understand that the child does possess rights and the personal power to exercise those rights. Counseling has the potential to be a liberating process in which the child can sense personal rights, the child's worth as a person, and an awareness that the child can have some control over what is happening in his or her life. The child does not have to be a victim.

What are these rights and how might they be more known by children as an outcome of counseling? Following is a tentative list of those rights. The list is tentative simply because it is incomplete. The list becomes expanded only in proportion to the counselor's awareness that counseling can be conceived as a process whereby human rights denied to the child are returned to the child.

The child has the right to distributive justice.

Distributive justice is based upon the concept that all children should have equal access to counseling; that all children should have equal access to the counselor's resources, skill, time, and energy. This is a fundamental right of the child as an American and is supported among counselors who afford every child equality of treatment, positive regard, and empathic understanding regardless of the child's race, gender, religion, values, handicap, or ethnic affiliation.

The child has the right to retributive justice.

Retributive justice is the rendering of justice to those who have been denied justice. Minority children have too often been denied access to those rights and advantages which the majority takes for granted. Rights and advantages which the majority has inherited simply because they are members of the majority. Rights and advantages which have been passed from generation to generation of majority group members.

Retributive justice demands access to rights that have been historically denied to minority children. It means realizing that something is owed to minority group children today because certain rights were denied to them in the past. Retributive justice is the realization that these rights must be returned to their rightful owners.

The child has the right to be treated with dignity and worth as a person.

Our society, and the counseling profession, often give lip service to this concept. We intellectually realize that we all should treat each other with respect. Life, however, conditions us to have more respect for the "haves" than the "have nots." You can have a reasonably successful career if you pay more attention to the "haves" than the "have nots." The counselor counseling the son of a local school board member will often extend him more time, energy and respect than the boy who is on welfare and lives in a home with foster parents who both work at minimum wage jobs. All any minority child wants is fair treatment; equal access to the counselor's time, energy, and attention and to be treated with dignity and worth simply because the child is human.

The child has the right to self-determination.

The child's right to reach for self-determined solutions to problems comes from the counselor's respect for the dignity and worth of the child as a person. This right of self-determination is a natural extension of the counselor's respect for the child's dignity and worth.

The child's right to make mistakes, to challenge, to grow, to develop is a right which cannot be denied. Far too many counselors overtly deny children this right of self-determination. Others do it covertly by manipulating the child until the right is no longer known to the child.

The child has the right to become voluntarily involved in counseling.

The only way that some counselors can hold a job is to require that referred children see them on a regular basis. These counselors are comfortable with this procedure since it protects their jobs and guarantees them a pool of clients. They don't have to provide quality services to attract and keep their clients. If children were given the freedom to decide whether or not to undergo counseling, then these counselors would be professionally embarrassed when their cadre of counselees suddenly disappeared.

The concept of having children themselves decide whether or not they should undergo counseling can be threatening to incompetent counselors. The competent counselor, however, knows that counseling will be a positive and helpful experience when the child is a voluntary participant.

The child's right to be voluntarily engaged in counseling will put many counselors on the spot. They must suddenly develop a counseling program with credibility; a counseling program in which children sense that their voluntary participation is not only a right but a necessary first step if the counseling process is to be effective.

The child has the right to acquire an understanding of counseling.

If the counselor is to be effective in helping minority children, it is imperative that they be oriented to what counseling is and is not, what the role of the counselor is, and what one can expect to get out of counseling (Thompson and Rudolph, 1992). Surely, if the child is to have the freedom of choosing or rejecting counseling, then the child has the right to sufficient knowledge and understanding of the counseling process. Unrealistic and inappropriate expectations can develop in the counseling relationship if the child is not informed about the nature of counseling and the role of the counselor. Well-designated orientation procedures delineating the role of the counselor, the purposes of counseling, and the counseling atmosphere necessary for developing counseling effectiveness, will all inform children and give them a foundation for their voluntary participation.

We further believe that children need to see counseling more in terms of the relationship than as a problem-centered process. Counseling then would not only emanate from a child's need for help but could also be based on a child's developmental need to communicate. Such a notion would question the commonly held idea that counseling begins only when the client experiences a degree of anxiety or discomfort that would make a solution to a problem more personally satisfying. But does ontological communion with children need to be based on the existence of a problem? Counselors can encourage children who have had exciting or pleasant experiences to share these in the framework of counseling. Sharing pleasant experiences with an adult is a developmental task deserving of the counselor's attention and worthy of being accommodated in a counseling program. Children, like all people, like to be listened to and understood, and they like to share their moments of glory and elation with others. The need to share may be defined by some as representing a state of disequilibrium, "positive disequilibrium," to be sure, but disequilibrium at any rate. Whether this is the case or not, counselors need to accentuate the positive motivations for counseling as well as the problem-centered reasons. By emphasizing the positive in an orientation, the counselor helps children to see counseling as a positive opportunity to relate with an adult in an understanding atmosphere.

The child has the right to confidentiality.

Maintaining and respecting the confidences of children is essential in counseling. Counseling (at least effective counseling) cannot occur unless the confidentiality of the relationship is assured. If a child cannot feel secure in revealing the self to the counselor, it is highly doubtful that counseling will be helpful and facilitating. Self-revelation and exploration take place only in an atmosphere of trust.

The need for keeping certain information confidential is clear. The child is hesitant to talk about problems until the child is certain that the counselor can be trusted. The child enters the counseling relationship voluntarily and more openly when the child knows that the counselor will hold in confidence what is said. Many of the normal developmental concerns of children revolve around their relationships with peers, parents, and teachers. It is essential that children feel completely secure about the confidential nature of the counseling relationship; otherwise, they are uncomfortable and conceal themselves, lest others, especially the persons most directly involved, learn how they feel.

Much of the reluctance and resistance to counseling which some children display emanates from a lack of trust in the counselor. Too many children have bared their souls to counselors in what appeared to be a confidential relationship only to find out later that what they revealed in a "moment of trust" was communicated to parents and teachers. In some communities the counselor is perceived as the last person to be trusted.

The issue of confidentiality is often expressed in the question, "To whom does the counselor owe primary allegiance: society or the individual?" We feel that the counselor's primary obligation is to the individual, but this does not mean a negation of an obligation to society. It is not an "either or" proposition. The counselor can serve society most effectively not by revealing confidences, but by developing a facilitative relationship characterized by trust. A relationship in which the child realizes and actualizes the self as a responsible and socially competent person.

Maintaining client confidences is not always easy (Long, 1981). Professional codes of ethics for counselors indicate that in those situations where information received in confidence indicates that the client may do serious harm to the self or to others, intervention by the counselor may be necessary. If a counselor feels the necessity to break a confidence, the counselor should certainly do some soul-searching to find out if the break is necessary, and if it is being done for the good of some organization or group or because of the counselor's insecurity, ignorance, and ineptitude (Wagner, 1981).

The child has the right to be different.

In the counseling relationship the child should experience the epitome of respect, acceptance, and understanding of the child's uniqueness and difference. This is a right implicit in the concept of counseling. A right which challenges the counselor to fully implement the counselor's belief in the dignity of the person and the counselor's deep respect for diversity.

The freedom to have ideas, values, and beliefs—the permission to be oneself—the right to be different—exist in a counseling climate that is marked by a deep respect for the individuality and uniqueness of the child. In the final analysis, each individual must discover personal uniqueness. It is in an atmosphere where uniqueness is fostered and difference is valued that the full discovery of self can be achieved.

The counselor accepts differences in the child because the counselor knows that where differences cannot be accepted, individuals cannot be. In an atmosphere where differences are valued and where the child feels that individual worth and contribution are held in high regard, the child sees that there is something that the child can contribute—that the child's meaning, feelings, and ideas have value and significance.

The child has the right to be accepted.

For the self to be freed for growth, it must be accepted as it presently exists. Acceptance of the child means an acceptance of the child's values. The counselor does not have to agree or disagree with these values, only accept them as representing the child's viewpoint. In being acceptant of the child's personal values—the counselor must recognize the child's right to *be* so that the child may *become.* When a child is not required to defend values the child is free to grow and change those values. Acceptance of the child means giving the child the opportunity of holding and expressing personal meanings without ridicule, attack, or moralization; the right to see things in a very unique and personal way. With this kind of acceptance the child is free to look at values without fear. Those values which are not psychologically sustaining will crumble in the process of talking about them.

True acceptance is unaffected by any differences in the child. It is not acceptance up to this point or that point and no further. It does not depend upon the child's acting or talking a certain way, socioeconomic background, religion or IQ, race, or gender. It is not dependent upon the child's meeting the counselor's values or standards of behavior. It is complete and unconditional.

The child's right to be must be deeply regarded by the counselor if the child is to move toward more self and socially enhancing values. Allowing a child to be will enable the child to examine that state of being and alter it as a response to effective counseling.

The child has the right to make mistakes.

Where mistakes are not permitted, the freedom and willingness of people to make choices are severely limited. Growth is facilitated when error is accepted as a natural part of the process of growth. Growth requires the challenge of new and different experiences, the trying of the unknown, and therefore, it necessarily must involve the making of mistakes. In order that people may grow and learn, they need opportunities to explore new situations and ideas without being penalized.

Counseling must be an open-ended relationship in which the child is free to move in any given direction. This demands enormous faith and consistency on the part of the counselor—faith in the child's capacity to choose and consistency in holding to that faith regardless of the choices the child makes. No child is incapable of making choices, although some children may feel that they can't.

The counselor conveys faith in the child and the child's right to make mistakes not just by what the counselor says but also through the counselor's attitudes, which indicate to the child, "You're free to choose." The child who feels free to choose and move in any direction discovers an increasing pride and confidence in making personal choices, and those choices will be characterized by experiences and goals which sustain the self and enhance others.

The child has a right to counselor genuineness.

Counseling has no room for facades. Children do not reveal themselves nor do they relate to people who play a role, who operate from behind a front. The counselor, because the counselor is human, facilitates growth in the child when the counselor is openly *being* the feelings and attitudes that are flowing within. Such genuineness on the part of the counselor does not imply that genuine means the impulsive blurting out of every passing and fleeting feeling and thought. Genuineness is recognizing persistent feelings and attitudes and expressing what one experiences.

The child has a right to know and respond to the counselor as a real person. Some counselors, in their effort to develop rapport with children, suppress their genuine feelings and attitudes and pretend to be someone they are not. Such behavior only serves to widen the gulf between counselor and children. By feigning acceptance and understanding when they are feeling anxiety, some counselors come across to children as unauthentic. The child has no less a right to counselor genuineness than the counselor has a right to expect genuineness from the child. By becoming more human and transcending one's professional role, the counselor can develop the kind of climate which nurtures trust and realness. However, being genuine does not obviate the counselor's responsibility to be free from judging the behavior of others by the counselor's own values. The counselor's personal values must not, however, intrude on the process of helping the child determine his or her values. These values must be chosen by the client. Counselor genuineness in the helping process will help children to discover the universality of their own individual values.

The rights of the child and professionalism.

Providing children with an opportunity to experience the preceding rights represents the counselor's respect for both the child and for justice; and if these rights existed for the child in their fullest sense we would see the demise of two currently polarized issues in counseling: (1) the importance of one theory of counseling over others, and (2) the proper role of the counselor.

The importance of a certain theory of counseling over others pales in significance when compared to the importance of guaranteeing the child inalienable rights as a person in counseling. If the rights of the child were addressed by different counseling theories, we might find some common ground on which to stand. Counseling theories are polarized essentially because they have adopted separate definitions regarding the nature of the person and the goals, processes, and outcomes of counseling. If we addressed ourselves to identifying the rights of children and the process whereby these rights could be realized, we would begin to move toward some needed theoretical integration. The rights of the child are more evident, understandable, and constitutionally defined than the grand propositions supporting the different theories of counseling.

By making counseling theories conform to the rights of the child, not only would those theories become more integrated because of the constancy of those rights, but another professional issue would begin to move toward resolution: the role of the counselor.

One way to move toward a better consensus regarding the role of the counselor would be to approach that role definition from a different direction—from the rights of the child. If the rights of the child were first identified, it would then be relatively simple for counselors to conceive a role which would enable them to function in the furtherance of those rights.

THE RIGHTS OF THE COUNSELOR

The rights of the counselor are neglected in the literature of counseling. The rights that have received attention are those pertaining to the rights of society (Stewart & Warnath, 1965) and the rights of clients (Hare-Mustin, Marecek, Kaplan, & Liss-Levinson, 1979). When counselors become more aware of their professional rights and organizations which employ them become more respectful of those rights, the quality of counseling will improve.

The right to counsel.

Professional counselors expect to spend the major portion of each working day in individual and group counseling (Boy, 1984). They are instead diverted toward being environmental engineers (Matheny, 1971), applied behavioral scientists (Berdie, 1972), teachers (Ivey, 1974; 1976), community psychologists (Goodyear, 1976), consultants (Karpius, 1978), evaluators (Sproles, Panther, & Lanier, 1978), diagnosticians (Shertzer & Linden, 1979), quasi-administrators (Shertzer & Stone, 1980), staff developers (Herr & Scofield, 1983), and computer specialists (Walz, 1984).

Those who state that the professional counselor should spend the major portion of each working day in individual and group counseling relationships (Arbuckle, 1975; Boy & Pine, 1990) also recognize the counselor's responsibility to consultation. Coordination is, however, viewed as a secondary responsibility. Their emphasis is on the counselor functioning primarily as a counselor.

Counseling takes time and some organizations do not appear to want the counselor involved in counseling because of the time that it requires; but when one looks at the client services provided by an organization, counseling is the one that most directly influences the behavior of clients.

Counselors have a right to counsel and that right must be recognized by organizations which truly are interested in the well-being of clients.

The right to a professional role.

The counselor's involvement in consultative activities occurs when these activities serve to improve the quality of counseling. In some organizations the counselor's involvement in consultation is designed to improve the quality of administrative services. Administrators prompt counselors to become more involved in consultation because such an involvement contributes to easing administrative burdens rather than facilitating the counseling process.

Administrators need to protect the time that counselors have for counseling. They need to identify counseling as the most important service provided to children and need to back up that commitment by decreasing, and eliminating, the counselor's involvement in administrative responsibilities.

Counselors have a right to a professional role and that right must be recognized. Such a right may not be in the best interests of administrators, but it is in the best interests of children.

The right to be fairly evaluated.

Some institutions create evaluation problems for counselors when they: (1) institute arbitrary evaluative criteria and impose these criteria on counselors; (2) employ criteria used to evaluate other staff as "suitable" for evaluating counselors without recognizing role differences between counselors and other staff members; (3) utilize a haphazard, disorganized, and unclear approach to evaluation; and (4) do not implement the evaluative process in a democratic manner (Boy & Pine, 1990).

Counselors consider an evaluative process to be fair when it includes the counselor in determining the goals, criteria, and process of evaluation. When the counselor is involved in determining the goals of evaluation, those goals will include priorities important to the professionalization of counseling; when the counselor is involved in determining the criteria of evaluation, the counselor has the opportunity to include criteria which are appropriate for evaluating the work of the counselor; and when the counselor is involved in determining the steps in the evaluative process itself, the counselor has the opportunity to contribute to the objectivity and fairness of that process.

The right to a politically free work climate.

In some organizations, some decisions are made not because they enhance the counseling process and contribute to the well-being of clients. They are made because of political favoritism or expediency. Political favoritism occurs for certain staff not because the staff member is exceptionally competent but because the staff member has maneuvered into a position whereby favors are gained. Politically expedient decisions are those designed to curry favor with individuals and groups who affect the institution. Counselors in such a work environment usually become disenchanted because an institution's noble mission becomes immersed in a sea of pervasive political influences.

The professional counselor has a deep and abiding commitment to serve human needs through the counseling process. It can be nourished in proportion to an institution's ability to create a politically free work climate. When this occurs, the counselor's work is done qualitatively and efficiently and the institution's reputation far exceeds one gained by political favoritism and expediency.

The right to fair administrative practices.

The best way for administrators to become more fair is to include staff in the decision making process. Including staff will take more time but the issue of fairness will be served. Staff members will feel that a sharing of the decision making process is an indicator of the administrator's respect for the opinions of staff and that they have a stake in the outcomes of decisions made. Creating such an administrative climate will cause the staff to perceive administrative practices as being fair and will contribute to improving and maintaining staff morale.

The counselor's right to fair administrative practices will be enhanced by administrators who live the importance of participatory democracy.

The right to equalized staff relationships.

Equalized relationships between and among staff members tends to be productive while unequalized relationships tend to be nonproductive. An equalized relationship is one in which staff members possess equivalent authority when dealing with each other or arriving at professional decisions. They deal with each other more openly when considering a decision and each other's input into the decision is mutually respected. When the relationship is equalized between marriage partners, labor and management, and between and among nations, all parties tend to engage each other more cooperatively and with a sense of mutual trust. When such relationships are unequalized, the level of cooperation and trust tends to be diminished and the outcomes of that relationship tend to be nonproductive.

Counselors who have equalized relationships with other staff members are free to communicate and contribute. Counselors have a right to equalized staff relationships and the beneficiaries of such relationships will be the institution and children served by that institution. Counselors tend to be more creative, energetic, and productive when they have equalized staff relationships.

The right to individualized professional values.

Counselors tend to seek employment in institutions which confirm their values while avoiding employment in institutions which contradict those values. There are often subtle value clashes between the counselor and the employing institution. These subtle value conflicts often revolve around: (1) the degree to which a child has the capacity to make decisions, (2) the degree of control that a counselor has over the behavior of the child, (3) the extent to which children are voluntarily involved in counseling, (4) the degree to which the child has the right to hold values contrary to those of the institution, and (5) the accuracy of a child's evaluation and diagnosis.

A mature work setting adheres to general values, but it also accommodates the individualized values of counselors, especially when those values are congruent with a theory of counseling. The counselor's right to individualized and carefully considered professional values must be respected; and the counselor's commitment to organizational values will be in proportion to that institution's respect for the counselor's individualized professional values.

The right to practice a theory of counseling.

A counselor's commitment to apply a certain theory of counseling is a serious professional decision. It is not made lightly. It is not based on counselor whims. It is a commitment based upon a counselor's understanding that a bona fide theory of counseling must meet certain criteria (Stefflre & Grant, 1972, pp. 4–7). A useful theory enables the counselor to find relatedness among diverse observations and experiences, compels us to consider factors that we previously overlooked, provides guidelines for monitoring our counseling behavior and effectiveness, tells us what to look for in client behavior, helps us to identify a process for improving that behavior, and helps us to make modifications in the counseling process so that it will better meet client needs (Boy & Pine, 1990).

A counselor's commitment to a certain theory of counseling must be matched by an organization's respect for the counselor's right to apply that theory. Organizations realize that there are several professionally respected theories of counseling (Corey, 1991) and when they insist on the application of only one theory, they are in conflict with research evidence supporting other theories, subvert the counselor's morale, and deny children access to theories of counseling which can be effective in meeting their needs.

THE USE OF INFORMATION IN COUNSELING

Behavior exists in the present and can therefore be dealt with in the present. This principle reflects the immediate view of causation. The problem of causation can be looked at in two ways—historically or immediately. These views are not mutually exclusive; they are both true. There is no doubt that a large component of a child's behavior is a result of the child's past experience or life history. How the child behaves at this time, however, results from the child's ways of seeing (the child's existing perceptual framework) at this moment in time. The existential view stresses that it is the way one sees the situation today, at this instant, which produces the person's behavior at this moment. If we can understand how a child is perceiving right now, we can help the child to develop insights and change behavior *even if we do not know how the child got this way.* That is, if human behavior is a function of perception and if perception exists in the present, it should be possible to change behavior if we can change present perceptions.

The key to developing facilitating and enabling relationships among children is what the counselor *is* and what the counselor *does* in the counseling process. Counselor behavior is a function of the immediate view of the child as the child is *now* in the relationship. This means moving away from a reliance on historical or external data. It implies that the counselor can effect change without knowing the case history of the child; it implies that change can be affected in children without necessarily changing parent behavior or the neighborhood environment. Rather than wrestling with cumulative records and test scores and seeing the child through an external frame of reference, it means becoming sensitive to how the child views the self *now*.

Many child counselors have learned that, no matter what a child has endured elsewhere, a positive facilitating *present* experience is enabling and growth-producing. Providing positive present experiences in the form of acceptance, understanding, and empathy does not depend on knowing what a child's past experiences have been. A child needs to relate with counselors who, instead of devoting their time and energy looking for the forces that caused the behavior, spend their time helping the child do something about it.

Information: Help or Hindrance?

Collecting and collating information so that the counselor can make a valid and accurate interpretation or diagnosis of the child's problem has often been considered an essential step in the counseling process. Many counselors believe that by collecting information about children they may come to understand them better, and that by giving information they may be more effective in helping the child to resolve a problem. As a preliminary step to, or an integral part of, counseling, the "information-getting-dispensing" procedure receives a major portion of the counselor's time and attention. Is the amount of time and focus given to collection, analysis, and dissemination of information justified in terms of effective counseling? Is information really a help to the counselor and the child or is it a hindrance?

Cronbach (1955) has historically delineated the polar positions on the use of information in the following statement:

> One function of the interview is to bring forth information about the client. The styles available to the counselor range from the highly directive to the completely passive.... The one counselor proceeds to get accurate information about those questions which he regards as likely to be important. He narrows the field of inquiry quickly. He is likely to prescribe tests which will yield trustworthy measures. The other counselor, however, leaves the initiative to the client. He lets the client choose the area of discussion and shift topics at will. He tends to avoid prescribing tests to answer specific questions. Is it not clear that the former counselor is reducing the bandwidth of the communication in order to obtain relatively faithful information? And that the second counselor uses a tactic which maximizes bandwidth even though it sacrifices fidelity (p. 3)?

We recognize that, for some counselors, the use of information may appear to facilitate counseling. However, we also recognize the use of information can hinder counseling, for there are many pitfalls inherent in the use of information.

The Limitations of Using Information in Counseling.

1. Information is often subjective and inaccurate. One of the major sources the counselor utilizes in gathering information are observations of the child's behavior. Unfortunately, these observations are often characterized by subjectivity and personal bias. A cursory glance at a random sample of such observations usually reveals that they tend to be more interpretive than objective.

   The "factual" information the counselor ordinarily uses frequently is not derived from a collection of facts. Evaluations and comments about children are opinions based on value judgments and cannot be considered as facts. Test scores reflect a sample of a child's behavior at a particular point in time and are, at best, estimates of performance and not facts. All in all, what the counselor usually possesses in the way of information are data which may represent someone else's reality and not the child's.

2. In the analysis of data, the counselor is a subjective element. Given the same information, several counselors will come up with several interpretations and diagnoses. The personality and values of a counselor will often enter into an analysis of information. The subjective perceptions, the background and the training of the counselor will also distort the counselor's interpretation of information about a child.

   The analysis and interpretation of information may be more reflective of the counselor than the child. Because of our self-concepts, we tend to select from our perceptual field those perceptions which we want and to screen out those perceptions we don't want. In handling and processing information, we frequently act on the basis of our own frame of reference and private perceptual filter. Our interpretation of client information may say more about ourselves than children.

3. Irrelevant information may be used by the counselor because it is the only information available. Significant information regarding the child and the child's problem may not be included in records or data and may not be found among other sources of information. In the absence of such information, the counselor will act on what is available. Although the information may have no relevancy to the

child and the child's problem, it may be used to explain the child's past behavior and employed to modify the child's present behavior simply because it is available and for no other reason.

This point was well brought forth by Vogel (1962). When a student is failing school, and before the parents are called in, the counselor and the teacher sit down and go through his/her records:

If the student's father drinks, the failure is blamed on that.

If the student is a younger child, the failure is blamed on that. If he/she is an only child, the failure is blamed on that. If he/she is an older child, the parents are expecting too much from him/her, and the failure is blamed on that.

If he/she comes from a broken home, that is the cause of the failure.

If he/she comes from a working-class home, the failure is due to cultural deprivation (pp. 144–145).

The use of psychological profiles derived from tests have a tendency to blind the counselor to the degree that the counselor becomes interested in children only as functions of their psychological profiles, not as fully-dimensioned human beings. Consequently, the counselor tends to develop a myopic view of the counselee—the child is perceived not as a person, but as the creature of the record—as an object.

4. Information gives the counselor a preconception of what the child is. In using information gathered from files, records, and other sources, the counselor works with perceptions external to the child's frame of reference. The image of the child which the counselor develops from the assimilation of others' perceptions may not be congruent with the child's self-concept and may present a formidable barrier which will prevent the counselor from entering the child's internal frame of reference. Information, rather than helping the counselor see the child's reality, prevents the counselor from fully understanding the child and from helping the child to understand the self.

5. The use of information distorts the existential nature of the counseling relationship. The information-using counselor is often perceived by the child as an information-gatherer and information-evaluator. The counselor's common practice of analyzing a child's personality and behavior places the counselor in the role of an evaluator. It is the naive counselor who believes that children are not aware of this

practice of compiling and summarizing information about the child. Children are aware of and are sensitive to such procedures and cannot help but perceive the counselor as an evaluator regardless of the counselor's efforts to dispel such notions.

6. The practice by the counselor of gathering and using information may constitute a threat to the child and prevent the child from revealing the feelings which cause behavior. The primary concern here is that some counselors have put themselves into the position of recording information, and writing evaluations and recommendations. The acceptance of this evaluative function by the counselor presents a conflict in roles. The counselor soon comes to be looked upon as the person who can do you good or do you harm. Children quickly learn that the counselor is the person with whom you have got to stay friendly or stay away from! Counseling relationships formed under these circumstances are not open and are characterized by a lack of authenticity and trust. What child will express inner feelings, private thoughts, or intimate perceptions with another person who is perceived as one who may use such intimate knowledge in a written recommendation.

   Children who are anxious about what will go on their records will naturally be anxious about revealing internal material to counselors and, consequently, will not become conscious of denied materials themselves. The dossier-building child counselor who becomes overly involved in using records make it dangerous for the child to deal honestly with the self and will block the child's expression of feelings which can help solve the problem.

7. Questioning is used by many counselors as a standard procedure for eliciting information. Because the counselor determines which questions to ask and when to ask them, question-and-answer relationships are markedly counselor-centered. In such a relationship the child can only await the area of the counselor's next question. The child has little or no opportunity to examine inner feelings and thoughts, and the various dimensions of the child's life, because the relationship primes the child to be more sensitive to the counselor's questions than to the child's feelings. The child responds, not as the child feels, but according to the area spotlighted by the counselor's question. Whenever the counselor structures the relationship by using questions, the counselor does not get to know the child but gets

to know about the child. Knowing the child is vastly different from knowing facts about the child.

Using Information in Counseling

Recognizing the fallibility and limitations of information external to the child, one may ask: Is such information any less accurate than the information the child derives from personal perceptions, the child's own internal view? Isn't it possible that the child will be an inaccurate source of information about the self? Can't the child be involved in self-deception? Isn't it prudent to provide an external referent against which to check the child's personal perceptions?

To the child-centered counselor, the issue is not what external source provides the most accurate information about the child. The counselor is more interested in the perceptions of the child even though these perceptions would be considered inaccurate by others. For the child the child's perceptions are truth and reality, they are "facts." The child's behavior is based upon these perceptions. The child's behavior will change when the child's reality changes. The counselor becomes involved in an empathic relationship with the child; through this the counselor experiences the child's reality and subsequently enables the child to make choices and to see the self in a new light. Information external to the perceptions of the child is not used by the counselor; it is of concern to the counselor only when the child indicates a need for this information. In such instances, the counselor would weave this information into the counseling relationship while maintaining its child-centered climate.

A Child-Centered Perspective for Using Information with Children

1. The child decides when information is needed, what information is needed, and how the child wishes to obtain it; the child should be provided the opportunities for locating information and discussing it with the counselor. There is not much point in the child using information unless the child wants it. If a child needs and desires information in order to make a decision, the child should have it.

2. Information is used by the counselor in such a way as not to break down or confuse the empathic quality of the counseling relationship. One way to preserve the empathic quality of the relationship is to enable the child to get information from other sources. This includes making the child's file available to the child if the child chooses to see it.

3. Information is presented in a neutral way without an authoritative tone on the part of the counselor. In giving the child information, the counselor's attitude is important. As the counselor communicates information, the counselor communicates respect for the child's capacity to interpret and use the information.
4. With the presentation of information, the counselor waits for the child to react to it with feelings. The counselor accepts the child's feelings and provides an atmosphere in which the child can freely search for the connection between the child's self concept and that information. The counselor provides ample opportunity for the child to respond to information through the expression of feelings.
5. Information is presented in terms that are understandable to the child and with due recognition on the part of the counselor that information will only be accepted by the child which is congruent with the child's self concept and the child's perception of reality.

COGNITIVE THERAPIES

The following therapies have been classified as possessing cognitive-behavioral characteristics by George and Cristiani (1986); rational-emotive therapy (Ellis, 1973); behavioral therapy (Wolpe & Lazarus, 1966); reality therapy (Glasser, 1965); transactional analysis (Berne, 1961); trait-factor counseling (Williamson, 1939); hypnotherapy (Erickson, 1983); neuro-linguistic programming (Bandler & Grinder, 1975); family systems therapy (Becvar & Becvar, 1982); and cognitive therapy (Beck, 1976).

Cognitive-behavioral therapies emphasize that an improvement in one's rational understanding of a problem will lead to behaviors which will logically solve the problem. Logical thinking plays a central role in cognitive-behavioral therapies, and so dominates the viewpoint, that there is a failure to investigate the powerful influence that our feelings have on our thinking and behavior. Cognitive-behavioral therapies concentrate on clearing up a client's falacious or inconsistent thinking so that the mind can exercise control over feelings (Beck, 1976). Central to the viewpoint is that feelings need to be controlled because of their potential to interfere with logical thinking. Therefore, cognitive-behavioral therapies concentrate on controlling those feelings which precipitate psychological disorders (Beck, Rush, Shaw, & Emery, 1979). There is no recognition that the person or child might also possess feelings which can exert an enormous influence on one's psychological stability. Positive feelings such as love, belongingness, caring, empathy, compassion are ignored in the research of cognitive-behavioral therapies, while the negative feelings of anxiety, depression, inferiority, anger, and hostility are well researched.

Feelings are far more difficult to identify, understand, and research, so the cognitive therapies instead concentrate on researching human behaviors. They can be more easily defined, observed, and quantified and, therefore, can be more easily researched (Patterson, 1986). Their research does little to help us understand the deeper feelings which lead to child abuse, murder, and rape, on one hand, and to love, caring, and peace, on the other hand. They instead concentrate on understanding and measuring behaviors without an investigation of the world of inner feelings as source for these behaviors. They want clients to control behavior by using their minds without recognizing that human behavior can be better influenced by first identifying and dealing with the feelings which cause the behavior (Rogers, 1951).

The cognitive-behavioral research concentrates on determining which stimuli cause which kind of responses but pay little attention to the degree to which feelings can be the primary precipitators of behavioral responses. The scientific requirement of precise definitions has led to cognitive-behavioral research which avoids dealing with feelings since feelings cannot be that precisely defined. Child-centered counselors, among others, recognize the power of feelings, because every working day produces clinical evidence of how feelings influence behavior. It is impossible to precisely define these feelings because of the individuality of their expression. Each person and child's inner world of feelings is so unique that the precise requirements of a definition are impossible. Furthermore, each person and child's subconscious influences on feelings are equally unique and also contribute to the impossibility of a precise definition.

Cognitive-behavioral therapies conclude that since feelings are so difficult to define, research about the influence of feelings on behavior is not a productive area of inquiry. They instead concentrate their research on behaviors since they are more easily defined, observed, and measured.

Cognitive-behavioral therapies emphasize that logical thinking will bring our emotional problems under control, while the child-centered view believes that our thinking will be more clear and logical when we discover how our feelings influence the clarity and logic of that thinking.

Both the cognitive-behavioral and child-centered views want the person or child to think better since improved thinking has the potential to solve problems. The basic question is, "How do we develop an improvement in our thinking?" Once again, the cognitive-behavioral therapies say that we can accomplish this by improving our knowledge of how the mind functions while the child-centered view emphasizes that improved thinking is accomplished by recognizing the powerful effect that our feelings have on our thinking.

If the demise of the cognitive-behavioral therapies is as real as Patterson indicates (1986), the fundamental cause of this demise is the failure to recognize the degree to which feelings contribute to how we think and behave. To ignore the existence of feelings because they cannot be defined, observed, and measured is a disservice to the advancement of knowledge. Knowledge advances when all phenomena and facts are taken into account when attempting to determine the cause of a reaction.

COUNSELING AND TESTING

Much psychotherapeutic practice operates on the principle of historic and external causation. The use of tests is a reflection of this principle. Testing is an evaluative procedure in which the client's behavior is sampled and measured against an external criterion. Counselors who use tests feel that they provide easily attainable and accurate information which can be used to understand the child. Test information is either interpreted to the client or used to help the counselor improve a relationship with a child. Tests are also considered as diagnostic tools to obtain information about behavior so that predictions about future behavior may be made (Hansen, Stevic, & Warner, 1986).

Many counselors believe that tests play a significant role in the therapeutic process. They feel that test data are indispensable and that effective therapy cannot occur unless tests are administered and interpreted. Tests are the most widely and commonly used tools in evaluating clients and as Gould (1981) points out, they possess the mystique of science because of the special status that test results enjoy.

Child-Centered Philosophical and Psychological Reservations About Tests

• Tests are designed and constructed on the basis of data external to the individual and attempt to evaluate the child against externally-established norms and standards. Since, in testing, the child's behavior is sampled and measured against external criteria, the result usually is the acquisition of information external to the perceptions of the child (Arbuckle, 1975).

• The use of tests contradicts a desired nonevaluative image of the child-centered counselor. The counselor who uses tests is often perceived as an expert who has highly developed skills and knowledge in an esoteric area. Some counselors foster this expert image among children.

• The child often sees the test administering counselor as an authority, and can become dependent on the counselor as an expert who is able to provide insights and advice. Shertzer and Stone (1980) point out that testing, because of the connotation of tests and the counselor's association with such instruments, can influence the child to become dependent upon the counselor for answers to problems.

• Tests may call forth anxiety, rigidity, defenses, or arouse new defenses. The evaluative nature of testing contains an inherent threat to the person or child tested. "Freezing on tests" is the layperson's description of the threatening nature of tests and the kind of anxiety that tests often bring forth. An anxious person or child will produce test results that are inaccurate.

• Test results may not represent the child's self concept. A self concept is the product of experiences and perceptions assimilated over a period of time. Test results often merely scratch the surface of a child's self concept. They do not have the power to penetrate the complex inner world of a child's feelings.

• Tests furnish the child with many opportunities to function at the cognitive rather than the affective level of communication. A counselor who emphasizes the importance of test results influences the child to believe in those results rather than helping the child to consider the inner world of feelings and how they influence behavior.

• In many cases, tests do not reveal any more to a child than is already known by the child. A child who is having difficulty getting along with family members does not need a test on family adjustment to show that the child has a problem relating to family.

• Tests are static instruments that cannot capture the fluidity and dynamics of behavior. A small sample of behavior cannot take into account the personal and environmental variables that will change present behavior, nor can it tap the elasticity of the larger universe of behavior. A test measures only a small fragment of total behavior and cannot encompass the multitude of variables that impinge upon an individual's behavior (Tyler, 1984).

• Tests are not sufficiently valid for making predictions about individuals and have limited value for purposes of selection and diagnosis. Statistical analyses of tests demonstrate that the validity of existing tests rarely exceeds .60 or .70 and the prediction of anyone's individual criterion score is accompanied by a wide margin of error. To cut the margin of error to 50 percent, a validity of .866 is required, a validity coefficient which is seldom obtained on standardized tests.

• Tests are not truly objective. They differ in terms of rationale and definition of the variable to be measured; they differ in content and format, and in the sampling upon which the norms and standardization are based.

• Six counselors may look at a child's test results and develop six different interpretations and conclusions. Although a test may to some degree be standardized, the counselor is not. Test interpretations may reveal more about the counselor than the child (Anastasi, 1982).

• Tests do not reflect the volitional element in human behavior. The child changes; the child is unpredictable. Even though a person or child's self-concept and behavior are influenced by an environment, they are influenced only to a degree. A child has psychological power and strength that no test can measure. The child can express feelings, change perceptions, control one's behavior, and behave in ways that influence persons in the child's life. A child's sense of personal responsibility and self-determination are human characteristics for which tests have not been able to account adequately (Rogers, 1980).

Many child-centered counselors hold philosophical and psychological reservations about tests which are similar to the preceding. Such reservations often run deep. Because child-centered counselors have reservations about tests doesn't mean, however, that test-centered interests will ever discover "the error of their way" and abandon commitments to the importance and integrity of tests. Child-centered reservations can, however, serve as a counterbalance to those who might become overly zealous in their attempts to create test-centered counseling relationships.

Tests are here to stay. They have become imbedded in the process of counseling and psychotherapy. Child-centered counselors need to review some established and workable methods for accommodating tests in the counseling process. Methods that will be sensitive to their reservations about tests while also enabling counselors to use tests in collaborative and constructive ways that serve client needs. Focusing on client needs is fundamental to the maintenance and enhancement of child-centeredness. Following are some well established recommendations about using tests that are designed to help counselors maintain a commitment to child-centeredness while also making use of tests in ways that have the potential to serve the needs of children (Seeman, 1948; Patterson & Watkins, 1982; Fischer, 1985).

Using Tests: Person-centered Recommendations

• The criticisms that have been leveled at tests are not new. They are limitations that have been examined not only by person-centered writers but by psychometricians who have no identification with the person-centered viewpoint (Anastasi, 1982). Psychometricians have long been aware of the weaknesses of tests and, in fact, have freely and candidly published the results of research showing the limitations and errors of their tools. Psychometricians have not claimed perfection for tests. They have studied their tools critically and scientifically to discover weaknesses and strengths. No group of professionals has urged more reasonable caution and restraint than the test makers and researchers themselves. Child-centered counselors must encourage an equivalent caution and restraint in environments which are more test-centered than child-centered.

• Although tests have their limitations they can be used in several ways consistent with a person-centered view. Person-centered reservations about tests are concerned with the way in which they are used. While tests are instruments of evaluation, they do not make the counselor an evaluator. While some counselors use tests to evaluate there is reason why tests must be used in this way. What then is the purpose of tests in child-centered counseling? Tests are used to assist the child in a self-evaluation (Patterson, 1986).

If the child wants and requests testing, tests may be introduced in child-centered counseling. However, it should be noted that a request for testing may be an indicator or an expression of a concern. Responding to the child's feelings regarding the power of testing may be more appropriate and helpful than actual testing (Pietrofesa, Hoffman, Splete, & Pinto, 1978). But, assuming that the child has reached a point where the child wishes to use tests to expand self-understanding, a choice has been made. The child has taken responsibility for the choice of testing; the counselor has not made the choice for the client. Although the child decides on the characteristic to be measured, the child does not choose the test itself; it is the counselor who is equipped by training to determine what test is technically the most valid and reliable instrument for the child's purpose (Rogers, 1951).

• Tests may provide an entry into counseling. Requests for testing may provide natural situations for the development of counseling relationships with some children. For example, interest inventories appeal to children of all levels of abilities and can sometimes be used to open the door to counseling. Because interest inventories are usually self-administering, self-scoring, and to a large degree self-interpreting, and because they have no "right" or "wrong" answers (the threat of success or failure is removed), they can be used by a child as a safe springboard to initiate counseling.

• The child-centered counselor who is still committed to not using tests can have another qualified person administer the tests if an organization requires testing. Doing this enables the child-centered counselor to continue being perceived as nonauthoritative among the counselor's group of clients. This child-centered counselor may interpret the results of tests since the person-centered view accommodates interpretations which are free from counselor judgments about the results.

• During test interpretation the counselor focuses on the child's feelings about test results and the degree to which the results are congruent with the child's self concept. The child-centered counselor is more interested in responding to the child's feelings about test results than the results themselves. By doing this the child-centered counselor remains consistent with the person-centered view and the process of test interpretation is reasonably blended with the application of child-centered counseling.

The counselor helps the child determine the degree to which test results are congruent with the child's self concept while also recognizing that test results, like the counseling process, may sometimes reveal aspects of the self which the child denies or distorts.

Empathically understanding what test results mean to the child enables the child to express negative feelings which interfere with the child's ability to make use of test data. The safety to express these feelings will enable the child to gain whatever there is to gain from those results.

• The reservations that child-centered counselors have about tests endure today. They often serve to ward off attempts to make the helping relationship a test-centered process which ignores the feelings and perceptions of the child. With these reservations in mind, the child-centered counselor can accept tests as a sometimes useful supplement to the process of counseling, especially when they are administered at the child's request in an atmosphere which focuses on the child's affective reactions to the test results.

PSYCHODIAGNOSIS

In recent years psychodiagnosis has become more routine for an increasing number of clients and patients (Seligman, 1983). A review of the literature, however, reveals no new information, procedures, or breakthroughs to account for the current increase in the use of psychodiagnosis. Other reasons, however, are identified. Patterson (1985) indicates that the tradition of behaviorism continues to stimulate interest in psychodiagnosis. Seligman (1983) links the interest to the accountability movement. Corey (1986) and Kottler and Brown (1985) state that the recent interest may be due to the insurance requirement that financial reimbursement cannot occur unless the client's problem is first classified through a psychodiagnosis. The purpose of this section is to review certain elements of psychodiagnosis to determine whether the controversy surrounding its use in the past has been resolved.

The Purpose of Psychodiagnosis

The rationale for psychodiagnosis emerges from the logic of an organic medical diagnosis (Patterson & Eisenberg, 1983). Since the human body is physically the same, for all persons, excluding gender of course, the logic of medical diagnostic procedures is obvious. When a patient's organic symptoms can be accurately categorized, a judgment can be made regarding what's wrong with the patient and what needs to be done to elicit a cure; and when large numbers of patients have the same patterns of symptoms, and those patterns can be summarized by a diagnostic label, we can more accurately link the treatment process to the diagnosis.

Some assume that a psychodiagnosis can produce an accurate psychological picture of a client with the same degree of accuracy that is achieved in a medical diagnosis. Others, however, tell us that a person's psychological characteristics are so unique and complex that they cannot be objectively identified or labeled (Rogers, 1951; Frankl, 1969; Arbuckle, 1975; May, 1981; Bugental, 1981). There is a great deal of difference in the accuracy of the process applied to identify a person's organic disorder and that applied to identify a person's psychological disorder. The body possesses physical qualities that can be seen, touched, measured, and objectively evaluated. These physical qualities can be altered and changed and the field of medicine is able to categorize and label the agents causing these changes. Psychodiagnosticians feel that they can evaluate the human psyche with the same degree of accuracy that medicine assesses the health of one's body.

Psychodiagnosis asserts that since all clients are different from each other, treatment processes must be tailored to meet individualized psychological needs that can only be known through a psychodiagnosis (Corey, 1986). Patterson (1985) presents the counter claim that although people are different in their outward appearance they are psychologically alike in their desire to experience loving, supportive, real and caring relationships. Such relationships produce psychological stability. When such relationships are not available people become psychologically disordered. Patterson (1985) indicates that successful treatment is related to the therapist's ability to create a therapeutic relationship rather than being dependent upon the assumed accuracy of a psychodiagnosis.

Belkin (1987) indicates that psychodiagnosis has the capacity to heighten the mystique of professionalism:

> The employment of diagnostic categories has found less favor than the approaches of the anti-illness movement in recent years, especially among partisans of the community health and humanistic positions. Such critics have argued that the main reason diagnosis is still so widely used is that it heightens the professional mystique. When a therapist is able to articulate what is "wrong" with a patient in a language that only other professional colleagues are able to understand, it invests the therapist with an authority that is lacking if he or she uses language that is comprehensible to lay people as well. Critics argue that this use of diagnosis insulates the practitioner from uninvited comments from the lay public (p. 4).

Psychiatrist Torrey (1972) says that the mystique of professionalism can also be heightened by the use of a diagnostic name or label—the magic of the "right" word:

> Every therapist who has ever had the experience of observing a patient's relief after solemnly telling him that he was suffering from ideopathic dermatitus or pediculosis knows how important the name is. It says to the patient that someone understands, that he is not alone with his sickness, and implicitly that there is a way to get well (p. 14).

Glasser (1984) indicates that a psychodiagnostic label enables the client to evade responsibility for a disorder since the client didn't cause the disorder just as a medical patient didn't cause a kidney to malfunction. The client is able to react to a psychological disorder with the same lack of responsibility and detachment as a medical patient. Glasser further states that it is precisely this lack of personal responsibility that is the root cause for psychological disorders.

One wonders if today's increased interest in psychodiagnosis is due to an enlightened professional need or whether it's being done more frequently "to satisfy the record keeping requirements of insurance companies" (Kottler & Brown, 1985, p. 161) which pay client bills.

The Tools of Psychodiagnosis

The two tools which are most frequently used in psychodiagnosis are personality and projective tests (George & Cristiani, 1986). Anastasi (1982) warns that these kinds of instruments are the least valid and reliable (along with aptitude and interest tests) when compared to individual measurements of intelligence and academic achievement tests. In other words, psychodiagnosticians are making weighty judgments about clients that are based upon instruments that have low levels of validity and reliability.

Patterson and Eisenberg (1983) identify the clinicians' face-to-face interactions and an "inner experiencing of the client" as appropriate psychodiagnostic tools without an acknowledgement that six clinicians may have six different "inner experiences" in face-to-face contacts with one client. The use of such overly subjective tools is alarming when one considers that evaluations emanating from such tools are sometimes used when making critical decisions about clients.

The instrumentation used in medical diagnoses reveals a vast difference in the technological sophistication of these instruments when compared to personality and projective tests. The accuracy of psychodiagnosis is dramatically reduced when we compare personality and projective tests with the diagnostic tests used in medicine.

The Methodology of Psychodiagnosis

If one looks at the nature of human nature, psychodiagnosis barely scratches the surface of a person's essence; that person's inner world of feelings, beliefs, perceptions, values, and attitudes, let alone the subconscious and unconscious material which continually influences how, when, and why we respond to particular stimuli. As Hansen, Stevic, and Warner (1986) have said, a psychodiagnosis "oversimplifies the client" (p. 391).

Existential psychotherapists tell us that the inner life of the person is vastly different from that depicted in a psychodiagnosis (Arbuckle, 1975; May, 1981). This difference is due to the length of a relationship between a counselor/psychotherapist and a client. That relationship may last weeks, months, or years. A psychodiagnostician's face-to-face contact with clients is limited to several hours, at the most. A psychodiagnostician knows what is obvious about a client while a psychotherapist learns about what is hidden. Knowing the client at this deeper level has a greater potential to produce an accurate picture of a client's disorder. A psychodiagnostician only sees the client's presenting problem because of the relatively short length of the relationship and the superficiality of the tools and procedures used to get to know the client.

The methodology of psychodiagnosis also fails to take into account cultural (Levine & Padilla, 1980), ethnic (Sue, 1981), economic (Kottler & Brown, 1985), and social (Corey, 1986) influences on a client's disorder. A psychodiagnosis must include these influences in order to understand a client's behavior, its causes, and the degree to which it can be judged to be disordered. The personality variables, perceptions, attitudes, and behaviors of Asian Americans, blacks, Mexican Americans, American Indians, and others are not easily accommodated in the methodology of psychodiagnosis because these characteristics are often seen as undesirable by Anglo American standards. As Corey (1986) has noted, "Certain behaviors and personality styles might be labeled neurotic or deviant simply because they are not characteristics of the dominant culture" (p. 303). Anastasi (1982) confirms the preceding when she says:

> Errors may arise when clinicians make diagnostic or prognostic inferences about a client whose cultural background, education, or socioeconomic levels differ markedly from their own (pp. 488–489).

A psychodiagnosis doesn't often include the client's opinion about what is wrong or what needs to be done. When it does, it is not given a high level of credence. The data derived from an external frame of reference is more trusted because of its assumed objectivity; an objectivity which is fictional because of the subjectivity of the evaluations and judgments made during a psychodiagnosis.

The methodology of psychodiagnosis errs in the direction of pathology instead of health (Kottler & Brown, 1985). Psychodiagnostic methodology prompts the clinician to identify what's wrong with the client with little or no consideration of what's "right" with the client. Kottler and

Brown further indicate that psychodiagnostic methodology contains no concept of indices of normal behavior against which the client's behavior can be compared.

There is no systematic or recommended procedure for correcting an inaccurate, wrong, or erroneous diagnosis (Kottler & Brown, 1985). Once the psychodiagnosis has been made, the label sticks. Rosenhan (1973) reports on eight experimenters who were admitted to psychiatric hospitals as patients after complaining, as instructed, that they were "hearing voices." Immediately after admission, the eight experimenters were instructed to behave normally as they would in their everyday lives. Regardless of the normalcy of their behavior from the point of admission, the eight experimenters were never considered normal regardless of how much contact they had with the hospital's staff of professionals.

Psychodiagnosis reduces the complex and mysterious nature of the human personality to a diagnostic label. The label is convenient and as Torrey (1972) has indicated, it contains the "magic" of the "right" word. Monahan (1977) indicates that a psychodiagnostic label can also prompt some clients to evade responsibility by imitating the behavior associated with a diagnosis rather than working to get well. The label enables a "self-fulfilling prophecy" to become expressed because the label comes from an "expert" in human behavior.

Psychodiagnostic procedures place the clinician in a dominant and authoritative role, thus encouraging the client to be dependent. The message to the client is that if he or she cooperates with the diagnostic process and furnishes accurate information, then a precise diagnosis can be made. The more the psychodiagnostician is perceived as expert, the greater the tendency for the client to become dependent (Boy & Pine, 1986).

The Psychodiagnostician

The psychodiagnostician's personality is assumed to be psychologically stable although it has the potential to produce even more problems than those associated with the tools and methodology of psychodiagnosis. The tools and methodology of psychodiagnosis can become exacerbated when influenced by impairments in the psychodiagnostician's personality.

The following factors can cloud a clinician's skills and cast doubt on psychodiagnostic conclusions: the theory of personality used to evaluate a client; the clinician who tends to be biased and expresses that bias by looking for behavior that fits a certain favorite diagnostic category; and the influence of the clinician's cultural, ethnic, and socioeconomic background upon psychodiagnostic conclusions (Corey, 1991).

Brammer and Shostrom (1982) have some questions about the person performing a psychodiagnosis when they indicate that he or she can: become preoccupied with a client's history while neglecting current attitudes and behaviors; rely on tests too quickly in the psychodiagnostic process thus heightening the client's expectation that these instruments will produce "answers"; become preoccupied with signs of pathology while ignoring those healthy and creative dimensions of personality; assume the mantle of "expert" by becoming telling and judgmental; and contribute to the process of reducing a psychologically complex human being to a convenient diagnostic category.

A psychodiagnostician's socioeconomic background, basic values, observational skills, and theoretical orientation will influence the scope and focus of a psychodiagnosis. A psychodiagnostician can also become so preoccupied with pathology that there is a failure to pay attention to the client's psychological strengths. Kottler and Brown (1985) conclude that different judgments can be made when evaluating the data derived from a diagnosis:

> Suppose a client presents symptoms of irritability, listlessness, low energy, failed performances at work, lack of sex drive, and loss of appetite; these symptoms may be diagnosed in a number of ways, ranging from anorexia nervosa to depression to an acute stress reaction. Errors are possible not only in the conclusions drawn about a case but also in the ways chosen for working with a client (p. 274).

In pointing out the lack of agreement that can occur among psychodiagnosticians George and Cristiani (1986) state that:

> The most common examples are the multitude of professional opinions expressed in evaluating individuals who are on trial for various crimes, and the studies of individuals who are readmitted to hospitals for various mental conditions and are seen by different psychiatrists or psychologists. The diagnostic reliability among professionals in these cases seems to be lacking (p. 223).

Anastasi (1982) gives different examples of how and when a clinician's judgment may be impaired or in error:

> A distinguishing feature of clinical assessments is their reliance on *judgment* in at least some aspects of the process. In this process, the observer often relies upon assumed similarity to oneself (p. 488).

and

... if clinicians are unduly influenced by their early hypotheses, they may look only for data that support those hypotheses. By the type of questions they ask and the way they formulate them or by subtle expressions of agreement or disagreement, they may influence what the client reports. Such biased data-gathering techniques probably account for the remarkably uniform etiologies found among the clients of some psychoanalysts (p. 489).

and

After exposure to a test protocol, a set of test scores, a case history, or a face-to-face interaction with a client, the clinician may assert that the patient is creative, or a likely suicide, or a poor psychotherapy risk, even though the clinician cannot verbalize the facts he or she used in reaching such a conclusion. Being unaware of the cues that mediated the inference, the clinician may also be unaware of the probabilistic nature of the inference and may feel more confidence in it than is justified (p. 490).

Arkes (1981) indicates that a clinician's theory of personality needs to be carefully monitored and controlled since it has such a dominant influence on one's clinical judgment. It may prove to be more powerful than the data gathered and could prompt the clinician to add or not add new data that would change both the psychodiagnosis and treatment plan.

Hansen, Stevic, and Warner (1986) are concerned about the issue of clinical overconfidence and its potential to be inversely related to accuracy:

Early research has indicated that as people are given more information, they may become more confident without being more accurate and also that the most confident judges tend to be the least accurate (p. 398).

CONCLUSION

The psychodiagnostic process has been inherited from the field of medicine (Belkin, 1987). Medical diagnosis is logical. When something ails us we want to find out what it is so that the healing process can begin. But medicine's logic cannot be applied to counseling and psychotherapy since medical and psychological disorders are different. Medical disorders can be differentiated into discrete groups or classes, each with a common etiology, symptomatology, course, and outcome; psychological disorders do not lend themselves to being differentiated the same way. Organic functioning can be measured with a reasonable degree of accuracy. The psychological characteristics of a person are far more abstract and illusive, and their identification is so deeply influenced by the psychodiagnostician's values, socioeconomic background, culture, ethnic identity, and psychological needs, that we cannot give a psychodiagnosis the same respect that we give a medical diagnosis. The foundation of a medical diagnosis is generally objective while the foundation of a psychodiagnosis is heavily subjective.

Counseling and psychotherapy's attempt to improve its methodologies must continue. But our attempts to emulate medicine in diagnostic procedures have not yielded the desired results. We must be willing to admit that the human psyche cannot be known, studied, measured, and evaluated with the same degree of accuracy as the human body. We must begin by becoming honest about what psychodiagnosis is and what it can accomplish.

Patterson (1969) was one of the first to point out that the analogy between medicine and psychopathology is weak:

> The two differ in many respects. The nature of the etiology is quite different. In the case of physical disease, though there are common factors of stress, there is always a specific ultimately verifiable, physical or external agent, whether chemical, bacteriological, or viral in nature. Such a statement cannot yet be made regarding mental disorders. In the case of physical disease, the process is primarily one of chemical and physiological malfunctioning. In mental disturbance, on the other hand, the process is primarily a psychosocial disturbance. In physical disease, patients having the same disorder follow rather closely the same course and in most cases with the same predictable outcome. In mental disturbances, on the other hand, there are wide differences in the course and outcome among those classified as having the same diagnosis. For the physical diseases there exist either known, or as yet unknown, specific remedies. Again, though the search and hope for such specific remedies continue, none has been found for the presumed different personality disturbances (pp. 8–9).

Child-centered counselors need to maintain a vigilance regarding the accuracy of diagnostic procedures and outcomes. They need to guard against the increasing tendency to categorize child clients on the basis of questionable instruments used by fallible professionals. Psychodiagnostic judgments about children can often create more problems than they solve.

REFERENCES

Anastasi, A. (1982). *Psychological testing.* (5th ed.). New York: Macmillan.

Aragon, J. A., & Ulibarri, S. R. (1971). Learn, amigo, learn. *Personnel and Guidance Journal,* 49, 87–90.

Arbuckle, D. S. (1975). *Counseling and psychotherapy: An existential-humanistic view.* (3rd ed.). Boston: Allyn and Bacon.

Arkes, H. (1981). Impediments to accurate clinical judgments and possible ways to minimize their impact. *Journal of Consulting and Clinical Psychology,* 49, 323–333.

Bandler, R., & Grinder, J. (1975). *The structure of magic I.* Palo Alto, CA: Science and Behavior Books.

Beck, A. T. (1976). *Cognitive therapy and the emotional disorders.* New York: Meridan.

Beck, A., Rush, A. J., Shaw, B. F., & Emery, G. (1979). *Cognitive therapy of depression.* New York: Guilford Press.

Becvar, R. J., & Becvar, D. S. (1982). *Systems theory and family therapy.* Washington, DC: University Press of America.

Belkin, G. S. (1980). *An introduction to counseling.* Dubuque, IA: Wm. C. Brown (p. 173).

Belkin, G. S. (1987). *Contemporary psychotherapies.* (2nd ed.). Monterey, CA: Brooks/Cole.

Berdie, R. F. (1972). The 1980 counselor: Applied behavioral scientist. *Personnel and Guidance Journal,* 50, 541.

Berne, E. (1961). *Transactional analysis in psychotherapy.* New York: Grove Press.

Boy, A. V. (1974). Motivating elementary school pupils to seek counseling. *Elementary School Guidance and Counseling,* 8, 166–172.

Boy, A. V. (1984). Are counselors counseling? *Arizona Counseling Journal,* 9, 26–30.

Boy, A. V., & Pine, G. J. (1968). *The counselor in the schools: A reconceptualization.* Boston: Houghton Mifflin.

Boy, A. V., & Pine, G. J. (1974). The rights of the client. *Counseling and Values,* 18, 154–159.

Boy, A. V., & Pine, G. J. (1976). Equalizing the counseling relationship. *Psychotherapy: Theory, Research and Practice,* 13, 20–26.

Boy, A. V., & Pine, G. J. (1978). Effective counseling: Some proportional relationships. *Counselor Education and Supervision,* 18, 137–143.

Boy, A. V., & Pine, G. J. (1979). Needed: A rededication to the counselor's primary commitment. *Personnel and Guidance Journal,* 57, 527–528.

Boy, A. V., & Pine, G. J. (1990). *A person-centered foundation for counseling and psychotherapy.* Springfield, IL: Charles C Thomas.

Boy, A. V., & Pine, G. J. (1986). Mental health procedures: A continuing client-centered reaction. *Person-Centered Review,* 1, 62–71.

Brammer, L., & Shostrom, E. (1982). *Therapeutic psychology: Fundamentals of counseling and psychotherapy.* (4th ed.). Englewood Cliffs, NJ: Prentice-Hall.

Brough, J. R. (1968). A comparison of self-referred counselees and junior high school students. *Personnel and Guidance Journal,* 47, 329–332.

Bugental, J. F. T. (1981). *The search for authenticity: Existential analytic approach to psychotherapy.* (Rev. ed.). New York: Holt, Rinehart, & Winston.

Cohen, C. & Naimark, H. (1991). United Nations Convention on the Rights of the Child: Individual rights concepts and their significance for social scientists. *American Psychologist,* 46(1), 60–65.

Corey, G. (1991). *Theory and practice of counseling and psychotherapy.* (4th ed.). Monterey, CA: Brooks/Cole.

Cronbach, L. J. (1955). The counselor's problems from the perspective of communication theory. In V. H. Hewer (Ed.), *New perspectives in counseling.* Minneapolis, MN: University of Minnesota.

Cunningham, H. (1967). The reactions of students in grades 5, 6, 7, and 8 to a voluntary counseling program. Mimeographed. Durham, NH: University of New Hampshire.

Deschenes, R. H., Fish, S. C., & Hislop, A. (1967). An elementary school counseling program: Rationale, role description and evaluation. *Perspectives on Counseling,* University of New Hampshire, 2, 10–16.

Ellis, A. (1973). *Humanistic psychotherapy: The rational-emotive approach.* New York: Julian Press.

Erickson, M. H. (1983). *Healing in hypnosis.* New York: Irvington Press.

Fisher, C. (1985). *Individualizing psychological assessment.* Monterey, CA: Brooks/Cole.

Frankl, V. (1969). *The will to meaning: Foundations and application of logotherapy.* New York: New American Library.

Gardner, J. (1971). Sexist counseling must stop. *Personnel and Guidance Journal,* 49, 705–714.

George, R. L., & Cristiani, T. S. (1986). *Counseling theory and practice.* (2nd ed.). Englewood Cliffs, NJ: Prentice-Hall.

Glasser, W. (1965). *Reality therapy.* New York: Harper & Row.

Glasser, W. (1984). Reality therapy. In R. Corsini (Ed.). *Current psychotherapies.* (3rd ed.). Itasca, IL: Peacock.

Goodyear, R. K. (1976). Counselors as community psychologists. *Personnel and Guidance Journal,* 54, 512–516.

Gould, S. J. (1981). *The mismeasure of man.* New York: Norton.

Hansen, J. C., Stevic, R. R., & Warner, R. W. (1986). *Counseling: Theory and process.* (4th ed.). Boston: Allyn and Bacon.

Hare-Mustin, R. T., Maracek, J., Kaplan, A. G., & Liss-Levinson, N. (1979). Rights of clients, responsibilities of therapists. *American Psychologist,* 34, 3–16.

Herr, E. L., & Scofield, M. E. (1983). The counselor's role in the development of staff competence. *Personnel and Guidance Journal,* 61, 300–304.

Ivey, A. E. (1974). The clinician as a teacher of interpersonal skills: Let's give away what we've got. *The Clinical Psychologist,* 27, 6–9.

Ivey, A. E. (1976). An invited response: The counselor as a teacher. *Personnel and Guidance Journal,* 54, 431–434.

Ivey, A. E., & Simeck-Downing, L. (1980). *Counseling and psychotherapy: Skills, theories, and practice.* Englewood Cliffs, NJ: Prentice-Hall.

Karpius, D. (1978). Consultation theory and process: An integrated model. *Personnel and Guidance Journal,* 56, 335–338.

Killinger, R. R. (1971). The counselor and gay liberation. *Personnel and Guidance Journal,* 49, 715–719.

Kottler, J. A., & Brown, R. L. (1985). *Introduction to therapeutic counseling.* Monterey, CA: Brooks/Cole.

Levine, E. S., & Padilla, A. M. (1980). *Crossing cultures in therapy: Pluralistic counseling for the Hispanic.* Monterey, CA: Brooks/Cole.

Long, J. (1981). Ethical issues in counseling children. *Counseling and Values,* 25, 243–250.

Matheny, K. (1971). Counselors as environmental engineers. *Personnel and Guidance Journal,* 49, 439–444.

May, R. (1981). *Freedom and destiny.* New York: Norton.

Monahan, L. (1977). Diagnosis and expectation for change: An inverse relationship? *Journal of Nervous and Mental Disease,* 164, 214–217.

Patterson, C. H. (1969). A current view of client centered or relationship therapy. *Counseling Psychologist,* 1, 2–25.

Patterson, C. H. (1985). *The therapeutic relationship: Foundation for an eclectic psychotherapy.* Monterey, CA: Brooks/Cole.

Patterson, C. H. (1986). *Theories of counseling and psychotherapy.* New York: Harper & Row.

Patterson, C. H., & Watkins, E. (1982). Some essentials of a client-centered approach to assessment. *Measurement and Evaluation in Guidance,* 15, 103–106.

Patterson, L. E., & Eisenberg, S. (1983). *The counseling process.* Boston: Houghton Mifflin.

Pietrofesa, J. J., Hoffman, A., Splete, H. H., & Pinto, D. V. (1978). *Counseling: Theory, research, and practice.* Chicago, IL: Rand McNally.

Rogers, C. R. (1951). *Client-centered therapy.* Boston: Houghton Mifflin.

Rogers, C. R. (1980). *A way of being.* Boston: Houghton Mifflin.

Rosenhan, D. L. (1973). On being sane in insane places. *Science,* 179, 250–258.

Russell, R. D. (1970). Black perceptions of guidance. *Personnel and Guidance Journal,* 48, 721–728.

Seeman, J. (1948). A study of client self-selection of tests in vocational counseling. *Educational and Psychological Measurement,* 8, 327–346.

Seligman, L. (1983). An introduction to the new DSM–III. *Personnel and Guidance Journal,* 61, 601–605.

Shertzer, B., & Linden, J. D. (1979). *Fundamentals of individual appraisal: Assessment techniques for counselors.* Boston: Houghton Mifflin.

Shertzer, B., & Stone, S. C. (1980). *Fundamentals of counseling.* (3rd ed.). Boston: Houghton Mifflin.

Spang, A. T., Jr. (1973). Understanding the Indian. *Personnel and Guidance Journal,* 51, 387–389.

Sproles, H. A., Panther, E. E., & Lanier, J. E. (1978). PL 94-142 and its impact on the counselor's role. *Personnel and Guidance Journal,* 57, 210–212.

Stefflre, B., & Grant, N. (Eds.). (1972). *Theories of counseling.* (2nd ed.). New York: McGraw-Hill.

Stewart, L. H., & Warnath, C. F. (1965). *The counselor and society: A cultural approach.* Boston: Houghton Mifflin.

Sue, D. W. (1981). *Counseling the culturally different: Theory and practice.* New York: Wiley.

Sue, D. W., & Sue, D. (1973). The neglected minority. *Personnel and Guidance Journal,* 51, 387–389.

Thompson, C. L. & Rudolph, L. B. (1992). *Counseling children.* (3rd Ed.). Belmont, CA: Brooks/Cole.

Torrey, E. F. (1972). *The mind game.* New York: Emerson Hall.

Torrey, E. F. (1974). *The death of psychiatry.* Radnor, PA: Chilton.

Tyler, L. (1984). What tests don't measure. *Journal of Counseling and Development,* 63, 48–50.

Vogel, A. W. (1962). Forget the records. *School Counselor,* 9, 16–18.

Wagner, C. (1981). Confidentiality and the school counselor. *Personnel and Guidance Journal,* 59, 305–310.

Walz, G. R. (1984). The role of the counselor with computers. *Journal of Counseling and Development,* 63, 135–138.

Williamson, E. G. (1939). *How to counsel students: A manual of techniques for clinical counselors.* New York: McGraw-Hill.

Wolpe, J., & Lazarus, A. (1966). *Behavior therapy techniques.* New York: Pergamon Press.

AUTHOR INDEX

SUBJECT INDEX